Wounded
by School

Recapturing the Joy in Learning and
Standing Up to Old School Culture

A Learner's Bill of Rights

Every learner has the right to know why they are learning something, why it is important now, or may be important to them someday.

Every learner has the right to engage in questioning or interrogating the idea of "importance" above.

Every learner has the right to be confused and to express this confusion openly, honestly, and without shame.

Every learner has the right to multiple paths to understanding a concept, an idea, a set of facts, or a series of constructs.

Every learner has a right to understand his or her own mind, brain wiring, and intellectual inclinations as completely as possible.

Every learner has the right to interrogate and question the means through which his or her learning is assessed.

Every learner is entitled to some privacy in their imagination and thoughts.

Every learner has the right take their own imagining and thinking seriously.

—Kirsten Olson, 2008

Wounded by School

Recapturing the Joy in Learning and
Standing Up to Old School Culture

KIRSTEN OLSON

Forewords by
SARA LAWRENCE-LIGHTFOOT
and PARKER J. PALMER

Teachers College, Columbia University
New York and London

Published by Teachers College Press, 1234 Amsterdam Avenue, New York, NY 10027

Library of Congress Cataloging-in-Publication Data

Olson, Kirsten.
    Wounded by school : recapturing the joy in learning and standing up to old school culture / Kirsten Olson ; forewords by Sara Lawrence-Lightfoot and Parker J. Palmer.
        p. cm.
    Includes bibliographical references and index.
    ISBN 978-0-8077-4955-5 (pbk. : alk. paper)
    ISBN 978-0-8077-4956-2 (hardcover : alk. paper)
        1. School failure—United States—Case studies. 2. Learning, Psychology of—Case studies. 3. Alienation (Social psychology)—Case studies. 4. Problem children—Education—Case studies. 5. Motivation in education—United States—Case studies. I. Title.
    LB1088.O47 2009
    371.15′23—dc22   2008054811

ISBN 978-0-8077-4955-5 (paper)
ISBN 978-0-8077-4956-2 (cloth)

Printed on acid-free paper
Manufactured in the United States of America

16   15   14   13   12   11   10   09   8   7   6   5   4   3   2   1

Dedicated to

All the learners who bravely shared
their stories for this book.

Contents

Foreword

I vividly recall one of the first conversations I had with Kirsten Olson soon after she arrived at Harvard's Graduate School of Education as a doctoral student. It was the first in a long-running series of dialogues that we have had over the years, and one that would stop me in my tracks. I can still hear in my mind's ear the intensity and passion in her voice, the hope and determination laced through her sentences, the language and metaphors she used to describe her views on education and schooling. At the center of the educational enterprise, she argued, should be learning. Of course. But what I found fascinating was the way Olson linked learning with love.

She spoke about "the love of learning," about "loving to learn," about "learning to love," about "learning as love." She spoke about the passion, pleasure, and desire that should be part of learning, the mystery and the magic, the energy and flow, the excitement and exhilaration. Love and learning were expressions of the heart and mind and body and spirit; they appealed to intellect, emotion, and the soul. Love and learning should begin with a student's deep curiosity, with asking questions; naïve, surprising, and impertinent. Love and learning should be nurtured by attentive and respectful teachers whose pedagogy begins with listening and a deep appreciation for the myriad ways that intelligence gets expressed, ideas get pursued, and truths get told. And schools should be caring and compassionate places where relationships of love and trust permit people to feel safe; where risk-taking is encouraged; where failure, generosity, and forgiveness allow people to discover their unique gifts and capacities.

As I listened to Olson—a wise, mature, worldly woman of enormous perceptivity and grace, a devoted mother of four children, a graceful writer whose currency of discourse has always been judiciously chosen words— I was struck by her language of love and her desire to discover people and places where love and learning were joined. A few years later she began, slowly, carefully, and methodically, to pursue her burning question. Her initial conversations were with a handful of people, all adults, whose lives seemed to be sustained by their curiosity, their questioning, and their desire to learn.

In her first foray into the field—in-depth interviews with an award-winning architect, a distinguished university professor, a gifted writer, a marketing executive—Olson certainly expected to hear stories of joyful and productive learning, stories that mixed seriousness, adventure, and pleasure, work and play, desire and commitment. Instead, she discovered the shadows of pain, disappointment, even cynicism in their vivid recollections of schooling. Instead of the light that she expected, she found darkness. And their stories did not merely refer to old wounds now healed and long forgotten; they recalled deeply embedded wounds that still bruised and ached, wounds that still compromised and distorted their sense of themselves as persons and professionals.

This surprisingly sad response from her first interviewees—a response that felt, at first, wrong and counterintuitive—spurred Olson into a 10-year-long investigation of school stories from scores of people of all ages, races, ethnicities, and socioeconomic backgrounds; people from public, private, and parochial schools; from urban, suburban, and rural communities; people at the top, middle, and bottom of the achievement/success pyramid, in school and in life. Olson proceeded with caution as she traveled across the country speaking with folks whose stories wanted telling, offering them a stage on which they could narrate their dramas and dreams and hear their voices. It did not take much to get the conversations rolling. Olson mostly listened, with her receptive antennae poised, her fury down, with undiluted attention. And their stories poured out unedited, tentative, and fluid. This was tender and treacherous work—an excavation project that required enormous sensitivity, empathy, and restraint from Olson, their narrator and muse.

This wonderful and probing book is filled with the stories Olson has shaped from the original narratives: powerful, poignant, passionate stories—stories that are at once fragile and strong, painful and enduring. They make us mourn the losses of laughter and opportunity in schools, weep at the lingering sadness and sorrow in schools, laugh at the absurdities, and grin at the moments of mischief and inspiration.

There are compelling currents that flow underneath these narratives of wounding. I am struck by the persistence of these wounds, by their embeddedness in people's psyches long after they have been inflicted. The original hurt can seem small—a teacher's obliquely obscene gesture, a cruel turn of phrase, a reward withheld, a blocked opportunity—or the wound may seem long and large—the sustained inattention to, and invisibility of, an "average learner"; the chronic neglect or misdiagnosis of a child with a learning disability. But whether big or small, these wounds can feel deep and dispiriting, and they can last a long time, sometimes forever.

I am also struck by the ways in which Olson reframes our view of the inequalities purveyed by schools. At this time, when the public discourse about schooling tends to focus on the quantifiable indices of access, achievement, and opportunity, when the measurements of inequality use a rhetoric that is literal and objectifying, when educators and policymakers tend to be preoccupied with "achievement gaps," with "high-stakes testing," and with statistically based assessments and accountability, Olson raises up another specter of injustice that is more randomly spread. She speaks about the wounds of schools that cannot be easily classified by race, class, or gender, by the disadvantages of disability or giftedness, by things visible or countable. Certainly Olson recognizes the pernicious forces of poverty, racism, sexism, homophobia, and xenophobia that cause disproportionate distortions and disaster in the lives of marginalized people. But she also, importantly, underscores the ways in which people who seem to thrive and excel—the perfectionist, the overachiever, the valedictorian, the brilliant athlete—may also be carrying around pain that dulls curiosity, limits creativity, stifles imagination, and ultimately may one day lead to inertia and depression.

In pointing out the pervasiveness of the wounding—across the boundaries of race, class, gender, and generation, for both high and low achievers—Olson raises fundamental questions about the purpose of school in our society, about the culture, structure, and organization of our educational settings, about our definitions of intelligence and the shape and depth of our curriculums, about the relationships teachers are able to establish and sustain with their students in school. She questions the appropriateness of school structures, norms, rituals, and routines that were set in place—cast in stone more than a century ago—that now seem dangerously anachronistic and alienating. And she asks us to consider the ways in which we might create more cherishing and inclusive school cultures that would incite learning and love.

Although you might think that a book focused on the wounds of school might feel overly despairing—too painful to absorb, too full of pathos and pathology for the reader—I found Olson's reporting and writing surprisingly hopeful. The first sign of hope: Throughout these pages we hear people telling their deeply emotional, formerly hidden stories, often for the first time. They become both the narrators and protagonists of their tales, and in so doing experience an emerging sense of agency. They hear themselves speak and discover what they believe, what they know for sure. In the telling of their stories they find release, insight, and a measure of redemption. The healing begins.

The second sign of hope: As Olson points out, the first step in making schools better places for learning is to unmask the dangerous undercurrents of abuse and harm—wittingly or unwittingly inflicted on students. Identifying and documenting the litany of lacerations helps people, both individually and collectively, experience the realness and legitimacy of their memories and reflections. It also offers insight into what steps might be taken to remedy the systemic injustices.

The third sign of hope: After offering up pages of pain and words of wounding throughout her book, Olson does leave us with selected tales of healing and recovery, and with lessons on courage, resilience, and responsibility. In this worldly-wise book, full of grit and grace, we are able to bear the pain because it opens up the path to compassion and healing. In witnessing the wounds, we can find our way toward wholeness. Just as Olson hoped, we can begin to see the love in learning and the learning in love.

—Sara Lawrence-Lightfoot,
author of *I've Known Rivers,*
The Art and Science of Portraiture,
and *The Third Chapter,*
October 2008

Foreword

The notion that schooling can wound us will not strike many readers as odd. And that is a great shame. Most adults I know at all well have personal stories to tell about wounds they received at school. I do not mean the kind of wounds we all got from accidents or small scuffles on the playground, or from personal humiliations at the prom. Nor do I mean the direct and indirect wounds that come from the tragic multiplication of Columbine moments in our world.

I mean the hidden and long-lasting wounds that result from the structural violence inherent in the ways we organize and evaluate learning, wounds that range from "I found out that I have no gift of creativity," or "I learned that I'm no good at sports," to "They drained off my self-confidence," "I emerged feeling stupid," or "They put me in the losers' line and I've been there ever since." Equally sad and profoundly ironic is the wound that may be the most widespread of all: the eagerness to learn that we all bring into the world as infants is often diminished and even destroyed by our schooling.

The wounds of schooling do not belong to students alone. They are frequently shared by teachers. After all, most teachers were called to their work by a desire to enhance, not inhibit, the growth of young people. I have talked with many teachers who are deeply wounded and wearied by the fact that, every day, as they work hard to build their students up, they watch the system grind them down. And then, of course, there are the parents, many of whom can tell stories about their sense of helplessness as they get distress signals from a wounded child: "Please don't make me go to school, today or ever again!"

Yes, there are teachers and parents who participate in the wounding of children, adults who have grown so numb (and dumb) that they have lost touch with the feeling-life of the child, adults who subject the children in their care to the same kinds of cruelty that led to their own deformation. But for every one of these, there are multitudes of conscientious and caring adults who want to help children heal their wounds and grow into people who are grounded, confident, and whole, capable of contributing in every arena of life, from family to workplace to the public realm.

The book you hold in your hands can help parents, teachers, schools, and children themselves find a path toward healing—and toward the kind of education that does not wound in the first place. Informed by data she gathered with rigor and care and analyzed with great insight, Kirsten Olson has written a book that is at once intellectually engaging and replete with usable resources and proposals for action. Telling vivid stories of both the wounded and the healed, she points to the problem and to its solutions, suggesting multiple ways we can bring new life and real learning to young people, and to parents, teachers, and a world in deep need of those same gifts.

May this splendid book be read, discussed, taken to heart, and put into action by a growing company of educational "wounded healers."

—Parker J. Palmer,
author of *A Hidden Wholeness*,
Let Your Life Speak,
and *The Courage to Teach*,
December 2008

Acknowledgments

There are so many to thank, so much gratitude to express in the writing of this book, it is hard to name everyone without feeling I am devaluing them as individuals. First and most important, I want to thank all the extraordinary individuals who, with bravery and boldness, came forward to tell me their stories of learning—both in and out of school. It is from them, and their struggles to make sense of their own histories, longings, lacerations, and recoveries around learning, that this book emerged. Listening to them as they recounted their understandings of their pasts, and their wishes for their futures, has been one of the great gifts of my life. Their stories transformed me, and altered my sense of the meaning of learning in human life.

From the beginning of graduate school I have been supported and enlivened by a group of extraordinary mentors and colleagues. Sara Lawrence-Lightfoot, my beautiful and inspiring mentor, has touched every word on every page of this book—from my soul to hers. As a guide, shaper, and meaning-maker she is unparalleled. Both a fierce lioness and a gentle nest tender, and someone who can really choose a piece of jewelry, I think of her whenever I am dressing for a special event. No one does it like Sara. Pedro Noguera, Stephen Brookfield, Patricia Albjerg Graham, and Herbert Kohl all served as beacons of light, meaning, and sense through many long and difficult intellectual and credentialing passages; my gratitude toward them and what they've contributed to my thinking is lifelong.

My dear friends Antonia Rudenstine, Maxine Effenson Chuck, Tony Wagner, Greta Olson, Erika Bjerstrom, Julia Horowitz, Deborah Sawch, Catherine Corman, John Moynihan, Marleigh Higgins, John Tarvin, Gannit Ankori Karlinski, and Trebbe Johnson have all, in their various loving and supportive ways, made this book possible. To each one, in private shares, I couldn't have done it without you.

Susan Arellano, my generous, brilliant, and profoundly sensible agent, has been a stalwart supporter and envisioner for many years; Jeff Garmel Knott was an incredible friend and an amazing legal whip on this project.

Brian Ellerbeck has been a calm and steady supporter and believer at the helm of Teachers College Press, filled with insight and an eye on the future; and Karl Nyberg, a comforting, knowledgeable voice in the wilderness of text. Brian, Karl, and Myra Cleary all helped me see that this thing could actually be done with a minimum of errors and mishaps. I thank you.

To some of my new colleagues at the Center for Courage and Renewal, especially Sally Z. Hare, Terry Chadsey, Pamela Seigle, Bev Coleman, and Marcy Jackson, your insightful generosity and the way you live your ideals in your day-to-day work is a constant source of inspiration to me. Finally, to Parker Palmer, one of the most benevolent and outreaching colleagues I have ever encountered, my sense of gratitude for your nurturing and understanding are vast. I am impressed by your to-the-bone understanding of so many things and the way clearness has come to you through guidance from the inside. Thank you for finding ways to make this clearness more present to us all.

Every day I work with extraordinary people in schools—passionate professionals who have a genius for seeing what is good in learners, what is hopeful in failure, and what it means to both demand and inspire. These folks show me that in addition to a very sophisticated set of learned skills, teaching is also a gift, a love, and an inspired passion. Some of special inspiration to me are Abigail Erdmann and Keira Flynn-Carson of School Within A School at Brookline High School; Sarah Miller, Megan Mehr, Winston Benjamin, and Beth Anderson of Phoenix Charter Academy; Christine Ozahowski of the Landmark School; David Rose of CAST; and Frieda Owen of the Wood County Schools in West Virginia.

A special thanks to those who spoke on the record and shared their learning stories and perceptions for this book with judicious, careful reflection: L. Todd Rose, Lauren Connolly, Jonathan Mooney, Bernard Gassaway, Abigail Erdmann, Emma Abby, and Thomas Skiba. Your generosity toward "uncoverage" and to this project overall is huge. You have truly been intellectual partners in the co-creation of this book. Along with them, my many wonderful students at Wheaton College have also been great teachers, always generous and allowing as their instructor found her way. I have learned about the patience of students first-hand from you.

Finally, to Richard Elmore, my intellectual partner and deepest love— thank you for endless support, understanding, and belief. Without your passion, patience, persistence, and our shared sense of purpose, my life would be lived in black and white instead of vivid color. Mango and magenta we are. And at last to Henry, Cole, Lily, and Sam—inspiring and reflective life co-constructors, and truly my best teachers. I am grateful for the vibrancy, wisdom, balance, and fun you bring to every minute. Thank you.

Introduction

Just as the wounder wounds himself, so the healer heals
himself.

—C. G. Jung, *Memories, Dreams, Reflections*, 1961

During one of my first seminars at the Harvard Graduate School of Education, we students were sitting around a table explaining why we were studying at Harvard, offering sketches of our backgrounds and trying to appear smart to one another in veiled, circuitous ways. Our teaching fellow, a founder of several schools and an instructor for 3 decades—a kind of wise elder at the graduate school with long, graying hair and glasses that bespoke much seeing—said, "I just didn't want school to hurt my children too much."

I've never forgotten that.

Big Changes in the Educational Landscape

I went to graduate school in education during a period of acute, precipitous change in educational policy in America. During the 1990s educational performance and definitions of "world-class" education in America were being "turned around," shaped up, and reconfigured, largely through accountability policies that emphasized scores on standardized tests and state-instituted educational standards. The emerging view of students and teachers as lackluster performers in a struggling division of a Fortune 500 company met with little opposition from many of my graduate school colleagues—in fact, it was largely embraced, unquestioned, as a particularly familiar cultural paradigm in which to castigate and undervalue the complex work of teachers and the extremely intricate, consensual processes of learning. ("If educators would just be more like businesspeople . . . ," many of my colleagues would comment ruefully.) In my early years of doctoral study, I attended, and sometimes unwillingly participated in, impassioned debates on Kentucky's breakthrough statewide reform initiatives on school testing and curriculum standards, or read nascent scholarly articles on Texas's TAKS test, which was to become the model for the No Child Left Behind Act a few years later.

Because I had gone to graduate school with the idea of studying education as a spiritual, transformative enterprise—at Harvard I heard Cornel West memorably say, "Education is soul crafting"—I felt bewildered and unhappy. Who was watching out for students, I wondered, in a discourse in which pupils were expected to snap out of it, quit goofing off, and pull up their performance in quantifiable, ever-ascending yearly increments— without a change in teaching methods, institutional culture, or ideas about education? Who was keeping an eye on the actual lives of pupils, who now had to perform well in every area of the curriculum, who could never get a bad grade, and who had to hit the Lotto on every standardized test if they wanted to go to a competitive college? Who was paying attention to the psychological and spiritual experiences of little kids, who in third grade sometimes spent weeks preparing for state exams and were taught with great acuteness how to respond to a state-mandated writing prompt, rather than to write, or how to "read all of the stem and every alternative" on a multiple-choice test?

My Own Children Start School

In the meantime, my own children were starting school. As I watched them explore the world and probed my own school experiences, I was deeply uneasy. Would my children's animation, enthusiasm, and vivacious spirits—their passionate life force—be lost as they went through school? How could I protect them from being judged—and judging themselves— based on standardized test scores? How could I insulate them from shame because they formed letters contrary to the Zaner-Bloser method? How could I keep them interested in the things they seemed to love, and spontaneously wanted to learn about, in face of the unrelenting and growing pressure to "hold them accountable" and "make them responsible for their own learning," which actually meant, comply with adult wishes? I didn't want them to complete hundreds of hours of mind-numbing worksheets before they left elementary school, and to come to accept this as "real education," or to begin worrying about college acceptances in seventh grade. Like all parents, I wanted my children to do well in school, but I also wanted them to *be well*, emotionally and spiritually, in school. I wasn't at all sure I could rely on their educational environments to take care of them—in fact, I had abundant evidence that although they were White, middle-class children with two parents at home and as yet no "identified" learning differences, they were at risk in a system that had at its center a frequently very off-putting notion of what "good" learning looked like and what "being a good student" meant. Perhaps most important to me, I wanted to nurture in them the thrill of wayward, passionate learning—the kind of learning that had, throughout my own life, given me the greatest joy. I didn't want that to be snuffed out under a mountain of five-paragraph essays, multiple-choice tests, and the dutiful outlining of endless chapters in a textbook.[1]

Going Deeper

Somewhat counterintuitively, I enrolled in graduate school in education. I was trying to crack—at least in my own mind—the genetic code of the institution, one that seemed so stubbornly, intractably resistant to change as the swirling world outside its doors morphed and altered almost daily. (This was the late 1990s, when schools were just beginning to realize that the Internet might have an impact on teaching and learning in classrooms.) In graduate school I learned, of course, how complex the answers could be to questions about what school does. (In academia you become convinced, finally and irrefutably, that no question ever has a simple answer, and that the way the question is framed—and who is asking it—always influences the answer.) As I took (seemingly) innumerable courses, and learned how to conduct educational research—much of which would have no influence on the practice of any teacher I encountered—I also studied the history of American schooling. This gave me great respect for the stability and resilience of the American educational enterprise—the love Americans have of their ideas of schooling—and also the urgent need for reconfiguring how we do and think about school.

Over several years, my own research interests also emerged. I began a project charting the emotional and psychological experiences of powerful, transformative learners.[2] I reviewed the surprisingly skimpy literature on the personal, individual experiences of highly engaged learners, trying to understand how extremely motivated, persistent learners had became avid and self-confident, and what those peak moments of learning were actually like from an emotional, affective point of view. Through lengthy, semistructured interviews I probed my subjects' early learning biographies, their first memories of school, how they regarded themselves as students, and their earliest experiences in school in relation to their lives as learners and thinkers now.

Almost immediately I began hearing stories about educational *wounding*. Although in this project I was speaking with very "successful" individuals (a research professor at a high-status university, a national-level marketing executive, a venture capital partner, a gifted and prolific writer, an award-winning architect—individuals who felt learning was at the center of their lives), as I tried to capture their educational biographies, nearly every one of them told me they felt they had a lot to recover from in their school experiences, and that their learning lives had developed primarily outside of, or in opposition to, their experiences in school. Theirs were private wounds, almost wholly undisclosed. I interviewed a successful professor at an Ivy League university who could remember the fabric of the couch he sat on when his sister finally helped him learn to read in fourth grade, after years of torment. I spoke to an architect who could recall every epithet flung at him in grade school because he was artistic (labeled a "faggot") and a late reader (called "stupid"). An insightful and fluent writer told me about the comment from his high school English teacher, "You're a fxxk-up, and you'll always be a fxxk-up," words that were intensely difficult for him to forget, even now in his 60s. In the literature on creativity, some researchers assert that deeply creative people often are unmoved or untouched by the workings of school ("It is quite strange how little effect school—even high school—seems to have had on the lives of creative people," writes Mihaly Csikszentmihalyi in his book on creativity and flow[3]). But the individuals I spoke to felt that school was not just benign or neutral—it had fractured them. Their creativity, their humanity, and their capacity to imagine were, at the very least, unsupported by their educational environments, and in some cases actively hampered by them. Their journey as adults was about, in part, "recovering" what they had lost in school, so that they could express themselves more fully as professionals and in their personal lives. This was a journey that required courage.

My project widened. I began to speak to many people about their learning experiences in school: normal, "ordinary" students, not just those with identified learning exceptionalities, differences, or other unconventionalities. I talked with pupils currently enrolled in public elementary and high schools, in elite private boarding schools, in charter schools that serve some of our most disadvantaged and challenged pupils. I interviewed my own college students. I talked with parents, professionals in midlife, grandmothers in their 70s. I worked with teachers and school administrators, and I heard their stories of challenge and uneasiness about some things they were doing in school. These stories began to fit together into patterns—patterns of laceration and rupture around common educational practices for which we seemed to have no language and were largely, in the education profession, in the business of denying.

Of course, not everyone I spoke to felt that they were wounded, but those who did also expressed a great deal of private shame about their wounds—they felt that their hurts were their own fault and they had little perspective on the ways in which the institutions of education might be dysfunctional and outmoded. I searched the educational literature for research that described these wounding educational experiences, and discovered that there was no book that conveyed, through individual learning stories, how school could be both vital and wounding. Education was critically important to the individuals who were telling me their stories, but also, in some cases, destructive, dangerous, and often unnecessarily searing and difficult. As Marcus, now a successful architect who had trouble learning to read, said, "Those memories will always be with me. I just hope they get easier to talk about. That shame about school is at the kernel of my being." Another interviewee, Jarrell, a school founder, described being "pierced" by school again and again. "I went to kindergarten as a happy child, with a vast imagination, and enormous amount of enthusiasm for learning. However, throughout the years in the traditional educational system, I lost a lot of my happiness, imagination, and enthusiasm. It all faded away and at an early age a robot was left, confined to the labels of the outside world. The school system was focused on organizing and labeling students based on so-called 'innate abilities.' If you get good grades, test well, and overall do well in school, you are intelligent, but if you do poorly, you are not intelligent. This greatly wounded my self-esteem and self-concept. This sort of societal construct pierced my self-esteem armor over and over again to the point of no-self-esteem and self-hatred."

Although no one I interviewed ever said schooling wasn't important—no one was disrespecting school or saying becoming educated wasn't critical—I was talking with people who experienced themselves as "school sick."

After graduate school and out in the job world, as definitions of accountability and powerful learning became organized, in an increasingly unquestioning way, around test scores, it seemed to me that more and more individuals—children, young adults, and instructors—were trapped in educational institutions that severely flattened and underestimated the complexity of what was being measured. Learning involves both joy and consent, and genuine engagement with the instructor and the institution. There was no room for this talk in the emerging discouse of reform. Instead a discipline and punish mentality, designed to produce better results, was spiraling everyone into a frenzy of uncritical, mindless test score jitters. As one third grader said, "I feel so scared of failing third grade. What if I can't go to college?" It wasn't that testing policies or accountability measures were all wrong—in fact, I see many powerful benefits and good outcomes of increased scrutiny of the performance of everyone in an educational system—but I increasingly encountered students who were having learning experiences that were stripped of every hint of spiritual meaning, pleasure, choice, or self-direction. Often after I observed a class, a teacher would say, "Something isn't working here, why am I doing this?" But these individuals had little opportunity to reflect on their school experiences or teaching practices in ways that invited deeper understanding about how the educational system might be making their students reluctant to learn.

Many people in schools, especially students, seemed to feel very unprotected and alone. How might administrators, teachers, parents, and students understand the impact of schooling more fully in terms of school's capacity to wound? How might students learn to protect themselves from being wounded in school? Would the learning stories that were being shared with me make a powerful and compelling set of portraits about the long-term impact of school, and a cautionary tale about how to guide ourselves through these systems with more sensitivity and sense of what ought to be? Most important, could we learn how to help those who were struggling in school by looking at how individuals "healed" and became more whole and productive?

With my own intensely engaged learning experiences in the background (these were never in school), and fueled by research on creativity and the state of "flow" in human consciousness, this book began to emerge. If engagement in learning is central to a happy human life, which I believe it is, and school alienates many individuals from that pleasure and possibility, then those school practices that wound and make individuals "learning reluctant," I felt, had to be examined and named so they could be transformed. It also seemed we needed a better shared language to describe "school sickness" and school wounds, not just from a special needs, clinical, or neurodevelopmental point of view. After all, so many of the wounded students I encountered were "ordinary," average ones—that vast group in the middle who "lived in the hump of the bell curve,"[4] neither causing trouble nor receiving terrible grades, but who also were overlooked, unengaged, and profoundly bored by much of what they did every day in school. "I was denied passion in school," said one young man I interviewed for this book. "What I really loved, from the time I was about 7 or 8, was making models of military battles. I was so into it. I once did an entire recreation of the Invasion of Normandy in the dirt outside my house, using pine cones to create the Atlantic Wall. But that never was a part of the curriculum. I don't think a single teacher ever knew."

Being denied passion is no longer acceptable in learning situations—it produces institutional despair and unacceptable educational underperformance. So without scrapping the entire system of schooling to which we are committed in America, this book seeks to draw attention to some of its more glaring affective warts and flaws. Does this 19th- and early-20th-century sorting and tracking institution still serve us well as a society? Does it engage most learners? What are the costs for most students in passing through American education? From the interviews that form this book, it became clear we need to rethink our institutional views of what good learning is—to move away from some of the old-fashioned ideas that many schools still represent and to become more explicit about honoring and valuing the spiritual and emotional aspects of learning. These are vital to the engagement, persistence, and performance of all learners, and we ignore these paradigms at our peril.

So Who Is This Book For?

This book is for any student who senses he or she may have been wounded by school, or is becoming reluctant to learn in school, and wants to understand more about this. (Are there other people like me? What have they done to help themselves?) It is for teachers who feel frustrated by the isolation and the seemingly intractable conditions of changelessness/too much change in their work, and want to hear about and find colleagues who are thinking about their work in new ways. It is also for parents who ask themselves how to keep their children intellectually and spiritually safe and well in school, and how to work effectively in school systems that seem to both invite and repel their involvement and interaction. As explained, this book originated in a research project I undertook a decade ago when I began interviewing adults about their earliest learning experiences and memories of school, and then asking them to describe the impact of those experiences on their lives now. Many individuals spoke of very traumatic experiences—wounding experiences—with which they still struggled in their adult lives. Students enrolled in school described—sometimes in humorously glorious detail—the many ways in which school seemed unfair, simplistic, or shaming to them. Wise, sensitive teachers also told me about their uneasiness in visiting some of the same injuries on their students that had traumatized them; these injuries were often inflicted against the teacher's will. Many of the people I have interviewed in the past 10 years have felt trapped and confused, and struggled to name their experiences. They felt alone in their memories and feelings, adding to their confusion. Because of school's long, powerful presence in our lives, and its central role in shaping what we can do with our lives, it has an inordinately powerful role in determining who we think we are.

This book is written to help readers come to regard their own school wounds, if they have them, with sympathy and understanding, to acknowledge and grieve their losses, and then to work to change the system for others. With our own pasts better understood, we are in a stronger position to nurture vital sparks of creativity and joy in ourselves, our children, and our students, and to live inside and outside of school with greater vitality and abundance. This book offers the possibility that by understanding the wounds of schooling—why school wounds and what might be done about it—we need not suffer these hurts forever.

Part I

BROKEN

In Japan, ceramics of high value are repaired using an ancient technique called kintsugi—filling cracks with gold-laced lacquer. Visually, kintsugi celebrates breaks, flaws, and points of weakness as opportunities to create new beauty. Skillfully done, kintsugi can make a broken piece of ceramic more prized than an unbroken one.

CHAPTER 1

What Are School Wounds?

A bird does not sing because it has an answer.
It sings because it has a song.

—Chinese proverb

"I Felt Sick in School"

Charlotte sits across the table, sun streaming across her lovely face. She is telling the story of her academic career, about her early experiences in school, and how she feels they affect her now. I met Charlotte after giving a talk at her high school on healing from the wounds of schooling. Charlotte contacted me and asked me if she could tell me her story, "for your book, so maybe it will do some good for others."

Charlotte is a student in a well-to-do town in the southeast. Both of her parents are artists and graphic designers who work hard to stay afloat in a community where many families seem to effortlessly afford European summer vacations, cars are not atypical birthday presents at 16, and private academic tutors are the norm for students in subjects in which they struggle. Charlotte looks backward at her own school life haltingly, with caution, her story emerging fragment by fragment in nonchronological order, like the early stages of an archeological dig. Tall, willowy, with long dark hair and perfect skin, Charlotte is pretty enough to be a model even without adornment and in casual clothes on an early summer morning. Describing herself as "compatible, thoughtful, and observant," Charlotte is clearly working to understand the complex pieces of her own educational biography and to put them together ways that are useful to her as she plans to head off to the state university in a few months. For her, troubles with school began early.

"From the second to the fourth grade I cried practically every night," Charlotte recalls. "I guess I was just born an anxious person," she reflects as she begins her narrative of frequent panic attacks, medications for anxiety, and struggles in school. "In second grade I was the queen of mixing B's and D's," she says. And although initially they were unconcerned because Charlotte seemed "normal," she says her parents noticed that she "wasn't much of a reader." In second grade, Charlotte's school suggested that she might have dyslexia.

"I got put into the pupil support center, and I was labeled from that point forward," Charlotte recalls. "To be placed into the support center you were first tested in this little room with no windows. I remember being scared. It was humiliating." To Charlotte, the support center, a collection of rooms and special education teachers at her school that offered special academic interventions for struggling students, was a place that "was all about shame."

Anxious and worried about their only daughter, at that point Charlotte's parents began a frantic journey to understand and to make explicable what was "wrong" with her, feelings greatly exacerbated by living in an upper-middle-class town intensely focused on academic achievement. In order to help Charlotte, her father began reading books on instructing children in reading so they could work on things at home. Charlotte remembers one of her father's efforts particularly. Her dad read a book about how children could learn to spell best by working with clay. "My dad got this big block of clay and I would have to make letters with it. The clay would stain my hands red. I felt like it was literally written all over me: You can't read. I would go to school with red hands and feel so ashamed." Her parents read book after book on reading and language acquisition, often strolling into her room to read her passages and asking her, "Hey Char, do you ever feel like this?"

After being assigned to the pupil support center, Charlotte felt she stood out and was made different from other pupils in ways that were excruciating to her and discouraged her sense of herself as a learner. Pulled out of regular instruction for academic support, Charlotte always left class during creative writing periods, her favorite subject in elementary school. Describing a downward spiral that heightened her anxiety and made her feel depressed and stressed about school, she says, "I stopped writing after I became a regular at the center for pupil support." Looking back, Charlotte says quietly, Mrs. Mitchell, the center's head teacher, "is one of the few adults from my elementary school who still haunts me to this day." Although she recognizes that some children are genuinely helped by these special services, "for me I felt trapped there—as if it was hopeless and I could never get out. I felt sick in school." The actual support in the center didn't seem to offer Charlotte much in terms of real gains academically and, as she recalls, mostly made her feel ostracized and different.

Her town, Charlotte says, is "incredibly intense about education. It's a place where academics is the key and the only key to success. If you don't have that, you're out." As a consequence, she says, "I felt like I never fit in. Kids were mean to me and I was bullied a lot. I didn't have many real friends in elementary school." The pressure of not being academically successful in an environment in which this was paramount branded Charlotte and etched on her a sort of world-wariness that, in spite of later successes and greater understanding, lingers.

Indicating what a difference teacher attitudes made, Charlotte remembers one teacher in seventh grade who seemed to understand her and encourage her in ways that few other instructors did. "She was wonderful. Although she was very strict, she made me feel like everyone had the kind of problems I did. One day she said, 'How many kids in this class can't spell *unbelievable*?' and about 15 kids raised their hands. It made me feel like everyone had some problems. We all had to stay after class for spelling practice."

Struggling through seventh and eighth grades, Charlotte entered high school with hopes of turning over a new leaf. She realized she could leave all her middle school friends behind and "no one would ever have to know I had been in the support center. I could pretend I didn't have any learning problems, and so I did."

In freshman year, she says, "I went crazy. I stopped being a student and caring about grades. I was lying and not communicating with my parents. My dad also moved out then. It all happened in that year. I got involved in drinking, drugs, sex." Some things still seem a little too tender to share several years later—there is a pause in the conversation, and Charlotte says she regrets her behavior then. "Although it made me more mature, I'm really sorry about a lot of things I did. Some things I *wouldn't* take back, because I learned from them. But I could do without *a lot* of my mistakes."

By tenth grade she had grown more stable, but still struggled in classes where teachers were insensitive or classroom materials and activities were not well adapted to her needs as a learner. "I had a history teacher who would hand out these huge packets of material in tiny type. Then we sat in a circle and were to go around the circle and read parts of the packet. When we got to me, I got all tense and choked up and he said in front of the class, '*Can't you read*?' From that point, for the rest of the year when we read aloud, he skipped over me. He just jumped over me. I never read out loud in that class again."

Charlotte says she learned how to survive as a student through good communication, objectifying her learning needs, and then talking with teachers about them. "Everyone thinks you are just careless and lazy when you don't do well in school. In many ways, I don't know how I made it. I came to realize that I had to talk with my teachers all the time about what was going on. Now I believe learning *is* talking."

Much more knowledgeable about education and her own learning differences, as a junior Charlotte went back to the pupil support center at her elementary school to be tested so that she could receive extra time taking standardized tests necessary for college admission. "I didn't have an Individual Education Plan until junior year. I had already taken the state assessment exams for graduation. That's when I had to go back to that little room for testing. During that retesting, I started to cry because I realized how much I relied on memory to do well in school. I had to build with blocks, get patterns to match up. I just couldn't do it. Almost all the things I knew I had memorized."

For a senior paper in which she explored learning differences and dyslexia—an effort she regards as trying to uncover more about the kinds of problems students like her have—she again returned to the pupil support center to interview students there about how they perceived themselves. "What hurts me most is kids who say, 'I'm 6. I'll be here until eighth grade.' These kids feel like they can't change their fate. And they do feel fated to be there, in the dungeon."

As she contemplates her upcoming freshman year of college, Charlotte reports on the mixed ending she had to high school. Highly focused on grades, although she says she's transcended that, she reported with disappointment on a senior paper her teacher said didn't have a thesis. She got a C.

"I still don't read," she says. "What I know about myself is that I'm observant. My parents have helped me see that doing well in school isn't the most important thing in life. They are both creative people, artists. My dad's favorite thing to do is sit on the subway in New York City and watch people. I am like them. I believe awareness is what matters most, being realistic, being observant."

Surrounded by friends now, Charlotte says that none of her friends really know the full extent of her experiences, however. "I have a lot of maturity now, a lot of wisdom because of what I've been through, so my friends are always telling me their problems and asking me for advice. I just don't know if they know me as well." A sense of isolation and aloneness hangs over Charlotte, even as her strength and maturity shine through.

"I believe we all have to find our own way," Charlotte says philosophically. "I just wish mine hadn't been so lonely. I think it is wrong for schools to expect that all kids will learn how to read, and read well, at the same time, and call kids failures who don't. When I went back to the pupil support center, I interviewed little kids and I told them, don't let anyone else determine your fate. You are not trapped here. Don't get trapped in other people's expectations."

"I Take It Offensive"

Delmar attends Phoenix Charter Academy, a small charter school that serves one of the poorest neighborhoods in the state of Massachusetts. At age 19, after 3 years of total disengagement from school, Delmar voluntarily returned to Phoenix to earn a high school diploma and do something almost no one in his family had done—to enroll in college. "People were kind of surprised when I decided to go back to school. But I'd lost people that I loved. I needed to make a change, to get focused." Strikingly handsome, soft-spoken, and introspective, Delmar says to me, "School has not been an easy thing for me to make work. I know it's important, but a lot of things have kept me outside the front door. Even now I'm doing the battle every day to come in here."

Phoenix Charter Academy, an academically rigorous high school that caters to students who have academic promise but have not been successful in traditional school environments, serves students who have been kicked out of or left almost every high school they've attended. Over 90% of the student body is eligible for free and reduced lunch, very few students live with both biological parents, and many students have interrupted schooling due to geographic dislocation, foster care, gang involvement, or legal troubles. Most have dropped out of other schools and nearly all have experienced significant school failure. Most students have attended at least two or three high schools and have a history of patchy attendance, a lack of academic engagement, and a feeling of being lost and anonymous in other schools—like no one noticed or cared if they came or went to school or how they performed. "In most schools you're just passing through," said one of Delmar's classmates. "They don't even know who you are, unless you're a real problem."

Delmar described some of his own school troubles more specifically. Never having lived in one place for longer than a couple of years, his gang had been his family since he was 13. The youngest of five brothers, Delmar didn't know his mother, and his oldest brother, "the closest thing to a father I have," was awaiting sentencing out of state when we initially met. After living the street life for most of his teenage years, and after several run-ins with the law, including getting arrested by the local police directly outside of his high school ("that was done to embarrass me"), Delmar realized he had to make a change in his life. "I wasn't going anywhere. I had to do something different or I'd be dead." A reflective, contemplative person, Delmar described some emotional hurdles he had to jump to enroll in school and stay in school. "I've had some challenges. Because of my background, my relationships with men, I know that when a man says something to me, even if it's a teacher, I take it the wrong way, I take it offensive." Delmar said he's learned to work on that, and when he's angry or moody, to stay away from people and not take it out on someone else. "I'm improving. I've got it more under control. I'm a confident person, a good-hearted person, but with a bad temper. I have had to learn to deal with that."

Traditional high school was largely a place of frustration and negative feedback for Delmar, in spite of his academic promise. "I was always able to do well in some subjects, but staying focused for long was a problem." School officials rarely took the time to understand what was going on in his life; he was frequently suspended for coming to school late because he had an overnight job at a gas station that made it difficult to attend school on time. "I had to work to support myself—there was no other way to live. But then I'd get suspended for tardiness at school, even if I wanted to attend, and then I'd get angry about it when I got in trouble." Describing his first days at Phoenix Charter Academy as "difficult—I had some problems with fighting at other schools," he credited his social worker, and the teachers on Phoenix's staff, with helping him find balance. "My social worker is someone I can call up when I'm having an off day. The teachers here—this is a really small school—are into my business every day. If I don't come to school, they call me up or come get me at my girlfriend's house. They expect me to do my work. They tell me I am going to succeed. They get mad at me when I mess up." These are very different messages from those Delmar received at his last high school. "They asked me to leave. They said it would be easier for everyone if I didn't come to school. I was a hood rat. I wasn't worth it."

Asked to describe himself as a student, Delmar says, "I'm improving. I am also determined, I stick with it. This is my second chance." Thinking about the big changes he has made in his life, Delmar said of his many roles and identities, "My homeys know I'm there for them, but I'm trying to make something of my life." With a 98% attendance record, at our last meeting Delmar was preparing for the state comprehensive exam in math and planned to graduate by the end of the next year. Recently he told one of his teachers, "I'm one hell of a student." But his memories of other school failures are "always there in the background. It feels like they're waiting to jump me."

"I'm in the Middle"

Luke says he looks at the clock constantly in his "standard" ninth-grade math class. A freshman at a large, middle-class comprehensive high school in suburban Seattle, Luke told me he's been in "regular" math and "average" English since he can remember. "I think it started really early, like maybe in the first or second grade. We took these tests that showed you what level you should be in. That's where I've always been, right in the middle. Not really standing out. Mostly school is kind of boring for me. We go over the same work again and again, everyone does the same thing. I try not to cause trouble but it is so, so boring. We never do things in class that I'm interested in."

Luke is tall, lanky, with rectangular glasses, longish hair, and a quiet, reflective demeanor. We met during a consulting project at his school that was focused on raising achievement in math. Luke's middle school, from which he had graduated the previous year, was trying to track the performance of kids who were in standard or regular classes to try to understand why the school was underperforming and students seemed disengaged. At school one day I met Luke's mother, who told me, "My kid is the classic Average Joe, the kids who no teacher focuses on. That is a lot of kids, you know." I interviewed Luke because in his unassuming, untroublesome, easygoing way he seemed a classic case of the kid who "lives in the hump of the bell curve," neither standing out in school nor causing serious problems. Luke described what school is like for him—has been like for him—for as long as he can remember, and how he tries to motivate himself to stick with it. "Mostly what I like about school is seeing my friends there, hanging out, skateboarding after school. I took a photography course in middle school that was pretty interesting, but that's the last thing I can remember that I really liked in school. The work is pretty dull. It's hard to do the homework; I have to force myself to do it. There isn't really very much homework, but it's so stupid. In math, we've been going over the same problems for like 3 years in a row. I was hoping it would be different once I got to high school but our teacher said we had to review concepts to get everyone to the same level. I feel like I've been doing the same problems for so long." So what do you do when you're bored? I ask Luke. "Mostly, I doodle and daydream. Some kids get rowdy and cause trouble, but I don't. I'm pretty quiet. It think that makes me stand out less," Luke notes self-reflectively.

With Luke underchallenged and not regarded as a discipline problem in school, his mother says that once or twice in elementary school she went to school board meetings to ask about special programs aimed at her "average" child. "My son, who likes playing Xbox 360 and on a little toy ukulele, and hanging out with his friends, hasn't figured out who he is yet—what he's passionate about. He's always been okay in school, not especially brilliant or anything. His grades are okay; we think he should be doing more homework and we paid for karate lessons for him in sixth and seventh grade but he never really got into it. Nothing seems to capture his imagination; nothing especially turns him on in school that I can tell. I worry about that."

The average child, who receives no special instruction or attention in school, is perhaps the most under-identified wounded child in our school system. As a principal of a suburban middle school in New York said, "If we look at a heterogeneously grouped class of 30 children, statistically we would expect to find about 25 average children. Some of these average children will have one or more very strong strengths and one or more very weak weaknesses. Yet all of these children, despite their divergent learning styles, strengths, and weaknesses, are lumped together under that increasingly meaningless label of average. Fortunately, most average children fill their round holes quite nicely. Too often, however, we provide little adjustment to the fit because average children blend in instead of standing out as squeaky wheels demanding our immediate attention."[1]

At Luke's school, as we school consultants dug into Luke's and his classmates' math scores and the achievement data, it didn't appear quite true that Luke and his cohort were average. In some cases he and his fellow students were just scraping by in terms of the math skills and concepts they had acquired, and in some cases (like Luke's) they appeared much more ready for challenge, but were not being compelled to engage by their learning environments. As an administrator observed, "Many of these average children barely succeed in one or more of the basic skills of reading, writing, and math. I refer to these children as 'marginal' because they succeed by the thinnest of margins, scoring just above minimum competency standards but far below mastery levels. Yet these marginal students often receive no extra attention, and no special programs to meet their needs. They succeed just well enough to fall outside the reach of mandated remedial programs. These children often are left to just get by each year as they move through the system."[2] Many are ready for challenges their classrooms cannot accommodate. Students who have strengths like Luke's, say, in videography and photography, often fall off the range of school's notice altogether.

Luke's mother has another perspective. "It seems like no one really sees Luke or tries to engage him at school. I know he has talents—he made a really funny video and posted it up on YouTube. He's singing on his ukulele. But is this something that comes out in school? No. I think teachers don't notice him. A few days ago I found him reading something online

WHAT ARE SCHOOL WOUNDS?

- "Everyday" losses of pleasure in learning
- Belief that we are not smart, not competent in learning
- Belief that our abilities are fixed, and cannot be improved with effort, coaching, intervention, or self-understanding
- Belief that we are "just average" in ways that feel diminishing
- Painful, burning memories of shaming experiences in school that produce generalized anxiety and shut us down
- Chronic, habitual anger toward teachers, and those in authority, due to past experiences of injustice, of not being "seen" in school
- Belief that we are intellectually or cognitively "less than" due to experiences in school
- Low appetite for risk taking intellectually; wanting to be right or "just get the assignment done"
- Overattachment to "right" answers, correctness
- Tendency to classify others, and ourselves, into dualistic, diminishing "smart/dumb," "artistic/not artistic" categories
- Unprocessed, powerful feelings about education and learning that we become aware of as adults, in our interactions with our own children or students in school

about how to survive a boring class. That really scared me. I'm glad he's not a behavior problem, but how do I get him to see himself as special?"

I asked Luke about the instructions he had read about surviving a boring class. "I read in a wiki about how to make it through a day of school. One of the things it said was in class not to look at the clock too much. It can make the class seem that much longer. Now I try not to look at the clock at all."

The Wounded Parent: "I Feel Helpless About Saving My Son"

Baron lives outside Washington, DC, with his wife and two boys. He and his wife met at an Ivy League university where they both were selected "because we were superb students—working-class African Americans who did really well in school." A freelance journalist and stay-at-home dad who supported his wife while she went back to school to get her divinity degree, Baron has been deeply involved in his boys' school careers since they were little. While his younger son seems to flourish in a district-wide program for gifted children, his older son Adrian's academic life seems "headed for the toilet."

"I am so angry and hurt when I see what education has done to my son," Baron says. "Because of his difficulties in math and some weak—no, actually dangerously incompetent—teaching, he has lost much of the self-confidence, curiosity, and excitement about learning he had as a child. In fact, school is just something he does, with very little expectation of learning anything important. The system has no place for his strengths. He tests well in English and other subjects but, really, testing does not measure his creativity, resilience, leadership, humor, perseverance, or so many other traits that actually determine how well you will do in life. Learning facts is good, but it is just not enough. It is not education," Baron says wearily.

Baron contacted me to share his story when an article I had written about school wounding appeared in a national education newspaper. His love for his son, and his feelings of helplessness, were apparent from his earliest messages. "I hope I can find the setting to heal my son's wounded self. I do not know if you have children, but let me tell you, nothing hurts as much as when you tell your child he really is smart, despite what the report card says, and he looks at you and says with tears in his eyes, 'Yeah. You're my dad. That's what you're supposed to say." And this is from a kid who really is smart. How does he heal? Will he ever?" Baron's son Adrian is 15.

Baron and I spoke recently about Adrian's progress and his transition from middle school to high school. "In our district you get to choose where you go to high school from several alternatives. We put together a list of several schools. We were looking for a program that would support and engage Adrian. But it just doesn't seem to be happening."

Baron described his son as "creative, imaginative, able to teach himself guitar and photography—a highly social kid, responsible and well liked." Adrian always stood out as an exceptionally sensitive and broad thinker, even as a baby. "He was a kid who would look at books for hours, examining the pictures, asking questions, coming up with these incredibly wise statements about the condition of the world. But he had a hard time learning how to read, and math has always been a disaster." After the events of September 11, 2001—the Pentagon attack occurred close by and his mother's ministry work with families who had lost loved ones was ongoing—Adrian "took a downturn." He was in elementary school and began acting out. "He would scream and lie on the floor in class. He began to have temper tantrums and had trouble sleeping. The real world had intruded too quickly into Adrian's elementary school world. He had trouble handling it. He worried that his mom was going to get hurt. Each night before bed he would pack up a little emergency kit of things the family might need in the event of another attack. He wanted to keep us all safe."

The therapist whom they consulted said it was actually good, and positive self-protection, for Adrian to "pack his emergency kit." Eventually

Adrian began to calm down and settle into school life again. But real engagement in school never happened.

Now in ninth grade, Adrian is a chronic underperformer. A complete set of diagnostic tests in sixth grade—something for which his parents scraped the money together because the school would not recognize Adrian's Cs as a failure to progress or to "meet his potential"—revealed that Adrian had ADD (attention deficit disorder) and was "highly metacognitive." Even though he was demystified to himself (pediatrician Mel Levine's term for students' coming to understand their own brain wiring and strengths and weaknesses better), Adrian's dad reported that he still really hadn't turned the corner in school. "Okay, Adrian has a lot of problems in math, although the kid is an amazing writer." (Adrian entered a citywide writing contest last year by his own choice, and although he didn't win, he easily wrote 12,000 words that were "pretty damn good," says Baron.) In fact, as the demands on Adrian's attention and short-term working memory intensified—typical for freshman year of high school—Adrian floundered. "Right now Adrian is getting a 30%—failing—in math, and is probably not doing a lot better in several other subjects. Last year the school tried an 'intervention' of putting Adrian in a special education math class, but most of the kids in the class spoke no English. It was useless. Adrian isn't quite bad enough to get an Individual Education Plan, but he sure isn't doing well in school. Why does school have to be structured to punish him so much, and to be constantly focused on what he is doing wrong? Why can't they see what he's good at?"

Adrian also resists taking his attention management medications—Adderall—because he doesn't like the way they make him feel. This makes his father and mother furious. "That's his part of the bargain, that's what he's supposed to do." This failure to take his meds also adds to the drama around homework in the evenings. "I ask him 20 times, 'Have you done your homework?' Twenty times he says, 'Yeah,' or, 'I'm getting to it,' but he just drags it out and drags it out. All this fighting. It's really getting to me." The complex nexus of Adrian's need to separate from his parents and establish himself independently—typical adolescent behavior—and the need for Adrian's parents to stay on top of him, creates a strong, combustible brew in their household each night.

Asked what he thinks the school could be doing better, Baron names a couple of things. He says they're more focused on managing kids' behavior than fostering their academic growth. For instance, several weeks ago Adrian was late to school and the assistant principal called Baron up and put Adrian in detention. Yet, when he received Adrian's grades at midyear, he found out that Adrian had missed 16 homework assignments in math since the beginning of the year. The school had never contacted him. "I mean, they can call me up because the kid is 12 minutes late for school, but the teacher can't let me know that he's missed that many homework assignments? What is that about? Where are their priorities?"

Also, the almost universally negative feedback Adrian gets from most of his teachers—missed or late assignments, missed steps in completing homework, punishments for "not applying himself" and "laziness"—is turning Adrian off to intellectual life and the hope of academic achievement. "The kid has a D average. What's the hope now that we can transfer him to another school? He's the kind of kid high schools don't want to get. And we don't have enough money to afford a private school." Lately Adrian's been asking Baron if he can get a job. Baron asked him what kind of job. "A job in a restaurant, washing tables. I could do that." Here Baron chokes up. "My son thinks that the best he can hope for right now is a job mopping floors and wiping tables."

I ask Baron about his worst fears for Adrian. "I'm afraid when he turns 16 he's going to drop out and just fall completely out of the system. And then what are his prospects? A young African American man without a high school diploma. Now there's an unusual story in America. Really, the school is just neglecting him, it can't deal with his differences. And because he's not a behavior problem, they really don't focus on any aspect of him. A couple of days ago I took both boys to go see *The Great Debaters*, hoping to inspire them both. Maybe I'm not a perfect parent, but I need to find ways to keep Adrian in—doing something for himself in school that's positive. But I don't know. It's pretty overwhelming."

The Wounded Adult: "School Is Not a Distant Mirror"

Finally, there was the interview with Marcus, an architect who lives in a well-to-do suburb outside of Chicago. Bursting with bright, incandescent energy as he talked about his professional life, as soon as Marcus began speaking about his early experiences of schooling, his body fell quiet and he began to murmur softly, in measured tones filled with emotion. "Those were incredibly shaping experiences," he said with pain. "The shame was intense. This is very close to the kernel of my being."

Marcus grew up in a dying industrial city in Rhode Island, with deep divisions between groups of kids, differences that school seemed to magnify and intensify. "I was the oldest kid in my family, Protestant, vaguely upper middle class, in a Catholic, working-class school. Forty percent of the kids were Irish, 40% were Italian—it was a tribal town. As a Protestant, we were the Other. I had no tribe. The better families of the town sent their kids to Catholic school, and my mother considered herself better than the kids in my school because she was originally from a tiny "better" suburban town nearby."

Marcus described his first feelings about school in terms of the building itself. "It was a grand Victorian edifice," he recalled about his grammar school. "It looked like a penitentiary. I remember the feeling of darkness and monumentality walking in there as a 6-year-old, feeling very small, with no power. The ceilings were incredibly high; the building had an immense set of stairs, and huge overpowering windows. In fact, the whole thing was like a stage set. I spent 9 years there. I was a fish way out of water."

Marcus's family could not afford to send him to private school, and as a sensitive, artistic, somewhat shy child, he just never fit in. Yet to those whom much is given, much is expected, Marcus said. "My mother always told me I was bright, very bright. She told me how gifted I was and how much she expected of me." Therefore, Marcus's torment at not belonging, and underperforming academically, was intense. "In kindergarten there were three boys to one girl, and the whole environment was very male and brutal. The kids and the teachers would ask me, 'What are you? It was really Catholics against Protestants, and I was one of the only Protestants. My parents offered me little protection. My father was an athletic, easygoing, highly sociable man who didn't have problems getting along with people. He just couldn't understand this kid he had gotten."

Marcus had difficulty learning to read. "I had trouble with text. I have a tracking problem," he said about his learning issues. "Although I was obviously a very with-it kid, very articulate, I just couldn't learn to read. I was shamed by adults about this. My first-grade teacher called up my mother and talked to her about it. I was a little kid, and I thought, if you can't read, you're dumb."

Marcus's mortification about his reading troubles was the focus of enormous internal attention and self-management. He tried to hide his problems from the adults around him, not only in an effort to deflect negative attention from himself, but to live up to his mother's expectations for him. At age 6, he felt the weight of expectations intensely. "I had to be perfect for my mother. My mother was prevented from going to college. That was my birthright, to go to college for her." Marcus created elaborate strategies for coping with his reading difficulties. "When we had to read out loud in first and second grade, I devised these strategies of counting kids to see which sentence I was going to have to read, working on that one, and then trying to get it out when my time came. If the teacher ever skipped someone or went out of order I was out of luck. It was terrible. I was nervous, edgy all the time. I still to this day can't read out loud easily.

In fact I hate to. I hate email because it involves reading, and I'm frantically obsessed with spelling and making spelling errors."

Although Marcus eventually moved from this school to a smaller, more nurturing private school (he was offered a scholarship "by some miracle!"), the intensity of those early memories and their effects on Marcus's life now are striking. "All this developed into feelings of shame for which I still think I overcompensate. The first time I read a book, a complete book, was in sixth grade. I only ever felt intellectually comfortable in graduate school. When I was put into high-tracked ability groups, I faked it. I felt trapped and couldn't get out, but I didn't have any choices."

Marcus has shared his feelings and earliest memories of school with only one or two people in his life, and only lately finds it easier to return to these memories with calmness and a sense of perspective. As he thinks back to grade school he says, "I will never forget. It's all very intimate, and not complimentary to me. I really hate thinking about it."

As he watches his own young son tussle unsuccessfully and unconfidently with words at age 6, "it's bringing it all back, the horrible helplessness and anger at everyone—especially at my first-grade teacher." But Marcus also knows he must find a way to deal with his feelings and memories as he tells me about a recent school conference when his son was in first grade. "Some of this came out when I was at my son's end-of-year conference last year. The teachers said my son was having trouble learning to read and I just went ballistic. It was like I had been let off a leash. I started screaming at them, 'My boy is a boy in an all-girl environment and you don't understand him. I'm the only dad who drops off his kid here every day in this female-dominated world. He will learn to read when he needs to read, so just let him alone!'"

Recalling his out-of-control moments in the teacher's conference, and his wife's angry and frightened reaction to his outburst, Marcus said, "The line between me and my kid at that moment just didn't exist. I was hypervigilant, hyperprotective. They weren't going to hurt *my boy*."

As Marcus and his wife struggle to decide whether to intervene in their son's learning life, and to engage in some diagnostic testing to determine whether he has a learning difference, Marcus wrestles with the unfinished business of his childhood. "I know I have to get this stuff under control," he says, "for the sake of my kid."

These Stories Are Emblematic

Charlotte's, Delmar's, Luke's, Adrian's, and Marcus's stories are narratives of school wounding—of "everyday" learning losses and lacerations experienced in school that have lifelong consequences for pupils. At the moment, these wounds are largely undiscussed and unnoticed in the discourse of school improvement and educational reform.

For the past 10 years I have been interviewing individuals about their experiences of schooling: not just individuals with dyslexia or identified learning differences (classifications that suggest our intolerance for the varieties of learning styles and aptitudes), but people of all different ages, racial backgrounds, and professions; from public, private, and parochial schools; and from rural, suburban, and urban schools, those currently in school or those long out of it. As an educational consultant, college professor, and researcher, I have heard stories of lost human capacity, of intense grief, of profound shame, and of a sense of "divided self" because individuals have few words (and we as a culture have few paradigms) for identifying and describing learning reluctance and school wounds. Yet, like the butterfly effect—the notion that tiny variations in the initial environment can have immense consequences for the long-term behavior of the organism or the entire ecosystem—emotional and spiritual experiences of disconnection, misunderstanding, or intellectual rejection in school matter immensely, not just for students individually, but for whole school systems. These undetected injuries can lay a pattern for learning, and for feelings about life, which for many people are hugely consequential. For many teachers and school administrators, they are at the heart of underperformance and disengagement from school. For individuals themselves, these experiences need to be understood, made visible, contextualized, and, if possible, healed.

Although I was drawn to this project because I wanted to investigate the affective experiences of joyful, self-generated, self-directed pleasure in learning, my investigations quickly turned to the mirror opposite of pleasurable learning, joy, and flow—the research path was full of stories of school wounding, shaming, and hurt. My interviewees told me about their experiences of becoming wounded or reluctant to learn, of becoming self-conscious and easily discouraged about their intellectual abilities, or perhaps most fundamentally, of finding themselves alienated from the pleasure of learning because of their experiences in formal education. If the desire to learn is one of the most fundamental and basic to human life—as the author bell hooks says of learning, "To be changed by ideas is pure pleasure"— Charlotte, Delmar, Luke, and Adrian have been misunderstood by school, and wounded in many of their academic experiences—even though the schools they attend are well meaning and relatively benevolent.

In their particular cases, Charlotte, Luke, and Adrian's teachers were committed, and their lives were not in crisis. Charlotte, for instance, was

~~~~~~
WHAT ARE THE EFFECTS OF SCHOOL WOUNDS?

- Students believe they aren't "smart"
- Students believe they don't have what it takes to succeed in school (and by implication, life)
- Students believe their ideas lack value or validity
- Students believe all their efforts, no matter how hard they try, are below standard
- Students believe they are "flawed people"
- Students feel ashamed of themselves and their efforts; they develop "learned helplessness"
- Students show less pleasure, less courage in learning
- Students have lowered ambition, less self-discipline, and diminished persistence in the face of obstacles
~~~~~~

enrolled in an educational institution reported to be one of the best in the southeast and at a geographic center of educational research, reform, and forward thinking. Delmar's teachers at his former high schools weren't intending to create obstacles to his success; his oppositional behavior and inability to conform to school behavior norms encouraged them to see Delmar as a hood rat. Little in their work environment prompted them to look below the surface of Delmar's life, or supported them in getting to know him better. Luke's teachers weren't pleased that he was "lost in the middle," but frankly, few had much time to deal with such low-level problems given the range of other issues that confronted them every day. Some students I interviewed were considered great successes in terms of educational achievement, but reported having underdeveloped intellectual lives now and were concerned about their aversion to taking risks. Adrian is a student who, in spite of receiving diagnostic testing and being nurtured by loving and attentive parents, stands in serious danger of dropping out of high school. "I am worried Adrian will never explore his gifts as a writer because he just thinks of himself as an academic failure," his father said with foreboding.

How can we understand the individuals in this book better, and contextualize their wounds in terms of contemporary educational reform? How can we help ourselves heal from our own educational wounds, if we have them?

But Aren't Schools Better Than They Were Before?

I am often asked if I don't think that schools are better than they once were, and looking at pictures of some grim old schools, and reading of the schoolmaster and his switch . . .

> I think perhaps in some ways many of them are. Why are
> they then, as I deeply believe, so much more harmful? The
> reason is simple. In earlier days no one believed that a person was
> only what the school said he was. To be not good in school was
> to be—not good in school, bad at book learning, not a scholar.
> [But back then] most of life was still open, and the growing child
> had a hundred other ways, in his many contacts with adult life, to
> show his true intelligence.
>
> —John Holt, *What Do I Do Monday?*, 1970[3]

Despite recent critical scrutiny, we still live in an era of unprecedented focus on academic performance and educational attainment, rather narrowly defined. From mandatory prekindergarten, to yearly No Child Left Behind tests, to high school graduation exams, to Graduate Record Exams and LSATs, the requirements of schooling in most people's lives are more intense and far-reaching than they have ever been in American history. For the past 2½ decades educational attainment and accountability have been at the forefront of our national educational dialog: Schools are responsible for raising the performance of every child in every school, parents must monitor their children's productivity and assess their schoolwork and study habits on a daily basis, and kids' productivity and achievement are now, by law, tested at every grade level and scrutinized not just by their parents but by teachers, school administrators, state-level policy makers, and the Department of Education in Washington.

Teachers, school administrators, and school systems are under unprecedented pressure to achieve measurable, quantifiable improvements in student performance, and multibillion-dollar industries cater to producing higher grade point averages, improved SAT scores, and better study skills, even for those entering elementary school. Every day we hear about the importance of high school graduation rates and the centrality of college graduation to achieving a nominally middle-class life. We know that "education is considered the most important issue" to some number of voters in political campaigns.[4]

To achieve or stay in a "middle-class" life, we also go to school for longer than we ever have, often placing ourselves in debt for decades to come. For years and years, sometimes well into adulthood, many students never disengage from formal education. Anecdotally, my college students wearily note, especially around the end of the semester, that an undergraduate degree is now just another hole to punch in the ticket of life; graduate school has become nearly mandatory. Many students anticipate some professional retraining beyond graduate school, sometimes almost immediately after completing the first graduate degree. Although this is a condition the radical school critic Ivan Illich called "school sick," the data on educational attainment and income bear out the logic of students' plans. The longer one is in school and successfully completes degrees, the greater the opportunities for higher income and the more abundant one's job choices.

Yet, as many philosophers have written throughout human history, the capacity to learn, the human desire to learn, and the experience of pleasure and struggle in learning are not easily measured by standardized tests and harnessed in highly prescriptive curriculums. As Parker Palmer says, if you want to catch sight of a wild doe in the woods, you do not do so by crashing loudly through the underbrush. Human learning is in part a mysterious and mystic experience, requiring both privacy and communion, challenge and pleasure, to reach its highest levels. The human capacity for inquiry, something my interviewees have convinced me is necessary for a fulfilled and happy human life, has a spiritual and emotional component that we do not discuss, and do not have "room" to discuss, in schools and in the work of school improvement. The necessity of basic accountability in school systems, and the need for intensive, highly structured interventions for students who often come to school many years behind, is indisputable. On the other hand, my interviewees' stories tell me, we also cannot engender a deep love of learning, a desire for inquiry, or a capacity for sustained and creative analysis by harnessing, filleting, numbing, overworking, and overtesting students in school.

It is not just standardized tests my interviewees reported being wounded by—although they certainly were full of critiques of the rigid, low-level cognitive assessments they found at every level of their educational experiences. They also were wounded by the sense that in our educational system learning is regarded a product, not a journey; that every learning experience can be assessed in a way that produces easy-to-report data; and that they themselves were unformed products ready to be shaped and stamped and graded within the institution.

My interviewees reported that many of their experiences of formal education actually had the opposite effect on them than intended by policy reformers. Rather than making them more dutiful, more competent, and more disciplined, they grew weary of school and learning. Many said that the long-term effects of schooling may have made them too conventional in their thinking, risk averse, overly intimidated by authority, or too likely to underestimate themselves. For some, receiving many negative messages about their behavior and abilities made them almost toxically rebellious, reflexively contrary, and acting on anger and hurts that have not been acknowledged. Finally, some of my interviewees described themselves as simply deadened—less enlivened by the world and its possibilities than they might be, sometimes engulfed by a sense of hopelessness about our own futures and the possibilities life seems to offer. One academically successful 18-year-old about to graduate from an elite boarding school said, "What's the point, after all? So that I can go to a good college, get a good job, live in a wealthy place like this, and put my own kids through this rat race? It all seems like so dog eat dog. Why bother?" These individuals are wounded, and very far from the pleasure and wonder of learning. Understanding why school can wound, and how to heal oneself from those cuts and lesions, is at the heart of this book.

Rather than a diagnostic manual of the kinds of educational difficulties encountered commonly in schooling,[5] this book looks at the unexpected spiritual and emotional effects of school wounding—the ways in which learning can and ultimately must be connected to pleasure and self-definition, and how our current thinking about education has led us far from a vision of this. My work over the years exploring the wounds of schooling suggests how deeply personal, internalized, and often hidden school lacerations are, and how directly they are related to reluctance in learning. While school personnel, teachers, and even other children unquestionably have grown more kind and conscious of the power of words to hurt the emerging learner, my interviews suggest that educational environments still have the power to shape self-concept, and to determine what we think of ourselves and our abilities, in ways that are unrivaled and often undeserved. For some, they experience a sense of shame that sticks with them for life.

School wounding comes in many forms, as the following chapters show. As our schools move from 19th- and early-20th-century educational paradigms of authoritarian discipline, rigid classification of students by ability, and passive, frontal, adult-centered teaching and learning patterns, my interviewees' stories suggest that students often have legitimate reasons for feeling reluctant or anxious about performing in school. They have been treated in ways that are demeaning, disrespectful, or devaluing of their fundamental humanity as learners. In this book I describe the ways in which individuals become lacerated learners, afraid of the experience of exploring new topics and subjects, and unsure of how to work effectively to overcome some of the learning obstacles the experience of going to school has erected in them. This is a profound loss, perhaps as important as any in human life.

On the other hand, my work also has taught me that learners have the capacity to heal from these wounds, if they are appropriately explored and contextualized, and to make educational environments more humane and less shaming. First, though, we must honor the value of engaged learning in human life.

CHAPTER 2

Kinds of Wounds

It has always seemed strange to me that in our endless discussions about education so little stress is laid on the pleasure of becoming an educated person, the enormous interest it adds to life. To be able to be caught up into the world of thought—that is to be educated.

—Edith Hamilton, *Bryn Mawr School Bulletin*, 1959

Learning as Pleasure

Very rarely do we read descriptions about learning as pleasure. High schoolers are told they are slackers in relation to their counterparts in Shanghai and Bangalore.[1] Fourth graders in Florida take the DRA and the SRI pretests before they move on to the FCAT (Florida Comprehensive Assessment Test). First graders are administered timed reading tests to assess fluency. Middle schoolers learn how to write the five-paragraph essay. Advanced Placement students are tutored online on how to ace the open-ended-response portion of the exam. The list could go on and on. In June, at the end of my own children's school year, I examined some of the photocopied worksheets, tests, and notes they had disgorged from their three-ring binders onto the living room floor to prepare for final exams: mighty packets on the sum of exterior angles in a polygon; absolutism in Europe; the meaning of "sine," "trough," and "antinode"; how to create a character outline for *Julius Caesar* using two quotations; Pope Urban II's speech at the Council of Clermont, 1095; a review sheet on proper use of the demonstrative adjective in Spanish. All this material, like so much seaweed on the beach after a storm, was dried out and disarranged. It would all be thrown out as soon as final exams were over. I wondered how it looked in their heads.

Although we don't hear much about it in the contemporary discourse on educational improvement, pleasure in learning is one of the transcendent experiences of human life, one that offers meaning and a sense of connection in ways that few other activities can. As the author and school critic George Dennison wrote in 1969, when observing children learn how to read, "The experience of learning is an experience of wholeness. The child feels the unity of his own powers and the continuum of persons. His parents, his friends, his teachers, and the vague human shapes of his future form one world for him, and he feels the adequacy and reality of his powers in the world. Anything short of this wholeness is not true learning."[2] Robert Fried, a contemporary voice for self-direction, passion, and pleasure as central to the learning process, notes, "You can be an advocate for 'whole language' or 'phonics' instruction (or a combination of the two). You can be pro- or anti- on school uniforms, sex education, special programs for gifted kids, community service for all, even performance-based diplomas or graduation exams. But if you believe that adults can 'make' children learn well—in the absence of or in defiance of a child's inner sense of confident engagement with the power of discovery and mastery—then, in my view, *you are placing that child at great risk of failure as a learner.*"[3]

In my own experience, pleasure in learning is also central to human happiness—to an engaged and vital life. I began this book with a desire to understand the experiences of highly capable learners, virtuoso explorers who showed unusual vitality in learning. I wanted to explore those moments of human consciousness when learning became transcendently enjoyable and autotelic—self-sustaining, disconnected from time, and profoundly pleasurable.[4] My investigations of those experiences were quickly diverted by the repeated and powerful descriptions among my research subjects of educational wounding and laceration in school.[5] Many of the most vital learners I spoke to described being discouraged and alienated in their formal school experiences. They had to escape school to begin learning, as one of them said, because it had to be "beyond duty." As Edith Hamilton, George Dennison, and Robert Fried note, pleasure and intensive, deeply engaged learning cannot be disconnected. While pleasure in learning has many "faces," and is not simple, easy to tap, or straightforward, for many the pleasure of learning is what makes love, work, and living fundamentally enjoyable. Even though "real"[6] learning involves uncertainty, struggle, fortitude, and confrontation with difficulty, it also inspires transcendent joy. A writer in his 60s told me recently, "To sit at my desk in the mornings and have an idea come to me in a new way, to rephrase something so that I understand it better, so that its meaning is illuminated—that is pure joy. The hours fly by like minutes." A 19-year-old teenage mother graduating with high honors from her charter high school said in her valedictory address, "When you are learning a lot and it is fun—it doesn't get better than that."

The connection between pleasure and learning is fundamental and universal, and it is what draws us toward new experience. As described by writer Elaine Scarry, it is one of the reasons we "consent" to education. "This willingness continually to revise one's own location in order to place oneself in the path of beauty is the basic impulse underlying education. One submits oneself to the minds [of teachers] in order to increase the chance that one will be looking in the right direction when a comet makes its sweep through a certain patch of sky."[7] Yet we seem to have almost totally lost sight of the importance of pleasure, inspiration, connection, and that experience of wholeness (George Dennison's words) in our current vision of educational improvement. Thus my interviewees' experiences of school wounding became the central theme of this book—how our educational improvement discourse, ironically, led us away from a central source of sustenance and energy around increased rigor in learning—the experience of pleasure.

With his usual powerful insight, the 1960s educational philosopher and radical school critic John Holt could have predicted this disconnection. He saw it when he was writing about institutionalized learning, even in a somewhat less punitive and test-obsessed time. "It's a well-established principle that if you take somebody who's doing something for his or her own pleasure and offer some kind of outside reward for doing it—*and* let the person become accustomed to performing the task *for* that reward— then take the reward away, the individual will *stop* that activity. You can even train nursery school youngsters who love to draw pictures to *stop* drawing, simply by giving them gold stars or some other little bonus for a couple of months . . . and then removing that artificial 'motivation.' In fact, I think that our society *expects* schools to get students to the point where they do things *only* for outside rewards. People who perform tasks for *their* internal reasons are hard to control. Now, I don't think that teachers get up in the morning and say to themselves, 'I'm going to go to school today and take away all those young people's internal motivations' . . . but that's exactly what often happens."[8]

"Completely Filled with the Joy of Learning"

On the other hand, experiences of joy in learning vivify and inspire us. One of my earliest interview subjects, Paul, a researcher in his late 50s, offered an exceptionally detailed and comprehensive view of the critical learning experiences of his life, and of his experiences of joy in learning. Like so many people who have shared their stories for this book, Paul was a late, struggling reader. He described himself as a shy, anxious stutterer who had very difficult and traumatic early school experiences. "The state of the art was so primitive then about understanding learning differences in emergent readers, I ended up in remedial everything by the third or fourth grade." He recalled his sister "saving" him. "I remember sitting on a couch with my older sister being coached to read and realizing that I actually could do this. I had in fact learned a lot about how to read."

A watchful, sensitive child, the joy that Paul took in learning throughout childhood was an individual and inwardly directed thing, not for public consumption. In the world in which he grew up in rural Wisconsin, "boys didn't do this. Being inquisitive and thoughtful wasn't cool." By fifth or sixth grade he had become an avid reader, "seeing the library as an erotic place of mystery. There was something about all those books that was quite delicious. Making choices on the shelves, seeing the books that were locked up in a cabinet. It was all a place of exploration." At home, however, books were not discussed and family members rarely read together. His "tremendously powerful reading experiences" occurred alone and mostly in solitude.

Paul became a very dutiful, competent, hard-working student in high school, outlining the dualistic choices life seemed to offer him in his small midwestern town: either become a 1950s version of a well-rounded boy—get good grades, be an athlete, attend church, do community work—or "give yourself over to the dark side," to some kind of vaguely defined intellectualism, which was regarded as "highly unconventional" and would have provoked suspicion and hostility among his peers and his parents. With the exception of one lively, unusual chemistry teacher in high school, it was not until college that Paul encountered teachers and mentors who provoked powerful intellectual experiences in learning. "I was only beginning to realize I had a strong mind and that I could do something with it."

But it took until his early 50s before Paul first experienced real self-directed, self-designed learning—learning that engendered joy. "This is the central thing—it's one of the most important experiences of my life. I guess I'm a slow developer. I've just now begun to understand and trust my own interests and capabilities." His learning journey was self-designed and organized around exploring the visual, an interesting choice for someone who had devoted himself to research, critical analysis, and expressing himself in print.

On a sabbatical in Paris and living by himself without commitments of family or career, "I put myself in a situation where I would learn something more or less completely unrelated to my professional work. I chose modern painting at the turn of the century. I had been living, for as long as I could remember, a very other-directed life, where my learning and writing were driven by my relationships with professional peers as much as or more than by myself. Now I would be totally on my own to determine what I would do and how. I entertained the possibility that this would be a colossal failure—I would get there and find myself completely paralyzed and depressed. What in fact happened was something entirely different. I woke up the next morning, gathered up my notebook, the Metro map, and my curiosity. I headed out the door. I developed a ferocious and insatiable appetite for the visual. I spent 4, then 6, then 8 hours in continuous communion with art and sculpture, interspersed with hours of reading art criticism, art history, and social history. By the last couple of weeks I was completely filled with the joy of learning, the intense eroticism of the discovery of the intersection of life and art in people of the period, and the feeling that I was capable of sustaining myself intellectually."

For Paul, deeply engaged learning had an erotic quality—a kind of energizing, transforming intensity that is unforgettable to those who have experienced it. As several other interviewees confirmed, during intensely interesting periods of learning, there is flow: Work is performed effortlessly and emotional entanglements fade into the background. Learning becomes so gratifying that individuals keep at it, even if no one is looking, noticing, grading, or giving a performance appraisal.

As the 20th-century French writer and mystic Simone Weil—herself a great and adventurous learner—described the relationship between pleasure and the motivation to learn, "Intelligence can only be led by desire. For there to be desire, there must be pleasure and joy in the work. The intelligence only grows and bears fruit in joy. The joy of learning is as indispensable in study as breathing is in running. Where it is lacking there are no real students, but only poor caricatures of apprentices who, at the end of their apprenticeship, will never have a trade."[9] In other words, pleasure in learning is essential to the stick-to-itiveness required of learning, and if pleasure is disconnected from cognitive tasks, we are wounded.

"But Please Don't Tell People It Should Be Easy"

When I sent an early draft of this book to Mel Levine, the pediatrician and best-selling author who has popularized the idea of *acceptable* variation in the capacity of humans to learn (and who has created useful, nonmoralizing structures for schools to understand difference in human minds in educational settings), Levine implored me please not to tell people learning should be easy, or free of setbacks or periods of self-doubt. He said, "There is probably such a thing as an optimal level of educational trauma—neither totally wound-free nor perpetually and deeply injurious."

~~~~~~

THREE "FACES" OF PLEASURE IN LEARNING

What are three kinds of pleasures that prompt learning?

Autonomous pleasure. This is pleasure that often is seen as an ideal: It arises spontaneously from the activity of learning. It is the immanent pleasure of a learning experience, self-sustaining and highly generative.

Social reward. This is the pleasure that comes from social feedback as a learner masters or accomplishes something. This is receiving a gold star, an A plus, a field trip privilege, a fellowship, applause at the end of a presentation, admiration from those around you.

Tension and release. This is the pleasure that comes after completing a stressful project. This resembles Freud's models of sexual arousal and satisfaction. Writing and completing a paper can be like this; studying for and finally taking an exam offers relief from tension.[10]

While all these forms of pleasure are critical, as educators we tremendously undervalue and understudy autonomous pleasure.

~~~~~~

Levine's caution is a good one—learning involves difficulty, struggle, and persistence. Or, as a wise 8-year-old said when discussing *The Door in the Wall*, a book he was reading, "Robin was learning patience. He found out that the harder it was to do something, the more comfortable he felt after he had done it."[11]

In American education, however, our conception of what motivates learning has been dramatically oversimplified and flattened, particularly under No Child Left Behind. The motivational world of the pupil is sometimes constructed as almost cartoonish. At my local high school, students were offered an ice cream social by their principal if they promised to take the Massachusetts Comprehensive Assessment Exams seriously. Many of the individuals who described their school experiences for this book said that it was in school that they began to experience learning as something almost painfully disconnected from themselves—*as something they must do*. Choice and self-direction were eliminated or were too narrowly defined, shame or fear of making mistakes became their strongest associations with new learning tasks, and a deeper understanding of what made learning vital and meaningful was rarely in view. Subsequently, almost without realizing it, they lost their pleasure in learning, and along with that self-confidence and fortitude—all necessary components of learning.[12]

When I speak to audiences about the wounds of schooling, I often present "common" types of wounds, those learning injuries typically encountered by those who have shared their stories with me. Although there are as many types of wounds as there are research interviews, this taxonomy helps individuals begin to think about what parts of themselves they may have been alienated from in their educational experiences—what they experience as lost. Perhaps you will recognize parts of yourself here.

Wounds of Creativity

> There was always something mechanical about school, a mold that I never quite fit into, never quite understood. My writing continued to be an outlet that I kept to myself. The pages of my journals were quickly filled, only to be thrown in the bottom drawer of my desk, a place where my most secret and personal thoughts lay amongst a box overflowing with scrap pieces of paper. A lid with the word PRIVATE written bold was jammed on top of this time capsule, keeping it safe, guarded.
>
> —Student writer, excerpt from college reflection, 2007

One of my college students, Claire, a poised, talented, and thoughtful sophomore, spoke poignantly of her first experiences of creative wounding in school. "I can remember it so well, the time that grading rubric was attached to a piece of my writing. Maybe it was in third grade. Suddenly all the joy of writing was taken away. I was being evaluated. I was writing for a grade, not for myself anymore. I was no longer doing it for me. It took me years to realize that, and I want to get that back. Will I ever get that back?" As many of those who have been traditionally schooled have experienced, school tends to reward habitual, routine, expected responses; the ability to summarize material presented by a teacher in a prescribed format is greatly prized; and the capacity to produce work that fulfills the demands of the task is highly desirable. Our recent test-based accountability systems greatly exacerbate these tendencies.

While there are at least 60 definitions of creativity in the literature, most creativity researchers feel that, at a minimum, creativity involves the capacity to produce something new and that adds unusual value or perspective.[13] Conventional standardized tests and teacher-centered curriculums inculcate and reward habitual, routine, expected responses. As Robert Sternberg, Dean at Tufts University and a renowned researcher on intelligence, says, "Try being creative on a standardized test and you will get slapped down just as soon as you get your score." By approaching knowledge and assessment as a process of producing the right answers, many curricular designs encourage conventionality and predictable thinking. My college students are wonderful at describing this. In an exercise in which I ask them to list every standardized test they have taken—usually an astonishing number—and describe the experiences of taking standardized tests, one of my students, Aliza, said, "It's actually when I'm stupidest, when I'm thinking the most simply and conventionally, that I do the best on standardized tests. I'm really pretty good at them if I can just keep my mind from getting too creative or inventive. And never, ever find something funny on a standardized test. When you are laughing you know you are doing something wrong."

Put another way, Sternberg calls creativity a "habit." He says that creative thinking and expression are not just about living in an artist's studio painting huge canvasses while listening to Mahler, but "routinely approaching problems in novel ways." Sternberg feels that we can learn to be creative—learn to think novelly and unusually—and get reinforced for being creative. We can also learn *not to be creative*. "Most schools treat creativity as a bad habit," Sternberg notes, devaluing problems that do not yield to simple multiple-choice answers.[14] Daniel Pink, in his 2005 book *A Whole New Mind*,[15] proposes that we are entering a new conceptual age in which creativity will be at the center of workplace skills—the ability to empathize and create beauty, coherence, and meaning are the attributes that will be most valuable in the new, post-left-brain world.

As the quote at the opening of this section describes, being creatively wounded is a profound rupture—it robs us of delight and sources of interior animation. When we lose our creativity, we also are stripped of our courage and our nerve. At the climax of May Sarton's classic 1961 novel on teaching, *The Small Room*, a young professor confronts a brilliant student who has been caught cheating. The cheating incident is about to end this exceptional student's career. Her professor asks plaintively, why did you cheat? The student replies, "The pressure, the pressure, the pressure. . . . The more you do, the more you're expected to do, and each thing has got to be better, always better. . . . When I came here I was in love with learning, literally. I was like a starving person who finds food. You can't imagine what my parents are like, how crazy anyone seems who wants to read . . . especially a girl. When I got here I thought I was in heaven. . . . I just got tired of being pushed so hard, tired of the whole racket, tired of having a brain, tired of coming up to the jump and taking it again and again. I lost my nerve."[16]

Another one of my college students, who was not diagnosed with attention deficit disorder (ADD) until late in high school, wrote about her wounds from schooling and her "rediscovery" of her own creativity in college. "When I was first diagnosed with a learning difference, I was in complete denial. I was mortified that I had a disorder that, in my mind, was associated with rambunctious boys like my annoying cousin, Tommy. A jumbled mess of emotions overwhelmed me, ranging from infuriated to complete relief. However, the years of frustration and failures had taken a toll on my confidence and I found myself unable to trust my own ability in the classroom. I continued to write but rarely shared my thoughts with others. Although I knew inside that my writing was powerful and artistic, I was unwilling to make myself vulnerable to someone else's critique. I had spent so many years feeling inadequate that I was not about to take another chance with something I cared about as much as my writing. And so this passion became my secret, the margins of my notebooks would be filled with my scrawled writing, later to be torn out and shoved into the leaves of my journal, often forgotten. It was enough for me to consider myself a good writer, even if no one else could see it. Some of my teachers, who encountered my writing, acknowledged my enthusiasm for words and applauded my efforts; however, I was still tested in ways that exposed my weaknesses."

After studying the now increasingly apparent connection between creativity and ADD and ADHD, my student found herself coming to prize her moments of unusual focus and consciousness, and valuing her writing as important and creative. "The more I studied the researchers who showed the relationship between creative expression and ADD, the more I found myself digging deeper into my past, stumbling upon moments that I had frozen in my mind. Now when I write a paper, my fingers fly across the keys effortlessly as words splatter down the page."

She described her own state of flow and intense focus and concentration: "It's hard to tell all about the place that I go when this kind of focusing happens. I imagine it as being enclosed in a glass case that is hard on the outside but stretches on the inside, maybe more like a glass bubble. My thoughts are free to fill up the space, expand, and escape if they choose. However, nothing can touch me or distract me while I am in my glass bubble. I can stay there for however long my mind lets me, often longer than an hour. This level of focus can happen randomly, like in the middle of class when I think of the first line of a poem and before you know it, class is over and I have three pages of scribbled writing staring me back in the face. When my mind wants to go somewhere, there is no way I can stop it. If I do resist my imagination, I get this feeling inside of me, kind of like a spring that is being pushed down and pushed down. The longer I keep pressing down the harder it is for me to concentrate on anything else. However, once I let it go I feel relaxed, like I am able to take a deep

~~~~~~

WOUNDS OF CREATIVITY

- Belief that our unusual or novel ideas or capacities lack value, or are too weird, too strange
- Sense that everything we do has to "add up to something" useful or explicable
- Judgmental internal voices that tell us: Who do you think you are to try that? You're no good at that—you can't be successful at that.
- Blaming internal voices that say: You haven't worked hard enough at that for it to be of value or to make sense
- Denial of what we are passionate about, or for what we have affinity, in favor of what is conventionally expected
- Denying our inner compass about what is valuable, what our vocation is, what we have to add to the world

~~~~~~

breath. This is my creative outlet; this is how I express myself best. Writing is my way of dealing with my learning difference. It is my passion, my escape. This realization is why I chose to do my final project on creativity and ADD. The thought crept into my mind and I was not about to push it away. Instead I embraced it, not completely sure where I was going to end up, but knowing somewhere deep down I would uncover another hidden piece of myself along the way."

Wounds of Compliance

> To understand the political structure of the school we must
> know that the school is organized on the authority principle
> and that its authority is constantly threatened.
>
> —Willard Waller, *The Sociology of Teaching*, 1965

A student in Arizona described learning to be a good girl in school, and the wounding experiences of compliance and faulty justice that were central experiences of education. "When I started kindergarten, I learned to do what the teacher said: line up, raise your hand, be quiet. I learned some tough rules about interaction with others. When little boys chased me on the playground and tried to forcibly drag me into the boys' restroom, I was terrified and ran to the teacher for help. The teacher, who was supposed to help me, to know that this was not right, told me to quit being such a tattletale. I learned to be afraid and that authority figures were hypocrites who could not be counted on. My parents taught me how to defend myself against predatory children on the playground. When I fought back, I was punished by the teachers. I became afraid of cruel children and afraid to tell my parents I was afraid. So I stayed helpless . . . in a confusing land of contradictory rules. Perhaps the teachers were trying to encourage self-reliance. Perhaps they were just being lazy or were unconcerned. Regardless, their collective response discouraged seeking them out for help and created . . . a fear of asking for help on the playground that often extended into the classroom. . . . As the years progressed my confusion mounted."[17]

With its factory-like organizational structures and construction of learning as lower-level testable events, American education has tended to favor predictable behavior, intellectually and emotionally. Although the degree of compliance expected by students varies according to social class and cultural setting—working-class and poor schools tend to be much more rule oriented and to emphasize the teacher as "boss," for instance—learning to put down your number 2 pencil when asked or to speak respectfully to the principal is one of the central socializing purposes of institutionalized education. But too much compliance can make us politically weak and interpersonally weary. "Let there be no doubt," says Lisa Delpit, an educational critic and race educator. "A 'skilled' minority person who is not also capable of critical analysis becomes the trainable, low-level functionary of the dominant society, simply the grease that keeps the institutions which orchestrate his or her oppression running smoothly."[18] We need to learn to comply in order to get along in our culture, but excessive compliance is the enemy of creativity and higher-level thinking. It is a dilemma around which many of my interviewees have wounds.

One of my students explained, at an emotional level, an experience of early "overcompliance" in school through the administration of standardized tests. "In the spring of 1998 I was in fourth grade. It was during this year that the new Massachusetts Department of Education decided to start running trial tests of its new system that was made to assess schools: the Massachusetts Comprehensive Assessment System [more commonly referred to as the MCAS]. During that year, students in grades 4, 8, and 10 across Massachusetts were given the MCAS test. My fourth-grade class was turned into a room of guinea pigs."

"While teachers told us it had no immediate effect on our grades, or us, they still stressed its importance for months. I remember teachers and my principal telling us that we needed to try our hardest on this test because the state needed to see what we knew. If you put 'test' and 'state' in the same sentence it is going to scare any child. I remember taking flyers home to my parents about the upcoming test and its importance. The flyers stressed the need for good sleep, a good breakfast, and low amounts of stress and pressure. All this happened way in advance of the test, so you can imagine that with everything I heard about this test, I was in tears the day before the MCAS began. I was scared to do poorly and I was afraid of what would happen if I did. Everyone just kept telling us to do our best, but I kept wondering, 'What if my best isn't good enough?'

"The days of the test finally came and I clearly remember it being very difficult. Since it was the first time the state had administered the MCAS, they didn't know what level they should be testing at, and they ended up aiming higher than most fourth graders could handle. I remember struggling a lot and becoming frustrated and discouraged on many questions. Every day for almost 2 weeks we would skulk into our classroom and moan as the teacher passed out the next part of the MCAS test. We jokingly referred to the test as 'the bubbles' due to the hundreds of bubbles we had to fill in. Every day we would exclaim, 'The bubbles are back!' before picking up our sharpened number two pencils and beginning another grueling day of testing."

Wounds of compliance often are rooted in fear: fear of breaking out of the roles we are assigned by the culture, fear of being perceived as different, fear of not being successful, fear of being an outcast. Although my student's teachers and principal regarded the first administration of state-mandated tests for fourth graders as an administrative (and political) event, for my student the emotional content and emotional effects of taking the test were foremost. My student had not forgotten it, even now in college. Another interviewee, Sloan, a visual artist in her mid-60s, described herself to me as someone who has been "hooked on compliance" most of her life. She called her journey from "straight A student cheerleader" of the 1950s to painter who composes mixed-media presentations on gender and gender roles, "the most challenging, exciting challenge of my life. Every day I'm shaking off some pieces of the old role, learning not to be good all the time." She says she is learning not to be afraid.

WOUNDS OF COMPLIANCE

- Feeling that obeying the rules, especially in school, is of paramount importance for approval, for acceptance
- Feeling that we will be rewarded only if we obey the rules, even if the rules seem unfair, unjust, or diminishing
- Fear of being punished for sticking out: "The nail that rises above will be hammered down."
- Feeling of dislocation from ourselves due to institutional expectations: "I learned that the rules of school were wrong, but I still had to go by them."
- Overreliance on external rewards for motivation: "I took this course only because it would look good on my transcript."

Wounds of Rebelliousness

> Learning how to *not-learn* is an intellectual and social
> challenge; sometimes you have to work very hard at it. It
> consists of an active, often ingenious, willful rejection of even
> the most compassionate and well-designed teaching. . . . It
> was through insight into my own not-learning that I began to
> understand the inner world of students who chose to not-learn
> what I wanted to teach. Over the years I've come to side with
> them in their refusals to be molded by a hostile society and
> have come to look upon not-learning as positive and healthy in
> many situations."
>
> —Herb Kohl, *I Won't Learn from You*, 1994

Rasheed, a successful wireless communications entrepreneur, described feeling perpetually underappreciated and rebellious in school. "The talents I had, interpersonal, ability to get along with others, enthusiasm, humor, didn't seem to count for much in my schooling. Very few teachers saw what I had to offer. In junior high school I became rebellious and acted out. I broke the law, encouraged other kids to get into trouble, tested the boundaries in almost every way. I made my parents worried and crazy and they lost faith in me, too. I was looking for meaning and appreciation. I couldn't find it in school. My mother even refused to attend my high school graduation. After that I just went through the motions to finish community college. As soon as I left school, the successful parts of my life began." Rasheed developed what he calls a "habit of rebellion" in school, and now even as an adult he struggles between "being a good boy, too good," and wanting to "break down the walls, break down the barriers."

Many educational systems make students rebellious and angry— creating problems in students they then must "fix." Recently when I was giving a talk at a large, comprehensive suburban high school, a young man, a graduating senior, told me about his recent experience in the school library. "I was working on my senior paper, with the document up on the screen. But before I started writing, I wanted to check the basketball score from the night before online. The librarian came around on patrol, saw me 'off task,' and told me I had to leave the library. I argued with her. She wouldn't listen to me when I said that I was wasting time just for a minute. The librarian reported me to my dean. Now I am banned from the library, I no longer have access to the computers for doing research. I may not get my senior paper in on time." Authoritarian discipline structures exacerbated this young man's response, denying him access to the learning resources he needed to be successful in school. Many of my interviewees, particularly boys, describe how and why they rebelled in school, and how they became their own "worst enemies." For some, in low-wage, dead-end jobs or prison, the habit of rebellion has become a critical obstacle. Rasheed—who experienced his first real successes after his conventional schooling was completed—began to reflect productively on his experiences and change his life only after he left school. Wounds of rebellion are a drain on educational systems; high dropout rates and school disengagement are products of inflexible and intellectually monolithic systems where students feel bored, alienated, and unseen.

As Bill Page, an educator who has written extensively on the rebellious, at-risk learner, says, while students who don't conform, don't hand in assignments, are oblivious to bad marks, and create havoc in school are the bane of a teacher's and a school system's life, many students who exhibit these characteristics are actually begging for perceptive, inquiring attention. "Teachers often fail to recognize the embarrassment, consternation, and defensiveness that is at the root of at-risk, rebellious behavior," says Page. "Understanding . . . cover-up strategies such as 'being bad' is better than 'being dumb' and recognizing that defiance of authority earns respect from peers, can give teachers new insights."[19] Page says that in 30 years of teaching rebellious learners, he knows that looking below the surface of superficially rebellious behavior is a critical piece of effective instruction. "As teachers acknowledge and accept the underlying causes of at-risk behaviors, they can focus on helping all students, including those most at risk, while improving their teaching effectiveness and building an inclusive classroom . . . instead of focusing on the problems these students create in orderly classroom management."[20] Looking below the surface of rebellion is part of healing these school wounds. No interviewee for this book, no student I have encountered, expressed absolutely no interest in doing well in school; mostly, my interviewees had been made angry and resentful by feeling poorly treated within educational environments. This, in turn, made them rebellious and difficult to deal with. Understanding the legitimacy of rebellious feelings is, in part, a path to healing.

WOUNDS OF REBELLION

- Sense that the only way to protect oneself is to rebel, to object
- In response to being unsuccessful, or being told we are not worthy in school, fighting, acting out, becoming hostile
- Inflexibility in taking another's point of view; being flooded by one's own sense of anger and injustice
- Fighting or acting out learned as an adaptive response, that becomes fixed and maladaptive, and self-destructive

Wounds That Numb

> The student's false self evolves in the acceptance of routine
> within a culture of schooling that obscures learning in pursuit
> of superficial rewards. There's a world of difference between
> the student whose "straight A's" are a reflection of engaged,
> thoughtful and creative learning, and the student who has
> psyched out his teachers and agreed to do whatever it takes to
> get all A's.
>
> —Robert Fried, *The Game of School,* 2005[21]

Wounds of numbness are the mirror image of wounds of rebelliousness—many students are numb and no longer enlivened by learning. In spite of its external rewards and the positive attention it brings, succeeding in school also can be an alienating and cynicism-inducing experience; wounds of numbness—burnout, passivity, depression—are "difficult to detect but very crippling," in the words of one of my interviewees. Because being an entrepreneurial learner is perhaps the most important workplace skill in our new information-saturated world, this wound needs much more attention and more effective interventions than we provide students now.

A mother recently described her highly successful, although intellectually unengaged 15-year-old daughter to me: "Melissa does very well on her tests—AP Spanish, world history, and honors biology—and completes all her homework like clockwork. But I feel like nothing really turns her on. Her older brother, a much less consistent student grade-wise, would struggle and flounder in some subjects, but he was crazy about biology. He designed an independent study for himself, got really close with the teacher. I feel like Melissa has no curiosity about anything. She has learning interest like this," she says, making her fingers into a zero. "Nothing."

Some students, battle scarred and weary, are simply numb from the effects of school; they have developed a protective carapace that keeps them from feeling too much about any academic assignment, any learning exercise, any project that will ask for more effort from them than they can muster. Some of my college students display this kind of low affect around learning: They lean back in their chairs during class, eyes half glazed, they multitask on assignments if they think they can get away with it, they talk online in class, and produce only enough work to achieve the grade they have determined is acceptable for them to maintain their grade point average. They are not agape to learning, but self-shielded from its effects, well inoculated from excitement, animation, or real engagement. Some of my students attribute their affect to the amount of testing and

~~~~~~

WOUNDS OF NUMBNESS

- Loss of feeling around learning: numbness, being zoned out, diminishment of vitality around learning
- Feeling detached from learning events; just going through the motions
- Losing interest in learning experiences you once enjoyed
- Loss of learning ambition, not much courage or bravery in the face of learning difficulty

~~~~~~

assessing they've endured since they entered school. "I hate Scantron," said my vivacious student Aliza about the company that invented the ubiquitous bubbled answer sheet read by computers for standardized testing. "Get used to it, though, because that's all you're going to get until you're out of school." Other students, numbed out, say school seems like a grind to them, even the self-reflective papers in which they are asked to analyze their own opinions. One student said to me last semester, "I just don't want to write about my opinions or reflect anymore. I prefer straightforward assessments." Like jilted and disappointed lovers, some of my students just want to be left alone.

When school is constructed as all about achievement and attainment, with little that we feel choiceful about or deeply engaged in, we become numb. We sometimes can be roused to resentment—"I don't want to know *why* it's like that. Just tell me how to do it on the test. Write out the first step, the second" . . . recalled Alec Resnick, an undergraduate at MIT who was tutoring a high school student in math. "The difference between the successful and unsuccessful student is that the successful student has adapted more effectively to the system, to playing the game," Resnick observed.[22] When school becomes a cynical labor where every intellectual move is based on a calculation about how it will affect our chances of getting into college or graduate school, or, on the other hand, we've already been branded a failure, we become numb to the pleasures of learning. Ultimately, we lose interest in ourselves.

Wounds of Underestimation

> Dear Mr. James,
>   I was in your 10th grade math class. I am writing to let you know how your attitudes and teaching methods have affected me. Many times, you rattled off formulas so quickly that if I failed to understand you, and tried to think about what you had said, I lost track and became

completely lost. After asking you to please explain more fully how to do the equation, I was spoken to like I was completely stupid. The one thing I did learn was not to ask for help in any of my classes; it was just too humiliating in front of my peers.

I can even remember going to you after class one day and making an appointment to see you after school. When the time came, I was there, but clearly you were uninterested. You completely ignored me and continued to write the next day's lesson on the board. I tried to speak up. You knew I was there, but the fear of you and your superior attitude kept me from saying very much. I left no more enlightened mathematically than when I'd arrived and continued to fail your tests.

To this day, I feel inadequate when it comes to math. That feeling kept me from attempting algebra and routed me into a general math class. That closed a lot of doors that I had always hoped would be open to me.

It also kept me from taking chemistry because you were teaching it. Your belief that the truly intelligent people would always do well on your tests and in your class is frankly foul. For years, I had little belief in myself. As an adult, I took my first university class—English. It was there that I finally learned my gifts and that I had brains. In your single mindedness and need to be right, you missed out on that.

Your former student, Debbie[23]

Along with conventional thinking and predictability, school can teach us to underestimate ourselves. John Taylor Gatto, an award-winning public school teacher for 30 years, described an incident that convinced him that school was a malignant, toxic institution for children, especially for children of color. He was a substitute in a third-grade remedial reading class, a classically "easy" teaching assignment because the students were considered unchallenging and the teaching tasks could be completed on autopilot. Gatto handed out worksheets and sat down to crack open the newspaper when "a little girl named Milagros Maldonado came up to the desk and said, 'I don't need to do this. I already know how to read.' There was a reader on the teacher's desk, and she grabbed the reader and said, 'Ask me to read anything.' I cracked it open to a story called *The Devil and Daniel Webster*, which is an extremely difficult piece of American Victorian prose. And she read it without batting an eyelash. I said to her, 'You know, sometimes, Milagros, mistakes are made. I'll speak to the principal.' I walked into the principal's office and the woman began shrieking at me, saying, 'I'm not in the habit of taking instruction from a substitute teacher.' I said, 'I'm not telling you what to do. It's just that this little girl can read.' And she said something to me that, at my dying moment, I'll still remember. She said, 'Mr. Gatto, you have no idea how clever these low-achieving children are. They will memorize a story so that it looks as if they know how to read it.' Talk about an Alice in Wonderland world! If that little girl had memorized *The Devil and Daniel Webster*, then we want her in national politics! The principal said, 'I will come in and show you.' After school, she came in and put Milagros through her paces. The little girl did well. Then she told Milagros, 'We will transfer you.' And when Milagros left, the principal said to me, 'You will never be hired at this school again.'"[24]

In addition to the assaults that come from being non-White in our culture, children for whom English is not a first language, or children who have learning differences, are especially vulnerable to wounds of underestimation. In his wonderful memoir of growing up "learning outside the lines" with learning differences, Jonathan Mooney describes many of the things he was called by his teachers, beginning in first grade. Most of them were something like, "lazy, crazy, stupid." My own college students confirm this.

Many of my most skillful, persistent, and successful college students are those who have learning differences. If they have made it through school and been accepted at a small, selective liberal arts college, they generally have unusual degrees of self-knowledge about how their mind functions ("I know how my brain works," said one student with severe dyslexia) and also have developed incredible endurance and self-discipline that have helped them overcome many intensely negative school-based evaluations. One of my students recently reflected on his own school experiences. "I personally have had a teacher tell me that I would be lucky to graduate high school. My third-grade teacher once told my parents that I would more than likely drop out of school before I had the chance to graduate because of my learning disability. This leads me to the point that I do not see any of my teachers before college having anything to do with how I regard myself as an intelligent person. However, I do see my parents playing a large role in how I see myself and how smart I am. My parents told me that if I worked hard enough . . . I would someday have everything that I wanted and more. . . . This gave me one of the . . . best work ethics in my class in every school I had ever attended." As I explore in the next chapter, American schools tend to have very narrow views of what constitutes intelligence and of those abilities that "matter," and many with wounds of underestimation have had to strike out on their own to discover their skills and talents—to learn to appreciate themselves.

Shawnee, another college student with learning differences, wrote about the school for dyslexic pupils she finally began to attend in the middle grades. "That school completely changed my life, because all through elementary school, although no one was really mean about it, I felt stupid. I got no grades on my papers. I was pulled out of class when everyone else was taking a test. Kids piled up star after star for reading books in elementary school, and I was always the one with the fewest stars because reading a book took me such a long time. At my new school, the headmaster explained on the first day, 'You are a special and powerful person, and you just need to learn how to cope with being in school.'"

In addition to labeling kids who learn differently as problematic, sometimes defective, most schools classify, track, and categorize students from very early ages. As an abundance of research studies confirm, these classifications tend to become self-perpetuating and self-confirming. My interviewees illuminate the ways in which grades, tests, and opportunities to learn are often arbitrary, or related to class, race, and gender. In the supposed meritocracy of schooling, these markers and estimations have profound impact, not just structuring how we fit into the learning hierarchy of an individual classroom, but "who" we are and whom we believe we will become.

One of my students recalled, "I can remember my first experience with tracking. It was in third grade. After lunch our class had reading time. Reading time originally was conducted with the entire class and all the students took turns reading out loud. One day Mrs. Par explained that we would be broken up into groups. Mrs. Par called my name and explained that I would be going to another classroom for reading group. I quickly realized I was being put in the group with the slow-reading, stuttering kids that I thought were stupid. This group was a collection of all the minority and working-class students. I said to Mrs. Par, 'I don't want to be with the dumb kids.' I was immediately raced out of the room and scolded for making the other children feel bad. But no one did anything about my self-esteem. So, I was now tracked into the lowest group, where my academic self-concept still remains to some degree."

Not only do these tracking decisions tend to become self-fulfilling, they are frequently based on social-class distinctions. A brilliant young student of mine wrote about the way not being a fluent reader, and his parents' working-class social status, created wounds of underestimation from which he was still recovering.

"I was a poor reader put in the low expectations group from third to eighth grade. This had a profound effect on my education. I had never been documented as having a learning disability. I was just considered a slow reader or lazy, and my parents were not providing honors-track pressure on the school or me. This lack of advocacy allowed the school to sweep me under the rug. As a result, the school did not have to provide any special education resources (meaning money) to prepare me to attend college, because I was deemed unsuitable for higher education. This was the situation for a select group of kids, most of whom were from my neighborhood.

"The active sweeping away of the slower students was somewhat covert. For example, if any special education director saw my spelling test scores, a red flag would have shot up. But my teachers manipulated my scores by always telling me ahead of time which 15 of the 20 spelling words would actually be tested. This was the case for me and about seven other children in one section of the middle school. This small advantage allowed our scores to remain good enough not to invoke serious attention but did nothing for our learning or self-esteem. I think the logic of my teachers was that they were protecting us from the disappointment of bad grades.

"By the end of my middle school years I had no idea how to get good grades. This caused me to become less focused on my studies because I felt doomed. I was essentially a D and F student receiving inflated B's and C's. Teachers reinforced my feelings of inadequacy and social immobility. In eighth grade all students take a test that rates your personality traits and interests in order to suggest career paths. I remember being very excited when my sheet recommended that I become a lawyer or judge. I went up to my science teacher, Ms. T ("T" being the first letter of a very long Polish name no kid could pronounce) and told her that I wanted to be a judge. She said, 'No, Neil, you should go into radio because you are always talking.' This comment cemented my understanding of where I was meant to belong.

"With the understanding that I was miserable about my current school setting, my grandmother, who had a little bit of money, offered to send me to a local private school for high school. Now this school was no Choate, but it was a good school. I was placed in lower level math and science classes when I arrived. I still had difficulty competing in even the lower-level classes. I eventually started to learn the basic skills I had not been taught in the lower track and became part of the average. By senior year, I was one of five students actually given admission to AP English. Unfortunately, the class was canceled because of the lack of acceptable students. As a senior in college I am still working on refining the skills I was not properly taught in my middle school years. Because I was ability grouped through most of school, climbing the hill of higher education has been far

~~~~~~

WOUNDS OF UNDERESTIMATION

- Sense that we are not fully "seen" or valued in school due to our social-class standing, race, ethnicity, cultural background, gender
- Sense that assumptions are being made about us based on identity issues
- Learning outcomes constructed to "confirm" rightness of these assumptions
- Outright denial of access to learning due to assumptions made about the learner
- Difficulty in naming of underestimation wounds, sense that underestimation is "normal," the way it is and no other way is possible

~~~~~~

steeper. But I am extremely lucky, because of the other six kids that I was tracked with through middle school, not one of them attended college. I actually see one of them every time I return home, working at the Mobile gas station next to my highway exit. He's there every Friday night, working the late shift."

Wounds of underestimation are the most common lacerations I encounter in my interviews. For any number of reasons—social-class standing, race, gender, immigration status, or learning differences—many, many individuals have found school a place that teaches them to value themselves less highly then they find, or suspect, they should. In the 1970s Ivan Illich, the great school critic, wrote that school's primary function was to "instruct us on our own inferiority."[25] Many with wounds of underestimation are spending significant energy healing from those wounds.

Wounds of Perfectionism

> What happens to people with adaptive perfectionism when they encounter life problems? . . . Certain dimensions of perfectionism result in depression when perfectionist people encounter life difficulties that highlight the fact that things are not perfect.
>
> —Gordon Flett and Paul Hewitt,
> *Perfectionism: Theory, Research, and Treatment,* 2002[26]

We admire "effortless" achievement in American culture, and school systems tend to laud those who seem to succeed in school without appearing to expend much effort or missing a beat.

Sometimes, however, those who have been successful in school, with its clear reward structures and scaled attainments, can have trouble once they leave school. Perfectionist systems (especially for high-achieving students) ultimately can be disabling in the world beyond school. Michelle, a human resources executive, was a nearly perfect student all throughout elementary and high school, and then on through college. In our interview she told me that she was so "perfect" in school that she frequently had trouble relating to other children. "I would pretend to complain about classes and homework, make things up, but really, I loved it. I got 100% on everything and I identified with adults." The well-behaved child of a large, church-going Lutheran midwestern family, Michelle always did well in school. School's strict orientation toward predictable tasks, learning expressed through clearly defined assignments, rule following, and an externalized reward structure suited Michelle's intellectual and personal style extremely well. She was an exemplary student and universally attracted the respect and admiration of her teachers. She went on to do very well at her state university, where she graduated on the dean's list with a nearly 4.0 average. "I was such a good girl in school. In fourth grade I would volunteer to stay inside during recess and correct other kids' homework for the teacher. I always felt very self-confident in school. I was very comfortable in that environment and understood how it worked."

After graduating from college, however, she says she found the professional world very "unpredictable," and sometimes almost frightening. "Real life was a drag. I was really annoyed with having to leave school and go out into the world of work. I thought about graduate school and continuing on being an academic, but I felt I didn't have that many ideas of my own to pursue. So basically, I've become another kind of teacher/administrator in my job, going through my to-do list and always seeking the perfection of completion. But that never happens."

In the hothouse culture of high-attainment high schools, competition and the push toward perfectionism are intense. In 2006 Kaavya Viswanathan, a sophomore at Harvard College, was prominently in the news after a spectacular fall from her perch as a perfect student. Viswanathan, the only child of well-to-do, upwardly mobile Indian parents from suburban New Jersey, was raised with a multipronged plan organized around a single goal: to gain entrance to Harvard. When Viswanathan was a junior in high school, her parents hired a college entrance counselor from Ivy Consulting, a firm that helped her put together her application materials for college at a cost of $50,000. The college entrance counselor, also a literary agent, thought that Viswanathan's writing about herself might make a good "chick lit" novel for young adult female readers. Viswanathan was introduced to a book packager who helped turn her ideas and writing into something highly saleable. Lo and behold, the book packager spun Viswanathan's original drafts—initially "too dark"—into something light and commercially appealing. Two months after Viswanathan entered Harvard as a freshman, she received a two-book contract with a reported advance of $500,000. The buzz in publishing was that Viswanathan "was too good to be true": She was beautiful, articulate, wrote well, was only 17, and was going to Harvard.

Viswanathan *was* too good to be true. Her downfall came from her own student newspaper, the *Harvard Crimson*, which revealed that passages from her book, *How Opal Mehta Got Kissed, Got Wild, and Got a Life*, were copied almost directly from two well-known young adult novels by another author. While the case was a feast for bloggers and commentators of every persuasion, whatever its moral, it was clear that Viswanathan had an immense desire to please—to fulfill her parents' and community's dreams of superhuman success. She fell to earth with an awful thud and suffered severely for her mistakes. Her publisher withdrew her book, she was on leave from Harvard, and her book contract had been canceled. Viswanathan perhaps felt pressure beyond what is possible for one person to handle: She needed to be perfect. She plagiarized, she says, "inadvertently" to meet the outlines of her contract. Perfectionism, and the demands of doing well, are unrelenting in a world that clamors for more success, more achievement, and more attainment, much of which in our contemporary educational era is expressed through academic markers and competitive success in school. All these are best produced mythically, seemingly effortlessly. In an article on the moral hazards of genetic cloning, and our cultural attraction to perfectionism, Michael Sandel wrote, "We appreciate players like Pete Rose, who are not blessed with great natural gifts but who manage, through striving, grit, and determination, to excel in their sport. But we also admire players like Joe DiMaggio, who display natural gifts with grace and effortlessness. . . . There is something appealing, even intoxicating, about a vision of human freedom unfettered by the given."[27] Perfectionism, in some sense, is about our wish to escape mortality.

Yet we are bound to the earth. Jake, a man currently in his mid-30s with two Ivy League degrees who underwent a job setback and a period of unemployment during his late 20s, told me, "I had a glass jaw, until a few years ago. I had to learn to deal with failure, and what to do about it. Frankly, that was something that rarely happened in school. It was all so clear what you had to do."

Wounds of perfectionism, like wounds of numbness, can lead one into academic alienation and, ironically, lack of success. When one has

~~~~~~
WOUNDS OF PERFECTIONISM

- Sense that what we have done in school is never enough
- Being activated by whatever the next goal is, always wanting to achieve "the best," or "the most"
- Fragility around failure; sense that failure or making a mistake will lead to catastrophe; feeling that any failure is a permanent blot on our record
- Alienation from our own learning lives due to excessive attention to goals of others
- Unwillingness to take risks in learning due to fear of mistakes
- Lack of pleasure in learning due to fear of failure
~~~~~~

wounds of perfectionism, anything less than perfection can lead to self-incrimination, depression, and renewed determination to reach the impossible. Failure leads to shame and self-loathing. Traditional schooling, with its strong orientation toward measurable outcomes, tangible grades, and clearly defined tasks, can exacerbate the perfectionist's drive for perfection, sometimes creating a cycle of underperformance. Being at the top of the heap academically in school, succeeding in every domain as no one else has been able to, is frequently the domain of the perfectionist—fragile and unfortunately vulnerable to depression and failure.

Wounds of the Average

> I'm in the middle.
>
> —Luke, a ninth grader, in Chapter 1

A concerned mother recently described her daughter Vanessa, a student who was a late reader in elementary school and subsequently tracked into regular instruction (like Luke in Chapter 1). Vanessa "blew off" elementary school and now seeks to establish herself as a serious student in high school, a difficult uphill battle because her teachers have already decided "what kind of student" she is and what sort of work she can produce. Vanessa's mother said to me, "I asked her what she was thinking about all that time in elementary school when she wasn't doing very well and wasn't paying attention." Vanessa said she was making movies in her head. Her mother describes how happy Vanessa is during those moments at the end of the school year when she can make a movie, cast her friends, and produce something that is really important to her. "Those are times when she is really happy, when she is really alive."

A child like Vanessa is, in the words of veteran educator Peggy Gonder, "typical of many students in classrooms across the nation. They are the 'kids in the middle'—caught somewhere between special programs for the gifted and the handicapped, but qualifying for neither. Sometimes we call them 'kids who fall through the cracks.' There are not enough resources to give them special attention. These are our 'average students' who are not challenged in school. Instead, they 'mark time,' doing the bare minimum required in class because they are not engaged by classroom discussions or assignments. Ordinarily, the problem is met with quiet discontent. Yet not living up to one's potential is not only an individual tragedy. Our nation's future . . . depends on educated people."[28] In other words, our nation depends on instruction and engagement of those students in the middle. There is abundant evidence that school wounds of the average are frequently unnoticed and unmarked, as this poem first presented at a PTA convention suggests.

> I don't cause teachers trouble,
> My grades have been O.K.
> I listen to my classes.
> I'm in school every day.
> My parents think I'm average,
> My teachers think so, too.
> I wish I didn't know that
> 'Cause there's lots I'd like to do.
> I'd like to build a rocket,
> I've a book that shows you how;
> Or start a stamp collection—
> Well, no use starting now.
> 'Cause since I found I'm average
> I'm just smart enough to see,
> To know there's nothing special
> That I should expect of me.
> I'm part of that majority,
> That hump part of the bell,
> Who spends his life unnoticed
> In an average kind of hell.

> "The Average Child," first presented at the 1979 National
> PTA Convention by Michael Buscemi, Quest International

Much of the research literature suggests that overstressed teachers and schools simply cannot focus on those who do not pose threats to account-

WOUNDS OF THE AVERAGE

- Belief that we can "only do so much," based on inappropriate testing or tracking in school
- Idea that our abilities are fixed and can't be improved through exceptional effort or focus
- Suppressed ambition and self-discipline due to our own low expectations of ourselves and those mirrored in our school environment
- Denial of our capacities, both internally and externally
- Feeling "unseen," unknown, undersold in school
- Not being very interested in ourselves

ability structures or create problems for teachers. While Peggy Gonder cites the problems of low expectations, tracking and ability-grouping practices, inappropriate testing, and passive learning models as all contributing to the problem lack of engagement, underperformance, and wounds of being considered average, in general these dysfunctions receive very little attention in the school reform discourse. Students who are wounded by "averageness" are highly reliant on parents and other supporters for sparking motivation and achievement. Reflecting recently on the wounds of being average, child advocate Stacey DeWitt recalled, "I sometimes choose to forget that [as an adolescent] I was average . . . , making Cs, failing to practice piano, going to the mall, and hanging out with friends on Friday nights. I didn't start to perform academically until I worked for a while, began to discover my true talents, and developed a love of learning. At that point, I went back to law school and became a very different kind of student. I started to perform when I found my passion. Before that, I was an average student at best, and luckily for me, my mom embraced the average—and therefore embraced me even though I wasn't winning awards."[29] DeWitt credits her mother with helping her see parts of herself that weren't evident to her in high school, just as Vanessa's mother struggles to preserve Vanessa's passion for movie making as she presses on toward high school graduation. "Sometimes I just hope she makes it through school, so she can go on to doing something that inspires her," her mother says worriedly.

Commonalities

While all school wounds are different, as my interviewees' stories make clear, they have some commonalities. They are produced in educational environments that are intolerant of cognitive, emotional, or identity differences, where feelings about being different provoke disapproval and shame. They are produced in school climates where there is pressure to comply to relatively narrow standards of performance, and where there is little choice for the learner in the educational task. They are produced in environments where schools are more focused on labeling and tracking students, and driving down differences between learners, rather than celebrating and acknowledging variation. School wounds induce alienation from ourselves as learners, reduce pleasure in our experiences of learning, and create internal oppositions or underperformance that many spend lifetimes trying to heal.

One of the great joys of our new Internet age are the daily blogs I read from individuals around the world about learning as pleasure. (I have a Google alert for "learning as pleasure.") In a recent blog, a mother, Heather, expressed her educational philosophy—her philosophy of learning as pleasure and unwounded learning—through her observations of her 8-year-old in the garden. The following is from "Living and Learning in the Garden," a post from the blog A Handmade Life. Like a lot of homegrown experiences of learning pleasure, it is modest, humble, and celebratory of human ingenuity and curiosity. It is a powerful vision.

"I guess I have some fairly unusual ideas of what constitutes an 'education.' I don't necessarily agree that having someone teach bits and pieces of disconnected information, a curriculum, to a child makes for a proper education. . . . So, while some parents might thrill that their kids have memorized the periodic table, aced a test in algebra, or are able to recite one of Shakespeare's sonnets, I tend to find pleasure in different things (although I do love Shakespeare). The other day E [the writer's child] was out in the garden and I mentioned to him that he might want to check if he needed to weed his garden bed. He went to have a look, pulled a few things, and then told me that the remaining tiny sprouts were lamb's quarter and he would leave those to grow so he could eat them. I went over to have a look, and sure enough, he had identified some tiny sprouts as the lamb's quarter that we had eaten often in the past. I said that I was impressed that he could recognize them when they were so small, and he told me that it was because they had a bit of a silvery look to the leaves—this made it easy for him to identify. Can I tell you how pleased this makes me? That an 8-year-old can recognize wild foods when they are tiny. I really don't see what can be a more essential part of an 'education' than how to get or grow our own food. . . . I often wonder how different schools would be if every one of them had a huge garden in the schoolyard, if every child had the opportunity to dig in the dirt, observe the insects and other critters, and taste the products of their own work. I'm so pleased to hear that some schools are starting programs like this and I hope that the children taking part are given the chance to 'just be' in the garden. I think there is a lot to be learned when we have the chance to just be" (http://ahandmadelife.blogspot.com/, May 2008).

Heather's simple observations, ironically, circle back to much of the newest cognitive literature on learning. The opportunity for self-exploration, for connection and meaning in learning, and for relevance in learning tasks, is redemptive and restorative to wounded learners. Heather and her son knew this by looking at lamb's quarter.

WHAT ALL SCHOOL WOUNDS HAVE IN COMMON

- Are produced in school environments that are intolerant of cognitive, emotional, or identity difference
- Provoke feelings of disapproval and shame associated with being different
- Originate in pressure to comply, with unsuccessful (or too successful) adaptations to the educational environment
- Produce alienation from self as learner
- Reduce pleasure in learning

⬦⬦

CHAPTER 3

Why Do Schools Lacerate?

Mass education was the ingenious machine constructed by industrialism to produce the kinds of adults it needed . . . the solution was an educational system that, in its very structure, simulated this new world . . . the regimentation, lack of individualization, the rigid systems of seating, grouping, grading and marking, the authoritarian style of the teacher—are precisely those that made mass public education so effective as an instrument of adaptation for its time and place.

—Alvin Toffler, *Future Shock*, 1970

Outmoded Institutions: The Legacy of Rip Van Winkle

One of my very first classes in graduate school in educational policy opened with the quote, "If Rip Van Winkle were to come back today after 100 years, the only institutions he would recognize would be prisons and schools."[1] It was a turning point in my vision of educational institutions, and has come to represent the way many now regard the conditions of their work in educational settings and the problems of school change.

As everyone knows, educational discourse is thick with theories about what troubles schools. Some policy analysts say teachers cannot do the work they are asked to do because they are undertrained and unsupported, while some claim that standards for success are simply too low. Some say that students today don't have the work ethic that they "ought" to or once appeared to have, due to the technologies they've grown up with and their tendency toward continuous partial attention and multitasking. Many professional developers believe schools have "gotten off track" and can somehow be turned around by a compelling, usually singular intervention—sometimes the one they are selling. Teachers' unions insist that their members should be paid more. Competition-minded reformers advocate merit pay for teachers based on results. Many learning theorists observe that the instructional core of teachers' work is weak, teachers work in isolation, and cognitive difference is poorly understood. A complex nexus of forces, assumptions, and ideas about the purpose of education makes it difficult to sort through these competing, sometimes contradictory, theories.

On one thing, however, most educational policy makers, teachers, parents, and students do agree. Almost everyone I speak with concurs that schools are fundamentally old-fashioned institutions. In their looks, in the way they manage time, in the way they control and influence people within them, and in the kind of learning "product" they produce—these are institutions designed for a different era and for individuals who, once graduated, were going to face radically different conditions of work. As Todd Rose, a young neurocognitive researcher I interviewed about his own learning journey in school, said, "These are agrarian institutions in a completely wired world; they just don't serve their purposes anymore."

Jeffrey Lackney, an architect who specializes in examining the effect of physical setting on learning, recently said of the classic American school, "Today's 21st century schools model 1950s architecture, use 1990s technology, and deliver 1960s curriculum."[2] Others are less modulated. David Rose, founder of a not-for-profit company that creates technology-assisted learning structures for students with learning differences, observed that the teaching and learning in most schools is like "stagecoach driving in a world where you have to operate a Ferrari."[3] In other words, lots of things about schools organizationally, culturally, and cognitively once may have made sense, but don't anymore. We just don't know what to do about this.

In *Horace's Compromise* (1984), a breakthrough book about the lives of teachers and students in high school, educator Ted Sizer remarked that "most Americans have an uncomplicated vision of what . . . education should be [and] this uniformity is of several generations standing."[4] The idea that schoolchildren should be divided into grades, that they should progress down a "line" of learning to an endpoint, and that their curriculum, movements, and thinking itself should be highly prescribed and graded, bespeak a 19th-century, product orientation toward learning. Humans are the product, learning is the intervention, and human beings, with a variety of beliefs, attributes, and inclinations, are the raw material to be shaped, imprinted, programmed, and shipped out.

Evidence is mounting everywhere that these ideas don't serve us very well, in terms of student engagement with school, students' readiness for college and work, and students' felt experience about the learning they did (or are doing) in school. Teachers find their profession off-puttingly isolating, lacking in community, mentorship, and teamwork, ever more complex and undercapitalized. Fifty percent of new teachers will leave the sector within the first 5 years of teaching, and teachers frequently experience mid-career burnout as they journey farther and farther from the sources of joy that originally drew them to working with children or young adults. As we know, employers also do not experience high school and college graduates as work ready, and colleges must offer remedial classwork to three out of five incoming first-year students nationally. In spite of increased standards, accountability, testing, and attainment pressure, actual performance of students in relation to our international peers is trending downward.

Yet we are terribly attached to an institution that does not, in the face of a great deal of evidence, serve us well. After studying the dysfunctions of the comprehensive American high school, one of my very thoughtful students said recently, "It's like we just can't imagine anything else. And if we survived it, then maybe it isn't so bad." Leon Botstein, president of Bard College, says that educational institutions are fundamentally "conserving" cultural and social structures—meaning that they are designed and meant to reproduce knowledge, understandings, and visions from the past. What are they conserving and reproducing?

Old-Fashioned Ideas About Knowledge

> Right before our eyes, all that the education sector has controlled, dismissed, manipulated, validated, embellished, fictionalized, and ranked within an aura of tradition and ritual may be accessed by point-and-click. We need to stop chasing exponentially expanding content. Inquiry, problem recognition and solution, creativity, knowing one's strengths and weaknesses, communication, and relationships are what students must be prepared for.
>
> —Vincent Hawkins,
> Director of Curriculum, Instruction, and Assessment,
> Springfield School District, Springfield, Vermont, 2007

In a book about the ways in which school is modeled around old-fashioned ideas of teaching and learning, my colleague Tony Wagner explores the kind of teaching and knowledge that is valued by most schools, even schools that are considered highly effective and are very good at getting kids into college. Taking the reader through learning walks of several prestigious upper-middle-class schools, especially those that are deemed "the best" by various ranking magazines and the media, Wagner finds that even the country's most admired schools "are not contributing significantly to this country's capacity for creativity, imagination, and innovation—any more than they are developing the problem-solving skills of our students."[5] In my work as an educational consultant, I am almost always interacting with school leaders and teachers on the problem of instruction that is too teacher-centered, and where the role of the student is defined as sitting passively receiving information and answering questions when called on. In terms of cognitive demand—usually classified in a taxonomy from least demanding to most demanding[6]—students in 80% of American schools[7] are typically working at the one or two lowest levels of cognitive demand: knowledge and comprehension. Students most often are being asked to do very low-level work: to recognize and recall material, facts, or terms, or to classify or paraphrase material. (Sometimes they are given huge mountains of it, making the work seem hard or rigorous, but this usually means an increase in memorization or application.) In assessment, there is an equally heavy emphasis on identifying and recalling information, and paraphrasing or clarifying material. I rarely see students asked to work in higher-level cognitive domains—analysis, evaluation, creation, and metacognition (thinking about their thinking)—and I usually find that teachers and students have trouble determining what higher-level content is and how to design and access it. We are deeply imprinted with the norms of teaching and learning by our own schooling, so that it becomes, in the classroom, invisible or normative to us. For many, low-level cognitive work is what real school is.

While being able to memorize, recall, and apply discrete "material" was once perhaps an adaptive model of learning, it is no longer. One of the reasons our forebears placed such an emphasis on rote memorization and low levels of cognitive work was that education took place in an era of information scarcity. Libraries, books, and even printed material were rare and precious. Being able to remember facts and details, and categorize information, was central to being well educated. We now live in an era of information overabundance and supersaturation, where more facts, ideas, and documents than we possibly can remember or interact with are available at our fingertips, 24 hours a day. Thus the logic of my daughter memorizing the state capitals or the name of every river in Connecticut, in a Google world, is increasingly debatable.

Emerging views of the nature of knowledge require new understandings of learning, instruction, and the student's relationship to the teacher—essentially new schools. Ideas about knowledge and teaching embodied in schools go back even further than the one-room schoolhouse and Horace Mann; philosophically they stem from the 18th century and the Enlightenment, when the intellectual project was to formulate general laws of knowledge—guidelines based on observation and experiment. Out of this quest for certainty came a kind of intellectual authoritarianism in

"END OF A PUBLIC SCHOOL CAREER RENEWS, NOT DESTROYS, AN INTEREST IN STUDIES"

The column below, from the Fredericksburg *Free Lance-Star* newspaper, was written by Addison Herron-Wheeler, a graduating senior at James Monroe High School.[8]

AS I ENTER the last nine weeks of my senior year, I am overwhelmed by an urge—not to ditch my studies and relax for the rest of the semester, but to pursue learning on my own to a more intense degree.

Now that I am finally almost done with the public school system, I am beginning to see it from an objective viewpoint for the first time. I realize that much of the material taught there is merely information that needs to be taught in order for the school to pass a benchmark in a certain area and earn more credibility points. The students are not interested in learning it, and, for the most part, teachers are not too thrilled to be teaching it.

I used to merely accept all this as a fact of life. Kids in school, even the super-smart ones, did not like to learn—at least, not the way public education had in mind. Teachers were paid to do their jobs, and they had to draw some pleasure from it, no matter how tedious it seemed. I thought of school as an annoying obstacle that I must overcome five days a week in order to do the things I wanted to do in my life.

In hindsight, I see how sad that perception is. I spent so much of my time doing something that I did not want to do, and now all that time is gone and I can never have it back. Yet if I had been idle all that time doing whatever I had wanted to spend all my time doing at various points in my life, playing with dolls or coloring all day, I would have been worse off than ever, because I would have no education.

It has been said a thousand times, but I really see now why the public education system needs to be reformed. Kids who have no intention of going on to college should be allowed the option of taking classes that enhance their interests, whether on sound production or tattoo art. People who love reading and writing should be given dozens of books and poems to read every day, and provided with interested and involved adults to talk about them with, in order to enrich their understanding of literature.

Maybe college will be like this—but the sad truth is, so many students get discouraged by the uniformity—and sometimes-pointless demands—of public school that they have trouble getting into college, or maybe never even want to give it a chance. And the cost of universities is such that many cannot afford higher education at all.

It is by seeing things this way that I have been able to view life with a clearer perspective. Over the years, especially recently, as I started to think about life after school, I almost gave up on literature and writing, the two things I know I really love, and the only things that have ever stayed consistent and solid as influences in my life. I now know, however, that institutions do not define literature. They can't, because it is an art form. No matter how many people try to define it or set rules for it or exploit it, it is still an art form, and there are still people who see it and use it as such.

No wonder I had such turbulent feelings—I was seeing everything through the eyes of one engaged in the logical, structured view of a public school student who was worried merely about her future in the most practical sense. Now I am accepting that my future could just as easily contain an award-winning novel, a rewarding career as a professor, a life of crime or an imminent death.

When looked at in that sense, a great book or an inspired line I jot down is just as important and meaningful as my future career, if not infinitely more so. With that in mind, I head into the real world, much more confident in what I love than I ever was in high school.

schools—if we could generate knowledge that was absolute and unchanging, without legitimate alternatives to it (a valuable philosophical project), the role of the teacher was to impart factual knowledge to vessels waiting to be "filled." This translates into teacher-centered classrooms and teacher-centered learning, with subject content and transmission of knowledge superseding values, skills, feelings, and relationships. Thus in many critics' eyes, schools became a new institution of social control.[9]

New Skills and Attributes Demanded

Obedience to authority, ability to tolerate boredom, capacity to thrive in a complex bureaucracy, the inclination to focus on a small domain of responsibility, and above all loyalty used to be attributes that were highly valued in the workplace. (Think of Willy Loman, the salesman in Arthur Miller's *Death of a Salesman*, or the longtime Maytag assembly line worker whose job has now been shipped overseas.)

Now what many CEOs and human resource directors say they are looking for in employees is self-confidence, persistence, and creativity about how to do the work better. They also prize the ability to grow in the job as the work changes, the capacity to change and adapt to new circumstances, the ability to make decisions under stress, the capacity to work with others—these are some of the keys to employability, many report. "It might sound a bit ironic, but new employees are of limited value to our company if they cannot grow out of the role for which they were initially hired," said Bill Engler, President of Diesel Power Equipment Company in Omaha, Nebraska. "Being versatile is the surest way to get yourself noticed. Even if you are in an entry-level position, demonstrating versatility will go a long way toward having management think about you when new possibilities arise," Engler said.[10]

Bill Gallagher, President of ADS Financial Services Solutions, a provider of systems integration and computer-based solutions for the financial industry, agrees that "hiring smart today means hiring versatile." Gallagher continues, "Our consultants work on an assignment basis, traveling every day of the year, forging new relationships—in an entirely new setting—with every assignment." Gallagher adds, "We'll take a risk hiring someone without technical expertise, but you can't teach someone to be confident or flexible."[11]

Confidence and flexibility have not been the attributes most prized and rewarded in traditional education. As so many have said, our ideas about appropriate behavior in school—ability to comply, hierarchical orientations toward knowledge, emphasis on low-level cognitive work, and learning to tolerate boredom—don't produce the kinds of entrepreneurial learning skills most needed by employers. I recently worked in a high school where some of the department heads were gravely concerned about the lack of students' initiative and drive. "The kids won't really challenge themselves," a department head reported worriedly. "They have inflated views of their own abilities." But when asked to consider the learning climate of students' pasts—constant, persistent testing since first or second grade, great concern with meeting state standards on every assignment and unit, and very highly controlled classrooms where students were asked to answer teachers' questions and otherwise not talk—the source of students' lack of initiative became clear. As the school critic John Taylor Gatto has said, "Lockstep schooling, driven by standardized testing, testing not to measure learning but obedience, was the mechanism used to drive out imagination and courage. It worked and still works superbly, but, like the little mill that ground salt when salt wasn't needed, this brilliant utopian construction is about to kill us."[12] Gatto says that these qualities may be our downfall.

Outmoded Ideas About Human Ability

One of my interviewees, Jarrell, felt lacerated by school because of the ways in which school evaluated his intelligence and ability. "I recall going to kindergarten as a happy child, with a vast imagination, and enormous amount of enthusiasm for learning," he said. "However, throughout the years in the traditional educational system, I lost a lot of my happiness, imagination, and enthusiasm. It all faded away and at an early age I was left confined to the labels of the outside world, largely based on the concept of intelligence. The school system was focused on organizing and labeling students based on so-called 'innate abilities.'" In Jarrell's view, this caused the school system to view intelligence and his abilities very narrowly.

Now the founder of an alternative school in Virginia based on "broad views of human ability," Jarrell continues, "While I remember the pervasive and destructive messages that were being embedded into me from school, I also received them from my parents, peers, relatives, and other adults. A very common reinforcer of the view of intelligence was when I got good grades, relatives, parents, and others would say, 'Oh Jarrell, what a great job! You are so intelligent!' But when I did not get good grades I often did not receive any response or acknowledgment from anyone, except my parents. This greatly wounded my self-esteem and self-concept. This sort of societal construct pierced my self-esteem armor over and over again to the point of disgust and self-hatred."

Over the past 30 years we have undergone a revolution in our understanding of human learning, human cognitive capacity, and human development. In his early, groundbreaking book on multiple intelligences, Howard Gardner[13] attempted to open the doors and windows of American educators' views of what constitutes "intelligence" and valuable academic performances. Gardner not only described verbal-linguistic and mathematical-logical abilities (the kind of intelligences school tends to value most), but he also made a claim for visual, kinesthetic, musical, interpersonal, intrapersonal, and naturalist intelligences. Subsequently, many other towering individuals in the field of cognitive performance, like Robert Sternberg of Tufts University, or Carol Dweck, researcher and author of *Mindset*, have attempted to widen commonly held views of the complex nature of ability and why effort in school is actually more important than traditionally defined ability.[14] But common notions of "smartness" still remain strongly embedded in school. As one of my interviewees said, many schools implicitly value a hierarchy of traits—ability to produce information or answers quickly, ability to remember material accurately, fluency with abstraction. Although not explicitly detailed, that these attributes are "still the ones that matter" is evident to most who inhabit the school community, and this mismatch continues even though they are only a very small part of the skill set desired in the world of work.[15]

In school we still rely a great deal on old-fashioned ability tests developed in the early 20th century, often no more comprehensive or penetrating than the practice of phrenonlogy—the study of personality through manipulating the bumps on the skull. Although IQ tests are unstable until late adolescence and largely discredited for determining a single, generalized ability quotient,[16] many schools still use these tests to sort children as early as first grade, and to determine performance expectations from that point forward. While one young woman told a story of being "saved" by the IQ test she took in fourth grade—she recently had moved from an elite private school to public school and her grades were plummeting, and after being given an IQ test she was determined to be "brilliant"—much more commonly I hear stories of people who have had the opposite experience: students who were informed that they were of only average or substandard abilities. Often these individuals went on to live their lives and make career choices based on the results of a single test, all the while unaware that the results might be misunderstood, inappropriately applied, or a "false negative." This was brought home poignantly when I interviewed a man in his 70s who could recall his "aptitude" scores on tests in fourth grade. Based on them he decided to become an accountant—a job he disliked and found dull—because he was never a good speller.

Jake, my student who developed persistence in the face of highly negative feedback from teachers, told me, "No teacher expected much of me. It was always a surprise to my teachers if I ever had a good test score." Jake relied on his parents and athletic successes to fire a sense of his own potential. Jake's capacity for hard work, and believing in himself and his view of his talents as broad and dynamic, ensured his success— not the messages he got about himself or his potential in school. We have been very slow to adapt our ideas of ability in schools, in part because the structure of conventional education supports and validates the sorting and labeling function. I was very heartened recently to hear a teacher say about some students, "They are doing well at this school because they have good conventional memory and attention skills, but they may not be developing the metacognitive skills they need." Most often I hear that kids are "smart" or "slow." I wish we could ban these dualistic words and ideas from our vocabularies.

From Teaching to Learning: We Aren't Good Diagnosticians

Although most individuals who work in schools are benevolently motivated and believe they have a good eye for seeing talent and potential in pupils, as Jake's story above indicates, the evidence is far from conclusive that they are right. As dozens of my interviewees have attested, teachers and other school personnel often casually, implicitly, and unknowingly wound pupils when they overfocus on single testing events, track kids into fixed ability groups, or decide "what kind of kid" someone is and insist on creating environments that reinforce this. As described in

Chapter 2, some of the most common wounds my interviewees describe are wounds of underestimation, where a string of bad test scores or grades, a lack of proficiency in academic English, or lack of understanding of the codes of school behavior tracks a student into underperformance for an entire school career. Perfectionism, where students become unwilling to take intellectual or spiritual risks in learning because they have cracked the code of school too well and are overly reliant on external approval for motivation and drive, is equally toxic.

In spite of somewhat greater familiarity with common learning differences, many teachers are poorly trained to recognize and cope with the many "kinds of minds," dispositions, and learning difficulties that children routinely present throughout their school careers. Most classroom settings do not support engagement with subtle individual learning differences, and teachers are trained to organize learning tasks around observable behaviors and testable events. Without ongoing training in tailoring instruction to individual learners (and support in doing so), "fault" for underperformance or disengagement from learning is frequently shifted to the child: The child is lazy, has an attitude problem, or refuses to work up to his or her potential. The child is enormously vulnerable in this system. He or she is almost always on public display, has little recourse in attending school, and has no shelter, no honorable way out, once they are there.

Like Charlotte in Chapter 1, who felt trapped in the pupil support center and without safe harbor at her school, I interviewed another young adult whose memories highlighted the immense impact that school's grouping and evaluative methods had on her sense of self. Although a perfectly rational practice—grouping readers in terms of fluency in first grade—for this individual the first-grade "yellow group" label has stuck with her into adulthood. "A major part of the first-grade curriculum is learning how to read. However, when I started first grade I realized that I was a little slower with my reading capabilities compared with most of my other classmates. The first time I realized this was when the teacher separated us into groups. We all had to meet with her individually and read a very simple first-grade-level book. She did this to assign us to our appropriate reading groups. The teacher would have the name of a color for each group so that the kids would not know what level that translated to. I was in the yellow group. Even though no one told me that yellow meant the lowest level, I could tell from the number of people in my group and their reading capabilities that I was in the lowest level. I felt stupid and embarrassed that I could not be with my friends who were in a higher level. Being in the yellow group has stuck with me all these years." Without an understanding of why the groups were formed, or that they were not value judgments forever (although sometimes they are), students are intensely vulnerable to school wounding.

Even the hardiest child and the most well-grounded parent have encountered moments when the child receives grades or evaluations that have the world-splitting force of moral judgment. My mentor Sara Lawrence-Lightfoot recalled how her parents were told by her second-grade teacher that "she just might not be college material"[17] due to some mishap in school. Lawrence-Lightfoot's parents were shocked and went home shaken and stunned. After they had had a chance to talk between themselves, they told their daughter they thought the teacher was absolutely wrong. Lawrence-Lightfoot is the first African American woman ever to receive an endowed chair at Harvard University, where she now teaches. My interviewees tell story after story about how in school we are much too ready to make hasty judgments about students' abilities, potential, and appropriate learning challenges, based on too little evidence and not enough training. We also often fail to appreciate a student's vulnerability in the moment—the yellow group moment—and the potentially life-shaping force of our evaluations on students for all their lives. "School can be a very harsh place to grow up," one of my interviewees said.

Schools Are Deliberately Designed to Sort and Track

Many theorists suggest that the purpose of schools is to mold and shape individual self-concept so that pupils will accept a particular place in society,[18] and that schools are implicitly designed to reinforce messages about race, class, and gender[19] and life expectations.[20] In other words, a central function of the structure of education in America is preparation for a capitalist society in which some will be winners and many will be losers. This means school *inevitably* involves sorting, tracking, and the scaffolding of human expectations, or, in essence, that wounding is necessary. The great school critic John Holt said memorably that schooling was like the meat packing business, designed to grade people like cuts of meat and send them off to the appropriate markets and customers.

Taking another tack, other researchers say that the middle class and upper middle class are highly attached to the institution of school explicitly as a sorting mechanism, as a way of justifying privileges of which middle-class members are already the central beneficiaries.[21] These critics suggest that the entire notion of schools as meritocracies actually reifies and reinforces class privilege—making those whom school rewards (those who already have a lot of benefits) feel they deserve the privileges they have.[22] I encounter this attitude frequently in my college students, who have been encultured in a system in which they are taught to believe that everyone can be successful if they just try hard enough and show enough initiative and competitive drive. In an exercise in which we compare side by side the costs of building an application that is likely to be competitive at a selective liberal arts college (sports lessons and clubs, community service projects, music lessons, SAT tutoring, AP tutoring) in relation to someone who does not have access to any of these things, my students are often stunned. The costs of "necessary extras" can total over $50,000 per child, conservatively—these are advantages simply not available to high school kids at an inner-city charter school for which I also work. One of my college students, who had interned in a college admissions office throughout her undergraduate years, described her gradually dawning realization that "merit" as defined by her institution was not as fair as she once imagined. Reviewing the data on the relationship between standardized test scores, family income, and access to extracurriculars deemed essential, she said, "Having worked in the Office of Admissions for over 3 years, I find it very interesting that [the same standards] are used for all students . . . I am now embarrassed and truly ashamed that I broke it down in such a way."

This set of ideas flies directly in the face of our visions of schools as places that find and celebrate talent, where everyone can succeed with pluck and hard work. It is hard for us to believe that our system of education actually could function like this, and from the outside, from a more distant vantage point, it may not seem like it does. Here is one of my college students wrestling with her own "privilege" as she was ability tracked all through high school, and the way her early high, prestigious track placement in school determined what learning she had access to. "I was most definitely tracked throughout my 4 years in middle school and my 4 years in high school. Upon entering middle school we faced evaluations in numerous classes that would determine which level we would be placed in for math, English, history, and science. I went through middle and high school in the same level classes and with the same students every year. Although we all may have recognized the pattern in the students who would walk into class each year on September 6th, I doubt that any of us acknowledged the system as characteristic of tracking. The reason why I feel this pattern was so 'acceptable' to students and 'unchanging' was because we were all used to the process. Because we experienced 'level-evaluation' in elementary school for the first time, we grew up taking classes determined by which level we 'placed into.'

"Thinking back to high school, I have realized more and more about how frequently tracking was implemented. As if a solid, permanent block of students, we moved from year to year together, as class levels, from classroom to classroom as what the school had determined to be all at the same 'intellectual level and capacity.' Students did not usually move up or down from level to level, and in the rare case they would, the student's entire schedule would have to be rearranged. Specific level classes are offered at specific times, and if you are in the same classes with the same people day in and day out, this will determine the time these classes are offered. Even if a student wanted to take regular class rather than an honors class, they couldn't because it didn't fit into their schedules. Each and every class offered at my high school was tracked, from woodshop and graphic design to biology and AP chemistry. Detracked classes were not an option for me as a high school student."

It is hard for teachers, administrators, and students who work within schools to "see" how these systems of privilege and advantage work because we are deeply invested in making the system work, have been shaped by it, or are benefiting from it. The economists Samuel Bowles and Herbert Gintis, who used economic data in the 1970s to show that school implicitly shaped what we think we can do, and what we expect for ourselves and others once we graduate (based on our socioeconomic status, race, and other factors), looked back on their work some 30 years later in 2001 and found it had held up very well. Their claims had been better documented and supported by other research than they ever imagined. While skill and talent are undoubtedly important in how we perform in school, Bowles and Gintis said that this accounts for only part of our outcomes. In the 1970s, "we advanced the position that schools prepare people for adult work rules by socializing people to function well, and without complaint, in the hierarchical structure of the modern corporation." Schools do this, Bowles and Gintis said, by something they called the correspondence principle, "by structuring social interactions and individual rewards to replicate the environment of the workplace."[23] In other words, education legitimates economic inequality by appearing to be fair and open to all, while actually acting as a very efficient means of reproducing social and economic status. My students and interviewees say that the difficulty is in recognizing this. This is hard to "see."

Inculcating the "Hidden Curriculum"

In the view of the radical school critics of the 1960s, the subject of my doctoral dissertation, schools were not gentle, apple-on-the-desk acculturating institutions, but were organizations explicitly designed to colonize, imprint, and shape from within the most vulnerable and least powerful individuals in our culture. As Bowles and Gintis suggest, or the Toffler quote at the beginning of the chapter states, school teaches us a "hidden curriculum" of values and ideas, and then convinces us not to question too fiercely the norms and values we are being shaped with. In some sense, school actually may be functioning *very well* to produce the "hidden curriculum"—the underlying skills, beliefs, and experiences that it actually intends and supports. Our problem now is that these skills and knowledge are not actually so useful to us as individuals or as a culture in a new era. But perceiving the hidden curriculum is an ongoing challenge.

One of the best descriptions of inculcation of the hidden curriculum I've read is a young teacher's exploration of her own journey from good test taker and teacher pleaser to conscientious witnesser of the psychological effects of schools. Kristan Accles Morrison's 2007 teaching memoir, *Free School Teaching*, explores the ways in which her school experiences taught her to be "insensible to my peers and the meaning of subjects, to disconnect from my peers and the subject matter . . . and [from] my very being and desires and experiences" (p. 21). Morrison says school taught her lessons in class position (high-track kids are taught and treated in very different ways than low-track ones), to become immured to constant outside evaluation, and to seek external validation for learning "even if it meant suppressing my urge to learn more and be stimulated" (p. 25). Finally, and most insidiously, Morrison describes how she was schooled in cognitive and behavioral dependence. "Outside evaluators praised me for my acquiesce . . . I knew that if I jumped through the assigned 'hoops' that I would graduate with tickets to the next hoop . . . I thus became a consumer of classes, degrees, and so on for the reasons fed to me by the greater society. Again, I was cognitively and behaviorally dependent. . . . Children are thus taught that obedience is paramount, that it often comes through suppressing one's true feelings, desire, and interest, and that if one chooses to disobey, it is best to do so in a surreptitious manner" (pp. 28–29).

Once Morrison became a teacher herself, she noticed how well she learned the lessons of the hidden curriculum. Although she was intent on not repeating the mistakes of her own teachers, she observed several things about herself she didn't like: that her own teaching seemed to be about "passing on to my students the lessons of the hidden curriculum that I had learned so well" (p. 32). She describes some key moments of realization. "I am in my third year of teaching. It is lunchtime and I am walking my kids to the cafeteria. We are required to walk quietly and in a straight line along the right-hand side of the hallway. Two of the girls in my class, I notice, are walking side by side, talking and laughing. I instruct them to stop talking and get in a straight line. They obey. I feel powerful" (p. 37).

Morrison observes that before attending graduate school and learning about the hidden curriculum of schooling, she had no language for her feelings of unease about some school practices, and no way of framing her own experiences. "The concept of the hidden curriculum was a true awakening for me. I have reexamined my experiences as both a student and a teacher and realized that I was a stellar pupil in learning some specific hidden curriculum lessons. I then in turn, naively passed these lessons on to my students. The lessons to which I refer are . . . insensibility, class standing, constant outside evaluation, and cognitive and behavioral dependence . . . . The educational critics I read . . . helped me to understand my life in schools—they gave me the words to describe my discomforts with teaching and made me aware of alternative purposes to education. I was able to see that education doesn't have to be conceived of in just one way . . . other visions existed."[24]

This process of "awakening" described by the radical school critics, Morrison, and many others is what many reformers are trying to enact around the culture and fundamental structures of American education. Although it is clear to nearly all that the system needs fundamental re-evaluation and rethinking, just what to do to bring about change often seems impossibly complex and difficult. Fortunately, due in part to the charter school movement and the many other innovative experiments in American education under way, some new, promising versions of school do exist.

New Ideas About Schools

> As a teacher, I feel that lecturing in a classroom within a brick and mortar schoolhouse is coming to an end. Instead, distance education will become a more common tool, and students will have a more customized education based on their talents, abilities, and passions in life. However, I often worry that I am still thinking "in the box" and my ideas and vision for the future are not great enough. The world is changing at a very rapid pace, and I want to ensure that I am doing all that I can to meet the needs of my 21st-century learners.
>
> —Dawn Shephard Pope, high school teacher, 2007

Other visions of schools are emerging.

A couple of years ago I wrote a profile of a breakthrough high school in Minnesota for the Bill and Melinda Gates Foundation. Seeking to find new models for educating high schoolers in a world where high school dropout rates are about 60% in some American cities and half of the public high school population consider the work they do unchallenging, superficial, and boring, the Minnesota New Country School (MNCS) represents a new way to think about educating adolescents.

Set in rural Minnesota, MNCS is a school designed entirely around project-based learning. It has no regular classes or courses. It is run by a teacher cooperative, which defines the teacher's role in the school, and it has no principal or central office. It has an extended, year-round academic calendar and uses Internet technology as a central instructional resource. It is rigorous—students are required to report to the school community on their projects every few weeks and to graduate they must complete an extensive, challenging independent senior project some describe as akin to a dissertation. Most important, says an MNCS founder, it is about "a different way to talk to high school kids. We are rigorous and revolutionary." Visually, MNCS is a school without walls—most of the 17,000 square feet of space is unpartitioned and, as one observer said, looks like a dot. com office.[25] The school is filled with open space and student and teacher workstations and meeting/work tables. And although it is without a conventional high school curriculum, daily course periods, high school bells, or high school homerooms, it has superb test scores and college graduation results. These are "farm kids with attitude," a founder says with pride. I visited MNCS early in its development; it now has become a national model for thinking about how to reframe the big box of high school education.

This is what MNCS looks like when you visit (but you should go online and look for yourself at http://www.newcountryschool.com):

- The curriculum—as evidenced by student work displayed around the school and that has been written up in local and national newspapers and education publications—is almost entirely student driven and student initiated. Student work over 4 years must fulfill the Minnesota Profile Standards for graduation, but those standards are only general frameworks for project origination.
- Students complete 10 projects a year (100 hours expected on each project) to meet the Minnesota state curriculum frameworks, in daily consultation with their advisors.
- Students organize their own workspaces and workdays, in consultation with their advisors; students account for and document their time daily. Projects generally take 5 weeks; students take 1 week off after the completion of a project.
- Students are organized into small (15–17 pupil) advisor groups and have strong advisory group relationships. These are mixed-age groupings, including pupils aged 14–18. Students often work with the same advisor for 2 to 4 years.

- School days, which include daily morning meetings, whole-school lunch periods (11:30 a.m.), and reading times between 12 and 12:30 p.m. every day for the entire school, are loosely but carefully structured.
- Much student work is rigorous, detailed, and sophisticated. Student work also tends to be unusually coherent, projects connecting thematically with one another through the years of high school and with other pupils' work.
- Public presentations of student work occur several times a year. Presentations by student to parents, community members, and other pupils and teachers are a necessary component of completion of a project.
- The daily atmosphere of the school tends to be one of quiet, serious intensity. Between 80 and 90 self-regulating and engaged students work in groups, in pairs, with their advisors, or on their own in pursuit of their own learning goals. During the period of my observation, I saw a minimum of off-task student behavior, or of adults engaged in oversight or disciplinary activities. Almost no kids seemed to be hanging out or uninvolved ("Adults are not the enemy here," a founding teacher told me); students also reported an unusual sense of friendliness and a minimum of exclusive, clique-oriented behavior among students.
- Students, advisors, and administrative staff members (of which there are a minimum) seem genuinely happy. ("School is so interesting!" "It's fun to go to school.") An air of contented seriousness characterizes the school setting.
- In recent years 100% of MNCS graduates have been accepted to higher education institutions; 90% took the ACT, and 20% of the seniors received merit-based scholarships for college. MNCS students' average ACT scores in 2005 were 23.3, compared with a national average of 20.9.
- Parents report an unusually high degree of engagement in, knowledge of, and satisfaction with their children's school experiences at MNCS.

When I asked a founding member of the MNCS staff what kinds of pupils, what kinds of adolescents, MNCS best serves, he thoughtfully replied, "This is a situation that really works for any kid, any adolescent who needs to exercise a choice about what he or she is learning. At first we have to teach kids [who come from school systems where they are acculturated to be passive around their learning] how to do this kind of work, but they catch on quite well. Any child who likes to determine their own learning—and I've never met a kid who didn't, when given a fair chance—does well here."

While untraditional in feel, MNCS serves many kinds of students well. "There is a myth that Minnesota New Country is for gifted students," says advisor and school founder Dee Thomas. Although she disagrees with that perception, "every student leaves here with the gift of knowing how to learn."

Compared with the Minnesota New Country School, and many others profiled at the Gates Foundation website (http://www.whatkidscando.org/specialcollections/student_learning/portfoliohome.html), which looks at small, breakthrough school models, many large, comprehensive schools seem outmoded and old-fashioned; organized around shame and blame, teacher-centered learning, and low-level assessment; and like low-level prison facilities.

As so many visionaries and other individuals involved in reframing schools and our ideas of education note, we are already in a new era of teaching, learning, and molding and shaping students. We are just waiting for schools to catch up. MCNS may help in pointing the way.

Part II

HEALING

Nobody escapes being wounded. We all are wounded people, whether physically, emotionally, mentally, or spiritually. The main question is not "How can we hide our wounds?" so we don't have to be embarrassed, but "How can we put our woundedness in the service of others?" When our wounds cease to be a source of shame, and become a source of healing, we have become wounded healers.

Our own experience with loneliness, depression, and fear can become a gift for others, especially when we have received good care. As long as our wounds are open and bleeding, we scare others away. But after someone has carefully tended to our wounds, they no longer frighten us or others.

When we experience the healing presence of another person, we can discover our own gifts of healing. Then our wounds allow us to enter into a deep solidarity with our wounded brothers and sisters.

—Henri Nouwen, *The Wounded Healer*, 1979

<hr style="border-top: dotted" />

CHAPTER 4

How Do
People Heal?

Why do some people emerge from grief strengthened?
Why do some others become strained, depressed, anxiety-
ridden?

—Nini Leick and Marianne Davidsen-Nielsen, *Healing Pain*, 1991[1]

"I Needed a String of Successes"

Todd Rose, a neurocognitive researcher at the Harvard Graduate School
of Education, has come a long way since his early experiences as a high
school dropout and stock clerk in a minimum-wage job in a small town in
Utah. Todd was the first child of youthful Mormon parents, who had him
when they were still in their teens. Todd's mom commented. "When we
had Todd, we didn't know what we were getting into."[2]

Although a loving and highly energetic youngster, Todd's childhood,
by his own description, was "turbulent. I was hyperactive and a bit destructive." From very early on in school Todd had trouble completing assignments, doing homework, following the rules of the classroom, and
feeling successful. He misbehaved and had poor social skills,[3] something
that is hard to believe when meeting this engaging and personable young
man now. "As a kid growing up, you want to be like other kids, to belong and to be liked. I thought I was like everyone else. I really didn't
know why people didn't respond positively to me." Without help or guidance from Todd's school in interpreting his behavior, he was constantly in
trouble. As Todd recalled ruefully, "Unfortunately, the feedback my parents got from school was terrible. My parents did the best they could but
they were young and inexperienced. The very same institutions that were

---

Note: The names, identifying details, and schools of the individuals in this book have
been altered to retain their privacy, with a few exceptions: L. Todd Rose, at the Harvard
Graduate School of Education; Lauren Connolly, at Wheaton College; Jonathan Mooney, author and learning differences advocate; Bernard Gassaway, author and educational consultant; Abigail Erdmann, teacher; Emma Abby, graduate student; and Tom Skiba, researcher.
I thank them all.

supposed to be looking out for my best interests ended up doing more harm than good when it came to helping me directly," Todd reflected. Although they understood that their son was special, Todd's father once said, "I always knew Todd was really smart. I just thought he was going to grow up to be a really smart criminal."

Common to many stories of school wounding and healing (outlined more explicitly in Chapter 5), Todd experienced school failure after failure. In seventh grade his class was studying poetry and his teacher offered a king-sized Snickers bar to the student who wrote the best poem for the class. "I had never had a king-sized Snickers bar before and this was a big deal. So I went home and spent 2 days at the kitchen table working on the poem. I thought it was a great poem. I said to myself, I'm going to win. So a week later when we got our poems back I was eager to get my paper. Not only did I not win, but I got an F. I thought, gee, it was at least worth something. So I asked my teacher about the grade and he told me, 'You couldn't have written that poem. There was no way you could have written that. It was too good.'" From that point on, Todd says, he just quit trying in school. He said to himself, I quit, I really just quit, although occasionally he would have small pockets of success. In his junior year he flunked every other subject but got an A in Advanced Placement European history, one of the most academically challenging classes at his high school. Ironically, this made people angry with him because it showed that he had some academic talent. He finally dropped out of high school without graduating—with a .9 average. "You have to work hard to do that badly in high school."

At that moment Todd didn't think he would ever return to school—his identity had become too deeply entwined with underperforming and screwing up. Although he had athletic talent, he had been kicked off every sports team he played on because of his low grade point average. He had held "innumerable" jobs throughout high school, performing well at them until he became bored and then behaving erratically. Academically, he was at sea. "Basically I became motivated to not do well—like what I could do well was not do well. In the literature we talk about islands of competence —in school I didn't feel like I had them. Everybody always tells kids like me, you're not trying hard enough. In a way it's a compliment because they think you have potential. But no one keeps on trying hard at things that they just aren't good at. No one." Shaking his head he says, "Kids that struggle are so much more sensitive to *moments*—especially bad ones. These moments shape their whole lives, their sense of themselves. Teachers' little comments had huge effect on me. School extinguished my love of learning, which is incredibly ironic because the thing I love the most now is the opportunity to learn. This is one of the reasons I love science so much."

About midway through high school Todd's family moved to another, larger town in Utah. At his new high school Todd decided that he would fashion himself after a high school football star from his old school. Todd said he figured that guy wasn't all that good-looking or smart, and thought he could be like him. "Imitation is a good form of learning. I tried to do exactly what this football star would do, to mimic his behavior and responses, so that people would like me. And it worked!" After he had become popular and well accepted in school, some patterns of change were established. If he focused, if he had a plan, if he followed through on his plan, he could be successful because he was highly motivated. "I could be a new person, I could rewrite my history. I could become Mike Anderson!" he said with a gleeful smile. Todd identified this geographic move, which allowed him to restart history, as critical to kids who are trying to pull themselves out of chronic underperformance. Todd said, "I learned from this. I learned I could do something. Something changed and that was really powerful learning; it began to build my self-confidence."

Another turning point in Todd's path of healing came when his girlfriend—now his wife—discovered she was pregnant and he learned that he was going to become a father himself before he was 20. "I was 19 when my wife and I had our first child. I remember we were sitting in the hospital, and I do remember as if it was yesterday. My wife was asleep from the delivery, and they brought in our son and asked if I wanted to hold him. I said okay. I didn't know what to think—it was all kind of overwhelming—and I just sat there and I realized just at that very moment that this is not about me anymore and things needed to change because there is a young lady and now a young child who are totally dependent upon the outcome of my life and that was so overwhelming."

The changes Todd needed to make to his life, though, were not achieved immediately—as he says, this is not a story of a miracle. After the birth of his son, while working full time, he studied for and received his GED, which he described as a small accomplishment. "The test is pretty easy." Then, after he had been talking for months about enrolling in college, his wife finally went down to a local university and enrolled him in evening classes. "She always had faith in me that I could do it. Our story is really one of growing up together, being best friends, and bootstrapping our way up for each other. Having someone who believes in you, really believes you can be successful, is also a key part of my story."

Now enrolled in college, at first Todd took only "easy" courses, things he thought he would naturally be interested in, like psychology and economics. His dad had advised him to take only courses in which he had a lot of inherent interest so that his motivation wouldn't flag. "That was some of the best advice I have ever gotten." To everyone's amazement, including his own, Todd began to get As. He also decided once and for all to take medication for his ADHD, with which he had been diagnosed in 7th grade. "Back then I wanted to be like other kids, so I wouldn't take the meds. I realized in college that medication really did have a purpose, it helped me focus." Having seen him screw up so much, his extended family kept waiting for him to hit the wall, he says, to not make it, to start doing poorly—but this never happened. "In college, as I began to prove myself, my professors began treating me like a success. In fact, I was the best student in their classes. This was something I had to get used to. I had one professor I didn't turn in a paper for and she approached me and said, 'That's not like you, Todd.' [Todd said he thought,] *No, that's exactly like me.* I realized I was changing, and people were seeing me differently. I think this is huge, to be in new environments where people start to treat you like you are a successful person. I could never be in any college classes with anyone from my high school. I would immediately withdraw if someone from my academic past was there." Seeing himself in a new way, taking on the identity and mantle of a successful person, was also a turning point in Todd's journey.

After several years of increasingly strong performance in college, the thought of graduate school crossed Todd's mind. "It was kind of a silly thought, really. It was sort of fleeting. I knew I really enjoyed psychology and neuroscience. In college I thought there would be a point where my intelligence was going to hit a brick wall and I'd take a class that was too hard—okay, this anatomy class is going to be the one, or this statistics class is going to be the one, and actually I excelled in those things and was invited to be a teacher's assistant."

Toward the end of college, with encouragement from several professors and mentors, Todd applied to a wide range of graduate school programs. Although it was kind of "a distant dream" to attend Harvard, Todd applied, never believing he might be accepted there. He sent in an application with the attitude, "Why not?" One day when he was away at school he got a phone call from a professor at Harvard that his wife answered. Todd came home and his wife had a huge smile on her face. She said, "Kurt Fisher called. He said you got in." Todd says he was speechless. He didn't believe it and was sure that the Harvard admissions office had made a mistake. He called Kurt Fisher [a professor at the Harvard Graduate School of Education] back, but said he was dumbstruck. "I'm sitting there and I didn't have a thing to say. I'm sitting there on the phone with this man I admire so much and I can't think of a thing to say."

Although graduate school was a huge adjustment—"I wasn't nearly as well prepared as I thought I was"—Todd discovered the intellectual passions that animate and give purpose to his life now. "I love science. The philosophy of science, the mind-set of science is so different from what I was raised with that I've just really come to appreciate that. I grew up not knowing anyone who wasn't Mormon. That is a school of thinking that starts with certainty—this is the one true Church, that is a certainty. Science is completely different—it starts on a completely different basis— let's assume we know nothing and begin with that. I really appreciate that. Ultimately, it's about whether you are willing to change your mind. What would it take to change your mind? That's what I'm interested in."

Now a researcher at the Center for Astrophysics at Harvard, after receiving his doctorate at the Harvard Graduate School of Education in the interdisciplinary field of Mind, Brain, and Education, I ask Todd what his dreams for the future are. (His wife was just accepted into a master's program at Harvard.) "I have big dreams. I want to be a scientist, I want to make a contribution there. And I also want to fundamentally change the way people think about kids with learning disabilities and how people treat them. Schools are such outmoded institutions, and there is so much garbage out there about how we evaluate kids. The evidence is so clear, we do know what we can do to help kids, but school environments aren't responsive to that. If I can change the way life in school is for kids, so they don't have to go through what I went through, that's valuable." In addition to his research and academic writing, Todd is also a compelling cognitive researcher on learning in schools.

I ask Todd if he had a moment of recognition, a point in his life where he came to see that there might be something wrong with the ways in which he was regarded in school—not just that there was something wrong with him. He replied immediately. He said the difference in the way he was "understood and framed" in various educational environments was very significant for him. "Back in public school in Utah, people got mad at me all the time for blurting things out, being rude, saying inappropriate things in class. I was the troublemaker, the bad kid, the stupid kid, the screwup." Now, he says, in graduate school, "I'm pretty much the same guy, doing the same things, but here I'm considered brilliant and witty and insightful."

For Todd that realization—he was the same guy, interpreted completely differently—was a moment when his outlook shifted, and his desire to change schools began to burn like a flame. "None of the things that happened to me," he says, his eyes filling with tears, "needed to happen. That's what's so sad about it. I want to change that."

School Wounds Are Often Invisible

Death and grief counselors tell us that the first work of recovery from injury is recognizing that our sadness, our grief, our sense of loss—our feelings themselves, in all their contradictory complexity—are real. We cannot comprehend loss, grieve, heal, or be re-energized unless we acknowledge that an injury has occurred. Acknowledging the wounds of education can be an unusually painful, mysterious, and opaque process, however; denial of school wounding is one of our most profound cultural discourses. Throughout our lives most of us have been taught to count our blessings for our education, to be grateful for the opportunity to go to school, and to attribute our educational discomforts and injuries to our own lack of ability. Most of us tend to profoundly personalize both our successes and our failures in school, seeing ourselves as the single source of both triumph and failure, and to look very little at the cultural surroundings that create them. ("I'm really smart, that's why I do well in school," not, "I was brought up in a family with abundant resources that enable me to do well in school.") Equally, our failures tend to be deeply personalized. Almost all the individuals interviewed for this book believed profoundly that their difficulties in school were caused by their failure to apply themselves, to exercise self-discipline, and to be committed to their own success. "I never really thought I had *the right* to feel wounded," said a grandmother in her 60s. "School was not mine to question."

David Stoop, a psychotherapist and founder of the Center for Family Therapy in Newport Beach, California, has done groundbreaking work on the "paths" of healing from significant psychic wounds—wounds of parental neglect and abuse, marital infidelity, and incest. He describes the problem of denial of wounds—both cultural and interpsychic—as a significant barrier to healing. He notes that denial of wounding actually intensifies our psychic hurts and impedes our ability to let go of our inner resentments, forgive, and move on with equanimity and resolution. "We must accept the fact that we hurt. We have suffered because of someone else's actions [or our own]. What makes it worse is that 'someone else' is usually very close to us. . . . The choice is always the same: to accept the reality or to deny it. Denying it—repressing it, pushing it down inside us—only intensifies resentment and stops the healing process."[4]

Grief and loss researchers Nini Leick and Marianne Davidsen-Nielsen also describe a grieving phenomenon they call ambiguous losses, losses that are "unclear" because their outcomes are difficult to articulate and tend not to be recognized by the surrounding culture and therefore often are not evident to the individual him- or herself. "A lack of recognition of loss is a source of stress. If the loss is accepted, the feelings of grief become accessible and the state of stress can be resolved in a healthy way."[5] One of the great struggles described by my interviewees is this sense that they have "lost" something in school—something undescribed and unrecognized by the culture—but the dearth of words to describe this, the lack of recognition of these losses, tends to turn them inward, to locate blame in themselves, or to deny these feelings altogether. My student Ross wrote in a self-reflective paper about his learning experiences, "I was always taught that if I was screwing up in school it was because I just wouldn't buckle down and work hard enough—that's what my parents told me, and that's what my teachers told me." Without a frame for comprehending experience, students understandably end up blaming themselves for their school underperformance. David Stoop points out that this exclusivity of self-blame leads us down the path of denial, with the final destination— depression and loss of pleasure in learning—unfortunately inevitable.

Cultural Denial

If cultural denial of school wounds is one of our most powerful educational discourses, evident in the approval received by those who work hard and play by the rules, and the disdain for those who are not successful, the sense that "school is supposed to be hard" (not necessarily intriguing, complex, uncertain) is strongly associated with the discipline and punish tone of the No Child Left Behind legislation and the Protestant roots of many of our educational ideas (knowledge is certain and the point of education is to induct students into these certainties). Although many individuals in this book were aware that through their school experiences they had become disassociated from pleasure in learning, or felt angry that their talents seemed invisible in school, many also received strong messages that this was their fault, their personal failing, and due to deficiencies of theirs. In the culture of school, where authority for learning is rarely seated in the student, pupils often are encouraged to suck it up, to conform, to keep a stiff upper lip, and to understand that "learning is hard, so deal with it."

The culture of school also encourages denial of wounding. If school underperformance or learning reluctance seems to the pupil him- or herself as more complex than simply being "lazy or careless," students are strongly discouraged from advocating for themselves or critiquing the

HOW DO WE DENY SCHOOL WOUNDS?

1. We deny that an injury ever occurred. "I'm fine. Nothing that happened in school was that big a deal."
2. We make excuses. "School sucked for everyone! I'm not the only one."
3. We blame ourselves. "If I had worked harder, been smarter, been more self-disciplined, I wouldn't have had those negative experiences in school."
4. We say the purpose of school is to learn our place in the world. "I needed a little pushing down."
5. We grant superficial forgiveness. "Oh sure, that teacher made mistakes, just like everyone else. I don't hold anything against them." "Oh well, I guess test scores didn't really matter." By granting superficial forgiveness we deny the reality of our feelings.
6. We attack those who suggest we need to deal with the feelings. "Aren't you just part of creating-a-victim syndrome? School is supposed to be hard."

The effect of denial is to devalue our emotional experiences and, often, to visit them on others. "It worked for me. . . . " Underlying this denial is often deep shame and regret.

system. They are told, in effect, that their wounds don't really matter, or that "this is the way it is—get used to it." That's the school system they are in, a globally competitive, flat world, so "deal with that, too." Todd Rose, who opened the chapter, was never encouraged to articulate his own learning needs in relation to the environment of school; by his own description he wasn't aware that he had unique learning needs in the first place, or that anything about him as a student was of special value worth cultivating or investigating.

This cultural denial of school wounds has practical implications: political fragmentation and interpersonal exhaustion. As a culture, because we don't yet have a discourse that allows us to frame school wounds personally—in terms of being denied pleasure in our own learning—we also lack a coherent larger critique of our systems of schooling that keeps us from questioning why educational environments operate as they do. We don't yet have language to frame our problems with institutionalized schooling in affective terms, except in somewhat atomized ways—we

COMMONALITIES OF HEALING STORIES

- Jonathan's mantra: "Good things come out of bad things."
- My deficits are the shadow side of my great gifts.
- I am good at learning from my mistakes; my mistakes tell me things I need to know about myself.
- I can always do better; I have high expectations for myself.
- Mistakes aren't the end of the world! (The painter Robert Rauschenberg's motto was: "Screwing up is good!")
- Challenges are wonderful—being labeled and told what you cannot do isn't.
- I define myself—not other people, nor the institution where I go to school.
- I am kindly toward myself.
- I know how my own mind works; I work with my strengths, and wisely and strategically compensate for my weaknesses.

join the homeschooling movement or enthusiastically embrace contrarian writers or reformers who speak to these issues.

As a practical matter we also tend to be totally preoccupied and consumed by the problems of individual children, or groups of children (as researchers and policy makers), and to focus less on the institutional and cultural conditions that lead to school wounding. When writing about parents and children with learning differences, student advocate Jonathan Mooney notes, "None of us have the hours or the stamina to question anything [about the educational system] because we are so preoccupied with [our own] children's immediate problems. There is not a moment to question our culture's ideas about schooling or learning, or to consider whether the idea of learning disabilities is contributing to educational or social inequality."[6]

So how do people move to recognition of their wounds, and then to healing? At this point, our efforts are still largely individualized, and the product of long, slow journeys through painful educational experiences in which individuals come to see their own narratives through the larger frame of the institution itself. The stories of healing in this chapter, however, have many commonalities: individuals whose profound academic failures and deficits seemed to overshadow most aspects of their existence, who slowly came to realize that their "deficits" were the shadow side of their great strengths, their gifts.

THE DENIAL DISCOURSE IN ACTION:
"KIDS SHOULD GET THEIR BUTTS IN GEAR"

In this online column from *The Flint* (Michigan) *Journal*, the author, Kelly Flynn,[7] says students should "get their butts to school, sit down, be quiet, do their work, quit whining, and make [their] parents proud." While Flynn raises some good points about the importance of effort and attitude in school success, she denies that schools themselves have any responsibility for school disengagement. It is the student's fault if he or she fails. This column is a pungent example of the discourse around denial of school wounds.

"It's Time We Put Some Responsibility Back on the Students"

I just read the following in an education e-newsletter, the ASCD SmartBrief: "Some 7,000 high-school students drop out of school every day, at a cost to society of $209,000 per student over their lifetimes. Between 20 percent and 42 percent of graduates require some remedial coursework before moving on to college-level work, and 60 percent of manufacturers say recent entry-level hires were unprepared for the work they were hired to do." The question facing educators and business leaders is: What can be done to reverse this trend? Well, I know one thing we can do.

Let's put some responsibility back on the student.

See, what we seem to forget is that it's all there for the taking. If you want an education in this country, you can have it. The information, textbooks, workbooks, journals, reference books, videos, technology and lab equipment are available, to one degree or another, in every single school.

And what's more, almost every school offers more than academics. Art rooms are filled with paints and paper, music rooms with pianos and sheet music, theaters with playbooks and props, and in many cases there are vocational classes to introduce careers like health care or journalism.

Even the poorest schools are full of information, and people who are ready, willing, and able—aching, actually—to teach a student who wants to learn. It makes teachers nearly weep with frustration to see bright, capable, talented children slide lazily along, refusing to partake of the bounty of knowledge that is offered to them.

All any student has to do is open the books, read the material, study for the quiz, write the paper, listen to the teacher, and try.

I'm fed up with the steady drumbeat from partisan groups that continuously, relentlessly, incorrectly, and nauseatingly bash the public school system in America, as if educators are solely to blame for low test scores.

We have sold the children in this country a bill of goods that says they are responsible for nothing, it is our duty to spoon feed them, if they don't like the system we'll change it, if they screw up we'll cover for them, and everything will be handed to them.

Whether it's an allowance or a grade, kids need to know that they have to work for what they want.

Education reformers rant that the public school system needs to "improve outcomes." Well, how about improving input? How about sending us some students who are eager to learn so that we don't have to force-feed them?

It's about time we tell the kids in this country: get your butts to school, sit down, be quiet, do your work, quit whining, and make your parents proud.

"My Creativity Is a Large Part of My Intelligence"

The Albatross

Often to pass the time on board, the crew
will catch an albatross, one of those big birds
which nonchalantly chaperone a ship
across the bitter fathoms of the sea.
Tied to the deck, this sovereign of space,
as if embarrassed by its clumsiness,
pitiably lets its great white wings
drag at its sides like a pair of unshipped oars.
How weak and awkward, even comical
this traveler but lately so adroit—
one deckhand sticks a pipestem in its beak,
another mocks the cripple that once flew!
The Poet is like this monarch of the clouds
riding the storm above the marksman's range;
exiled on the ground, hooted and jeered,
he cannot walk because of his great wings.

—Charles Baudelaire, *Fleurs du mal*, 1857

This past semester I had the pleasure of instructing Lauren, an enormously talented young woman from New England whose writing gifts and engines of self-expression were exceptional. Lauren was a poetic, accomplished writer at age 20, but she had struggled a great deal in school, and had very nearly not made it to an academically challenging college. In fact, but for extremely supportive and patient parents, and moving to a smaller, more nurturing educational setting in high school, she might have been a student whom the system lost—who never began to realize her potential.

Lauren began her learning story like this: "In preschool my parents were called in for a parent teacher conference to discuss how I was doing in school. Mrs. Brushy informed my parents that all my teachers enjoyed having me in class and my lively, humorous personality made me stand out from the other children. However, Mrs. Brushy mentioned that there was something that concerned her. She told my parents that my vocabulary was somewhat weak. For example, every time I was asked to name a picture of an apple, banana, strawberry, or pear, I would respond by saying, 'FRUIT!' When my parents heard this they fell into hysterics, picturing my braids bouncing up and down, and my bright blue eyes widening as I declared my confident answer. Of course they knew they were not the parents of a baby Einstein, but they did not want to be. They admired my unique personality and all the quirkiness that came with it."[8]

This was the pattern of gently voiced concern in Lauren's parent–teacher conferences in her elementary years. "In the first grade I took my spelling quizzes at Mr. Morris's desk, my little feet dangling off the edge of his large executive chair. I felt special. My mom told me it helped me concentrate, when I questioned why I was allowed to sit at the teacher's desk while the other children stayed at their assigned tables. Looking back now, I'm happy I associated this accommodation with positive feelings of being 'special.' Not until later did being 'special' become a negative quality."

In second grade Lauren's problems began to worsen. "I often found myself being scolded for talking during class. I became lost within my imagination where I was transformed into a savage, orphaned child who had to subsist on mud cakes and honeysuckle. While I enjoyed many aspects of school, my strengths were in my creativity, my ability to understand and relate to their and my desire for adventure. However, as I grew and matured so did the culture's expectations of acceptable behavior. Girls were encouraged to be quiet and reserved, smart and studious. Playing pretend was no longer an acceptable activity to engage in and after sixth grade I found myself abandoning the one thing I had found comfort in for so many years, my imagination. Without my imagination, school was dull and frustrating. I continued to enjoy learning but found that the only subjects I excelled in were English and music. I have always had a passion for music and singing, and knew from a young age that I had talent. I remember how the other children would fall silent when I sang out loud in front of the class, and when I got my first lead role in the school play. I was proud of this talent.

"Soon the demands of schoolwork and sports became too much to handle and I had to drop out of the Periwinkle Performers theater program I had been enrolled in for the past 3 years. My focus turned back to school where all my insecurities were waiting right where I had left them. I now understood why I went upstairs to the 'study skills' room and worked with Mrs. Ferris on math and reading. I now understood why I left my homeroom class to go to Mrs. Goldman's homeroom for math. I now understood why, after 8 hours in school, I had to go straight to the yellow house of my tutor where I spent another hour working on, take a guess, math. I remember my tutor's sharpened pencils writing neatly on the yellow lined paper. Inside this yellow house, written on this yellow paper, was the only place where math made sense."

Lauren's memories continued. "I kept my frustrations about school hidden from my parents and friends. The corners of my tests were quickly folded over to hide my grade before I even got the chance to look at it. I can still feel the lump that would lodge itself in my throat upon seeing a failing grade, the disappointment that weighed on my shoulders threatening to break my back. I avoided telling my mom about the results of a test in the hopes she would eventually forget. I wished I could save her from the disappointment when I confessed that despite the hours of tutoring and extra help from my teacher, I still got a bad grade. Even though my tutors responded to these grades in a gentle, kind way, I still felt as though I had failed everyone, including myself. I wanted to scream at everybody: tell them that it was not my fault, but I truly believed deep down that it was. Many times I wished I could trade my musical talent for academic talent. I remember thinking, 'What's the point of being good at something that doesn't even matter?' Although I received testing all throughout my elementary time in school, there had been no conclusive findings. After freshman year in high school and a D- in math, I went back for more testing. This time the results were different.

"I remember standing in the kitchen, waiting for dinner preparation to be finished. 'So the lady called from Chestertown, the one that did the testing a few weeks ago,' my mom said, glancing up from the cutting board. 'Yeah?' I said, because I felt very cautious. 'Well, she said you did really well, but she found that you had ADD [attention deficit disorder]. We've decided to put you on Ritalin to see if it helps.' She was smiling and I couldn't figure out why this was making me smile, too, which made me mad because at that moment this was the worst news I had ever heard. I immediately went into defense mode, getting angry with my mom for telling me this lie. 'I don't have ADD,' I screamed, as my mom's smile quickly dropped from her face. I was silent for a long time, my gaze focused intensely on an invisible spot on the countertop, allowing me to avoid seeing everything else. I was embarrassed by these three little words that now defined me. If this was true, then how come I had spent so many years frustrated? Why had I been made to feel stupid time and time again and only been told to 'try harder'? I had been trying. For over 10 years I had been trying and now I was finding out that I had a neurological disability accompanied by words such as 'slow processing' and 'testing anxiety.' I declared that night to my family that I didn't want anyone to know that I had ADD.

"Since I was diagnosed with ADD, my performance and attitude toward school have changed dramatically. I realized that my frustrations had come from my inability to concentrate and focus on allowing myself adequate time to understand that information. I was allowed to take my tests and quizzes in a separate room where I could sit for as long as I wanted without being distracted by other students who would be turning in their papers before I got to the second question. I continued to work closely with my tutors, who supported and applauded my smallest achievements. One tutor in particular, Ms. Chanda, changed my mentality completely. She tutored me in math and made it her mission to not only help me understand math, but also she used to tell me over and over how smart I was. She would attend my basketball games and concerts and always seemed to find a way to make me feel as though I was one of a kind."

Lauren's story is also an example of healing that was supported by a nurturing, well-informed school climate. "My understanding of my intelligence has made me want to become a teacher. I know better than many other people what it is like to struggle in the classroom and experience years of increasing frustration. Although I have had my setbacks and challenges since I arrived as a freshman, I believe I am finally beginning to feel that I know what it is like to be regarded as 'smart.' I am learning something new every day and am genuinely interested in the material I am studying. I no longer feel as though my efforts are being wasted on meaningless substance that will only make me look stupid once I am tested on it.

"As a teacher I hope I instill in my pupils the messages that were instilled in me: appreciate who you are, recognize what you have to give, and never, ever give up on yourself."

For Lauren, coming to realize that her "weaknesses"—her unusual ways of seeing herself, her expressiveness, the richness of her imagination—were strengths was a turning point in her painful journey through elementary, middle, and high school. Beset by messages about the ways in which she did not seem to reach her potential in much of her schoolwork, Lauren described going inward, becoming covert about her writing and about herself overall. Like Todd Rose, whose story opens this chapter, it was not until a change of scene—going to college, and engaging in work that actually was choiceful and meaningful to her—that Lauren began to achieve her true potential and that her gifts as a writer began to express themselves and be recognized. At a different stage of life than Todd, Lauren also is beginning to feel for the first time that who she is as a learner is not simply a damaged and wounded self, but someone who has immense capacity for creative expression. This is a huge change for her; Lauren painfully described being told by a college guidance counselor that her college essay "could not have been written by her," because it was too articulate, too well put together, that it must have been plagiarized. Like Todd's being denied authorship of his poem in seventh grade, Lauren's wounds of underestimation were only beginning to heal.

"I Felt I Was Bad, Almost Morally Defective"

Shame and anxiety had filled my life, were my life, for so long.
—Jonathan Mooney, learning differences advocate

Learning activist and best-selling author Jonathan Mooney also writes frequently about his journey of healing—from "intense screwup" kid to deeply engaged and successful adult. When I interviewed Jonathan for this book, he said his story of school began with an inchoate soup of bad feelings. (Mooney has chronicled his own journey of healing in his two books, *Learning Outside the Lines* and *The Short Bus: A Journey Beyond Normal*.) Severely dyslexic and diagnosed with attention deficit hyperactivity disorder in elementary school, Mooney did not learn to read until he was 12. To this day his spelling abilities—his phonetic awareness and orthographic memory—are still in the 7th percentile. Jonathan often opens his speaking engagements with kids by initiating a spelling contest, which the kids always win. Then he goes on to tell them how he graduated from Brown University as an English major with honors and won a prestigious fellowship upon graduation.

Mooney was a severely troubled child, who describes his anxiety and self-loathing as seizing him, like "a beast that crawled up my stomach and into my lungs and my head."[9] For Jonathan—and Todd and Lauren and Bernard, later in this chapter—his troubles with school started early. "My struggles in school started the first day in kindergarten. At recess there were these small metal bikes that I had never seen before, and I loved them. The rules were that you had to ride them in a practical pattern tracked on the concrete; I couldn't follow the lines, so I was banned from all the bikes. I also couldn't tell time. One day, when it was my turn in the time-telling circle, I guessed 10 o'clock. I was right. From that day on, no matter what time it actually was on the toy clock the teacher held up, I blurted out, 'Ten o'clock.' All the kids laughed. I learned quickly that it was better to be the funny kid than the stupid one.

"In second grade we all had desks lined up in a row like workstations in a factory. I tried to sit still, but I couldn't. Five seconds into class my whole body was moving—hands, feel, and arms . . . I was pointed at, ordered to stop moving, to control myself. Miss C., my teacher, yelled, 'Jon, what is wrong with you?' The rest of my day was spent out in the hallway, my spirit evaporating in the thin air. I was the bad kid, the stupid one with the terrible handwriting, spelling, and reading."[10] Jonathan, like so many of my interviewees, felt morally defective for not doing well in school. "That feeling ate away at my sense of self like battery acid."[11]

Jonathan's path of healing, although more vivid and fully articulated than most, encapsulates the journey of reclaiming the self that many of the subjects of this book describe, from one of self-loathing, blame, and profound shame, to recognition that an injury has occurred, to grief and anger about what has been lost, to acceptance and re-engagement.

Jonathan vividly sketches his inner turmoil during his "desire to be normal" period. "High school was a constant battle between the [conformist] . . . side of myself and another side that tenuously believed I had a valuable mind," he recalled. A gifted soccer player with a strong and unconventional family behind him, particularly his mother and sister, Jonathan tried hard to succeed in traditional ways in high school: He dated a cheerleader, was a jock, and got an athletic scholarship to college [he attended this college for only 1 year]. He began to hate soccer, however, and by the time he had landed the scholarship to play soccer in college, he was profoundly conflicted about the game—feeling that it represented what people knew of him and how they identified his successes, but that this identity was unreal to him. He got injured, did poorly in his first year of college, and dropped out. He dreamed of transferring. Wanting, like Todd, a complete change of scene and change of life, Jonathan applied to Brown University in Providence, Rhode Island—a place where he thought he would never be accepted. He flew to the campus to demand an interview. After waiting outside the admissions office doors for hours without an appointment, he was finally given a hearing. Jonathan was accepted to Brown.

At Brown, he says, he discovered himself authentically as an intellectual for the first time. He took hard courses and majored in English, something he was told would be too difficult for him—yet he triumphed. During his first days at Brown he met another student who also had been diagnosed with learning differences, and together they wrote a book called *Learning Outside the Lines*, which became a bestseller. For Jonathan, his process of recognition of his wounds came with success—yes, some conventional success—but also a deeper and more critical examination of what is considered "normal" and the effect of the school system on others. "My mom had told me that the system was broken but I realized . . . that I hadn't always believed that. I believed I was broken."[12]

At Brown University Jonathan became immersed in critical theory and ideas of social justice, theories that challenge conventional paradigms of school and the function of education in a capitalist society. "My mom was always a Marxist, and had these kinds of theories about school, but at Brown that whole part of my consciousness expanded." From this critique of the institution of schooling, Jonathan began to see disability itself as a social construction and to believe about himself that his so-called learning deficits were also his greatest strengths. As Jonathan says, he found his inner warrior. "Whether we know it or not, the warrior developed over years of fighting for our identities in school—surrounded by families who fought side by side with us—and in our struggles in the workplace and society. In the end, this is who we are."[13]

Jonathan's transformation from denial of his wounds—which he dealt with through drinking, unsafe behavior, and attempting to be conventionally successful—to recognizing that his wounds were real and honoring them allowed him to begin to accept who he is. "It's been a long, hard road to get to where I am today, but I'm here—a twice-published, dyslexic author, an energetic public speaker, a father. [I am in this place] because of my enthusiasm, my awareness of others, and responsibility to make the world a better place for that kid [whom I once was]," Jonathan told me.

Now Jonathan is an activist for people with learning differences, has his own mentoring project for students with learning disabilities (Project Eye to Eye, http://www.projecteyetoeye.org), and is a widely published and acclaimed author. His activism is based on his nuanced and deeply personal critique of the institution of schooling. "The battles for children who are different are brutal for everyone who tries to wage them. . . . [People] get exhausted. . . . There is not a moment to question our culture's ideas about schooling or learning, or to consider whether the idea of learning deficits is contributing to education or social inequality."[14]

For Jonathan, his long journey to self-acceptance and activism has come from the attitude drilled into him by his family members, his wife, and now himself: "Good things can come out of bad." Jonathan says he repeats it like a mantra.

"You See What They Think About You When You Act a Fool"

> According to my birth certificate . . . I was born a Colored
> baby. All this time I thought I was born a Negro or Black.
> —Bernard Gassaway, *Reflections of an Urban School Principal*, 2006

In the 1990s, Bernard Gassaway was one of the most successful urban high school principals in New York City, winning several awards for leadership, innovation, and excellence when he was principal of Beach Channel High School in Rockaway Park, New York. Now in an urban school leaders doctoral program at Teachers College, Columbia University, Bernard began his story of school wounding and recovery with a striking anecdote about his youth, one that indicates the distance he had traveled from 14-year-old boy running the streets of Brooklyn to senior superintendent of New York

City public schools. "Back then, in Bedford Stuyvesant, I was hanging out with a group of homeboys who were headed for trouble. One day when I was supposed to be in school [three other boys and I were] scurrying like little mice through this apartment. We were looking first for cash . . . then we began to assemble the goods to be sold, televisions, a stereo, and jewelry. I kept my eyes on the homey with the money. I didn't want him to stash any. All of a sudden, a shadow appeared at the front window of the apartment. . . . It became clear that the shadowy figure was a cop."[15]

As one of seven children whose mother raised them single-handedly "with great love and old-fashioned discipline," Bernard recalls school as not terribly challenging intellectually. "I can remember schoolwork being very easy, finishing all my homework before classes ended, and being given extra work to do at the back of the room that the teacher rarely checked." Although he was highly capable, his elementary school teachers seemed to focus relentlessly on Bernard's behavior, not his academic promise. "I am sure I held the record for the most suspensions in elementary school. It seems as if I was suspended every other week. As per school policy, I stayed home during my periods of suspension. I was probably suspended more for defiance of authority than fighting. Two suspensions in elementary school stick out in my mind. I was suspended for 5 days. I returned to school on Monday. I was then suspended on Tuesday for another week. My mother tried disciplining me the only way she knew. Literally, she tried beating the hell out of me." Nothing seemed to help. Bernard eventually was required by his school to see a child psychiatrist at Brooklyn Jewish Hospital, where he says he remembers playing board games. "Looking back on my elementary school experiences, I believe the school officials lowered the threshold for what they would accept from me. I will never doubt that some of their actions were justified. However, there were times when it seemed as if suspension was their answer for the smallest infraction." In some sense, Bernard says, "I was a victim of my schooling."

In spite of the trouble Bernard caused behaviorally, his academic gifts propelled him to the top of his sixth-grade class. At the beginning of sixth grade, he was placed in the highest performing sixth-grade section of the school, much to his disbelief. "I was not happy. I could not relate to the teachers and the students. All of my friends from around the way were in a special class called 6-109. It was a smaller class for disruptive students. I wanted to be placed in that class. So I began my journey of disruption. I worked at that—it required a strategy. In 1 year I moved from the top class to the bottom class to finally, 6-109. Students in the top class were not my cup of tea." Bernard was committing "suicide by educator," a process he described poignantly in his own writing. "Children who seek suicide by educator deliberately act in a disruptive manner towards teachers or children, provoking confrontations, failing grades, suspensions, expulsions or arrests. They feel disconnected, uncared for, stressed, confused and angry. . . . To them, school is irrelevant; failure is common; life is rough; fights are frequent. They lash out at school officials both verbally and physically. Anything or anybody may become the target of their anger. School personnel are not trained to deal with the level of anger they are experiencing with children; as a result, they often respond to them with punishment, suspension, failure or arrest."[16] Punishment, Bernard noted, only leads to more failure and more punishment. "It's a cycle that doesn't work for kids. It's the cycle we're in in too many schools."

Bernard is especially sensitive to the ways in which children get labeled and typecast in school, and how this labeling affected him. At one point Bernard received an award for outstanding academic performance, and he and his mother arrived at the awards ceremony unsuspecting of the circumstances. Bernard had been given an award as a special education student, for students with emotional disturbances who also performed well academically. When Bernard saw kids coming in to the reception area in wheelchairs, he thought he was in the wrong place. After the ceremony was over, when he and his mother got outside the venue, his mother laughed at Bernard's apparent consternation. "You see what people think of you when you act a fool." Bernard began to feel the sting of his status.

"I loved the wisdom of my mother for laughing. But when I won this award, the label of emotionally handicapped became relevant to me. I don't recall ever receiving an evaluation to receive this classification. They, the school officials, did whatever they wanted. I do not doubt that my behavior gave them cause for concern. However, an emotionally handicapped classification was arbitrarily assigned to me. The same was true for many of my contemporaries."

In seventh grade Bernard provoked a teacher physically and got "slapped around" for his provocative behavior, not only by the teacher but by his mother. Bernard became more truant and continued to skip school frequently. He was, in his own words, hurtling toward self-destruction. "I was on a path, sure, a path to dying. I was a kid who had leadership potential but who was not acting like a leader. Some homey would say, let's go do this, and I would say, yeah, let's. I was following along." His mother, at this point, was also frantic about what to do about him, and was at her wit's end. One day around then she told him, "I'm just going to leave you in the hands of the White man." She meant, really, the police.

After a series of increasingly serious crimes and arrests, Bernard faced a Black judge for the first time in his life. Apparently seeing some potential in Bernard, this judge decided Bernard needed a total change. Bernard was sent away to a correctional youth camp in upstate New York. He credits this move, and the judge who put him there, with saving his life. "I am one hundred percent convinced that my journey to Annsville Youth Camp [run by the New York State Division for Youth for the most difficult juvenile delinquents] in 1975 saved my life. I was quickly approaching the 'I don't give a fuck' stage. This is the most dangerous stage for any person, especially a juvenile. Nothing matters. You don't even care if you live or die. So the judge essentially gave me a second chance at life when he took me off the streets of Brooklyn."

One of the reasons Bernard says the trip away from home to the youth detention facility had such an impact on him was that the people there, the adults, were kind. He described a teacher he had there. "Nearly 32 years ago, while serving [my] sentence, I met a teacher who taught math in a way I could understand. Before I met him, I was totally turned off to math. My teachers did not explain it in a way I could understand, so I shut down. Here's what I remember about this teacher. He wore his hair in a ponytail. He wore jeans and a t-shirt. He cared about us. He made us feel special. He took some of us fishing. He was nice. He was cool. He was patient. I never forgot his impact on my learning experience."[17]

Additionally, he says, all the adults at the facility were concerned about the well-being of kids, and tried to make connections with them and genuinely help them. This literally transformed Bernard's life. "When I returned home two things were clear: I had to get serious about school and I had to find a new group of friends." When I asked Bernard what he thought made his story so different from so many others, of kids who were not saved, he said, "Divine intervention. I am not kidding."

Returning from the youth detention camp, Bernard began to buckle down in high school and put some distance between himself and his old friends. He started playing basketball and working at an after-school job. Slowly, gradually, he began to advance on all fronts and his prospects for himself began to change in his own mind. Bernard's sister was attending college, and a student from his high school, one of his friends, went to college. Bernard began to consider higher education for himself. With the help of a physical education teacher and a social studies teacher, Bernard applied to three colleges and was accepted at all three. Now transformed into an "almost overly serious, super-diligent student" (his wife met him in college and she remembers him as being constantly at the library), Bernard enrolled at LeMoyne College in Syracuse, New York, where he became head of the Minority Cultural Society and, eventually, a standout graduate. From there, he received two master's degrees and began to work as a teacher.

In the late 1990s he became principal of a huge, troubled urban school in New York City. Because of his own background, his own perspective on "troubled," disruptive kids, Bernard was able to institute reforms at this school that were remarkably successful. Due to his exceptional work at this high school, he was appointed Senior Superintendent of Alternative Schools and Programs for the City of New York. Unlike some educators who believe that more discipline is better for troubled kids, Bernard explains his approach as a principal and school leader. "I'm a mediator, always willing to listen to kids. I try to work with them positively always—I told my staff, don't come to me if you want to be negative. I always try to approach kids from the vantage point of their dignity, honoring their self-respect, their need for autonomy and also to be understood."

Bernard reflects on his past and says, "I have some survivor guilt, about the things I did and the fact that I made it and so many others didn't. The fact that I lived past 17—after that everything is a gift." An optimistic, reflective, and profoundly modest man, Bernard is on to his next professional role, earning a doctorate and pursuing school leadership at a national level.

As a principal, Bernard was intensely committed to caring about, respecting, and understanding the children under his care, and they rewarded him with increasingly higher achievement, with renewed energy in participating in school, and by ushering in a new era at a formerly troubled high school. Bernard is now committed to saving other children like himself from committing what he calls "educator suicide," in his own work as a college instructor, consultant, and possibly urban superintendent again.

"Adults create these awful, chaotic environments for kids in which they can't be successful. Then they blame the kids for messing up. It isn't fair. We have to teach the adults to take responsibility. Kids don't have a choice about their life circumstances."

A Break in the Clouds

For some, healing school wounds begins when they experience success—sometimes for the first time in a long time, sometimes for the first time ever. For Todd Rose, who opens this chapter, gaining acceptance socially—and finding a girlfriend who believed in him—and then having a few early academic triumphs began to change his view of himself and his own capabilities. For Lauren Connolly, parents and college professors who consistently supported and lauded her writing helped her come to see her means of expression as a central and critical part of her personality—this was a "gift" her learning "differences" gave her. For Jonathan Mooney, hitting rock bottom in his first year of college, flunking out and leaving behind his soccer identity, and finding out that people around him still loved and supported him gave him the inner strength to apply to Brown University and be accepted. For Bernard Gassaway, being sent away to a juvenile detention facility and gaining some perspective on his life from committed teachers allowed him to begin to chart a new course for himself.

These were, and continue to be, hopeful but arduous journeys of healing, requiring courage and perseverance. Every individual interviewed in this book has struggled with the sense of having private and often profound gifts that are unseen by the world—this is palpable in every life story. The grit, determination, and perseverance that have been required to understand and grapple with those gifts—blessings that school did not appreciate—and to bring them to the world was long and tortuous work. Every individual in this chapter spoke about the depth and profundity of their wounds, and the ways in which healing from them has given their lives purpose—determination to change the paradigms through which children in school are seen. Every person in this chapter is now an activist: Todd is working at the national level to influence the ways difference is regarded neurobiologically in school; Lauren wishes to become a teacher who can nurture the love of learning and writing in other students who might be like her; Jonathan has created an international mentoring program for students with learning differences to better understand their own "normal"; and Bernard wants to use his life experiences to reframe the paradigms of school leadership.

The next chapter outlines in greater detail the individual steps of healing, incorporating more of Todd's, Lauren's, Jonathan's, and Bernard's stories, and suggests the path the reader might take him- or herself in understanding where he or she is in the path of recovery and reconciliation.

CHAPTER 5

Stages
of Healing

Not everything that is faced can be changed, but nothing can
be changed until it is faced.

—James Baldwin, *The Price of the Ticket*, 1985

Profound Gifts Nearly Lost

Todd's, Lauren's, Jonathan's, and Bernard's stories are of profound gifts
almost extinguished by a hostile school climate that is overly fixated on
measuring a narrow range of intellectual capabilities, expressed in ways
that are adapted to the needs of the institution, not necessarily the learner.
Todd, Lauren, Jonathan, and Bernard were very nearly lost due to their
school wounds. Their paths of healing—from private shame about their
perceived deficiencies, to anger and grief about their own losses (a place
where many get stuck), to "forgiveness," acceptance, and re-engagement
with a determination to transform the conditions that contributed to their
own troubled histories—outline the several stages of recovery that many
of my interviewees describe.

While many interviewees tell different narratives, of how easy it is
for the shame of nonperformance to re-emerge ("it was all my fault"), or
self-doubt to rear its head even after years of success and acclaim ("I had
just completed a series of talks about our work in our department and
I was seized with the idea that I was stupid," one marketing executive
told me), the path of healing is neither straight nor linear. Darik, a police
officer who was once "one of the worst juvenile offenders in the neighborhood," and who suffered from immense negative feedback in school,
says his educational failures are still the emotional background of much
of his life. "Depression and anger still haunt me—I'm really working on
being consistently happy," he told me during our interview. The path of
healing from school wounds resembles transformation after any profound

psychic laceration—it is long and twisting, the road gets fogbound, and we wander into the underbrush and get lost. But the healing stories in Chapter 4 and throughout this book also indicate that we can get better, we can move on, and we can experience new joy and engagement with our learning and life. This emerges, in part, out of our recognition of and growth out of grief.

As described in Chapter 4, the discourse around denial of school wounds is profound and powerful. "Just be grateful you were able to go to school"; "I'm sure that teacher didn't mean to say that"; "That's just the way school is. What can be done about it?" Many of us get stuck in this denial discourse. Yes as emphasized by counselor David Stoop, *to be in the state of denial is to be stuck.* "If we head down the Path of Denial . . . either we will deny that the hurt occurred at all or we will blame ourselves for what happened."[1] Either option, according to Stoop, leads to emotional shutdown and depression.

One of my interviewees, Mariah, was informed early in elementary school that based on general intelligence tests administered in third grade, she was of "only average" ability. Intuitively she felt that the tests were wrong, but she developed terrible test anxiety that stayed with her throughout middle school and high school. She "flubbed" her SATs, which didn't allow her to attend a highly competitive college where she felt she really belonged. All her life she has felt she never achieved her academic or intellectual potential. She suffers from intense self-doubt and often feels depressed. "I never feel like I'm going to live up to what's possible for me." Mariah is on the path of denial, where she blamed herself for test results that told her what to expect of herself, and decided, "They don't really matter anyway. Who cares? It's all water under the bridge." Mariah also has, in the research literature's terms, learned helplessness—a sense that her efforts on her own academic behalf will not pay off, so it becomes useless to try. Shutting down emotionally, being in denial, according to grief counselor Stoop, is actually a coping mechanism we use to protect ourselves from the pain of the injury. He notes that individuals in denial are not just trying to fool other people, but are also trying to protect themselves from experiencing the pain of their injuries. Stoop observes, "An interesting thing about denial is that its main purpose is to protect us from the truth. I used to think that people in denial were trying to fool me. And they are doing that to some degree. However, denial's main purpose is to fool oneself. We choose denial because we cannot face the truth. . . . We are mostly protecting ourselves from having to deal with the pain of what actually happened."[2]

The Blame Trap

> If you could kick the person in the pants responsible for most
> of your trouble, you wouldn't sit for a month.
>
> —Anonymous

To whom we attribute responsibility for our school wounds matters enormously, of course, and the healing, growing stories of the individuals in Chapter 4 indicate the need for a balanced, nuanced view on this.

On the one hand, we need to be able to critique many of the attitudes, structures, and instantiated beliefs of the educational system that wounded us—without denying personal responsibility for some of the negative outcomes and attitudes that made school difficult for us. This is a fine balance. Todd speaks about being constantly disruptive in elementary school, acknowledging he was a difficult pupil for his teachers to handle, but also believing that the school should have had a more informed and less punitive attitude toward him. Likewise, Bernard critiqued his school for constantly suspending him for bad behavior, while at the same time recognizing that sometimes school administrators had to take action—he fought too much on the playground and was oppositional in many of his interactions with teachers. (And as a school principal himself, he had to make many of the same decisions about students like himself.) Blaming others for our misfortunes and wounds can deny us a sense of personal control—we feel helpless to change our situations or our behaviors, and surround ourselves with resentment, anger, and negativity. As cognitive psychologist Albert Bandura's concept of self-efficacy makes clear, our beliefs about what we are able to do, and how effective we are at changing the course of our own actions, dramatically affect our outcomes.[3] We have to take responsibility for our part in our own wounding.

On the other hand, many of my interviewees placed the blame for their school wounds too much on themselves, and the world helped them to do this. School personnel frequently tell kids with learning differences, for instance, that if they would just try harder they would do better in school. This reminds me of something my husband, a researcher on school performance in the NCLB era, says: "If schools knew how to do it better they'd already be doing it." Kids, like teachers who struggle under the accountability laws of NCLB, are not holding back personal and private knowledge of how to succeed in school simply to thwart adults. Most of my interviewees told stories of desperately wanting to do well, and of

STAGES OF HEALING FROM SCHOOL WOUNDS

Self-blame and private shame

Points of light/moments of insight

Grieving: Anger and sadness

Reconciliation: Activism/engagement in change

being injured because they felt they were not able to. For many, then, feeling unfairly blamed and misunderstood leads them to become oppositional and defiant, reducing their chances of acquiring the skills and knowledge to actually succeed in school. It is a vicious cycle that often has a deeply personal tone. Darik, the police officer who struggled terribly in school, was accused by his father of deliberately doing poorly in school to embarrass him, the school principal. This made Darik feel so angry and so helpless, he then really did begin to instigate trouble. As he said, "Why not?" In my interviews, rather than students craftily "denying" high performance, I more frequently have heard tales of boredom, disengagement, and self-blame, even self-blame for the boredom. ("I am sure that if I only paid better attention, Ms. Merrithew's closing the blinds and using the overhead projector after lunch to teach honors geometry would be more interesting. I need to try more.") The discourse of educational responsibility instructs individuals to blame their school wounds on themselves—not to also critique the institution, its methods of testing, and the way it shapes opportunities to learn, or to consider the interpersonal or social factors that affect school performance.

The outcome of self-blame is the same that of as denial: It leads to depression. As Darik said, although he has come such a long way in his journey toward recognizing his own strengths and feeling more confident in himself, being happy is still an elusive project. Grief theorist and psychologist William Worden outlines four essential "tasks" of grieving: recognition of the loss, release of the emotions associated with the loss, development of new living skills, and reinvestment of emotional energy in new projects and new ways of living.[4] In essence, Worden echoes the words of several interviewees: The project of experiencing the emotions associated with our school wounds is essential for healing and moving on from them. Cultural denial of our wounds makes these first steps difficult.

Commonalities of the Healing Process

Stage One: Self-Blame and Private Shame

> Shame has to do with who we are. When we do something
> wrong and feel badly about it, that is guilt. When we conclude
> that we are a terrible person because of what we have done,
> that is shame.
>
> —David Stoop, *Forgiving Our Parents, Forgiving Ourselves*, 1996[5]

As already described, given the immense cultural denial of school wounds, and the overattribution of school success and failure to individual, personal attributes, those who do not perform well in school tend to have deeply personalized understandings of their own experiences. These are private and tend to be shared with few. "I never wanted to tell anyone how stupid I felt," said one interviewee in his 40s. "I know that if I had tried harder, I wouldn't have flunked out." Because we personalize our wounds and assume that they are due to some inherent qualities in ourselves ("I assumed I was broken," said Jonathan Mooney), we often conclude that we are simply bad people, inadequate to meet the demands of our environments and lacking some vital stuff that is necessary for complete living. (Ironically, of course, this can cause us to try less hard and take on fewer challenges, actually intensifying our cycle of failure and shame.) Many individuals look for a way out of this cycle, this internal labyrinth, by avoiding academic situations they aren't good at, ceasing to try, deliberately "not learning," or rebelling in school and getting kicked out. They can develop a numb, defiant attitude, or become perfectionistic and intent on meeting the external world's every demand, another way of relinquishing control of our own standards. At the heart of each stance or way of coping is self-blame and private shame.

The quotes from my interviewees about how this dislocation and private sense of fragility feel are too numerous to capture. A second grader told his mother in tears as he got off the bus with one of his first marked papers: "I got a -2. I'm less than nothing." A third grader approaching her first state-mandated test at the end of the school year said, "I feel like I may not pass third grade. I'm so embarrassed." A graduating high school student with learning differences told me, "I had to cheat all through school to maintain a C average. It was a nightmare. I am such a fraud."

For Todd Rose, what he recalls most is a sense of trying so hard and just not getting it, and feeling like he was letting everyone down. "I wanted so much to be like every young kid, to have friends and things like that. I didn't understand why people didn't like me and didn't want to be around me. When you are little you just think you are behaving in the same way as everyone else." For Lauren, her kindly parents and tutors gave her support and encouragement and still she did not meet standards. "I kept my frustrations about school hidden from my parents and friends. The corners of my tests were quickly folded over to hide my grade before I even got the chance to look at it. I can still feel the lump that would lodge itself in my throat upon seeing a failing grade, the disappointment that weighed on my shoulders threatening to break my back. I avoided telling my mom about the results of a test in the hopes she would eventually forget. I wished I could save her from the disappointment when I confessed that despite the hours of tutoring and extra help from my teacher, I still got a bad grade." Bernard, too, expressed his sense of hurt at being misunderstood through anger, but now he is able to say a lot of his actions were about shame. "I still feel bad about a lot of the things I did."

For Jonathan Mooney, who wrestled with his mortification and sense of being wounded more explicitly than most, this period of private laceration lasted until he went to Brown University, where he finally was recognized for his intellectual brilliance and unconventionality. There he found other like-minded students who also had struggled all their lives with living under the veil of normalcy. Jonathan felt the strictures of self-blame begin to lift a little, just as the press to be normal and to fit in began to ease. Jonathan's second book, *The Short Bus,* is in fact an interrogation of the cultural idea of "normal" and a persuasive meditation on what we lose when we insist on "normal."

Stage Two: Points of Light and Changes in Self-Definition

For most individuals, that first sense of light breaking through the clouds of private shame and self-blame, or anger and resentment about school demands, came through an experience of unexpected success. For Todd, the former high school dropout, beginning to succeed in college classes was a turn in the path toward what he had always dreamed of, but had not dared to hope for—becoming a research scientist and expert on human cognition. For Lauren, her sense that her college professors recognized the beauty and vividness of her writing vindicated years of hiding out and covert creativity—she says she felt she was "being fully myself" for the first time. For Jonathan, being admired as an intellectual and beginning to swim in an academic environment where he could express himself with greater honesty and completeness helped him begin to capture and reclaim parts of himself that had been lost—to believe these facets of himself were even worth saving. Finally, for Bernard, moving from street hustler and juvenile delinquent to honors student and college-bound wage earner was like light breaking through the heavy cloud cover of his previous experiences. Bernard said that beginning to believe that he was able to do well in high school, to be someone who was "responsible enough that I would lock up the store at the end of the day and keep the keys"—this success helped him begin to see himself in new ways. "Maybe I wasn't going to die a street hustler," Bernard reflected. My interviewees noted the importance of getting out of old, unsuccessful environments—of the need for a change of scene for healing to begin. They needed to move to a new school and be away from peers and teachers who saw them as unsuccessful screwups, to be placed in learning environments that were receptive to their unique gifts, or to be taken off the streets by a tough-love judge.

Although we can't engineer success for those we'd like to begin to heal, or to heal ourselves, my interviewees describe how they needed to get beyond the "average, ordinary, nothing special" or "stupid, crazy, lazy" labels they'd been given in academic environments. Todd Rose's story emphasizes this point again and again: He became socially successful only after he left his elementary and middle school, doing well in college classes only if no students from his former high school were there, and escaping teachers who expected nothing but obstreperous behavior and poor academic work. Bernard talks about the power of labels and the need to escape them. "Boy, colored, Negro, nigga, nigger, Black special ed, dropout, juvenile delinquent, criminal, homeless, gifted. As a former New York City schoolteacher, assistant principal, principal, district administrator, and senior superintendent, I have struggled with the realization that children today suffer from the negative impact of labeling in the same way I suffered when I entered the same system as a student some 40 years ago. Why do we refuse to stop the harmful practice of labeling children?" As institutions, schools often are committed not to an effort model of growth in students, but to an entity paradigm in understanding human ability, and are designed to sort and label kids. For those who experience significant failure, or sometimes equally distorting, the label of "average," engineering success without an external intervention (try harder, be more careful, develop good work habits) is not easy.

For some interviewees, hitting bottom was a moment when—inadvertently—light began to peek through the cloud cover of school failure. When Todd was accused of lacking the ability to write the poem in seventh grade, or Lauren was informed that her college essay was too accomplished to have been composed by her, or Jonathan was charged with plagiarizing a paper in middle school, they hit bottom. The system seemed totally against them. These were low moments for each of them, when their sense of justice was sorely tried. On the other hand, they also began to see that the institution itself was simply unfairly stacked against them—this was the birth of a critical consciousness, that those evaluating them were highly fallible. In these discordant, seemingly hopeless moments lay the seeds for another essential tenet of those who heal from significant school wounds: Do not let the institution, teacher, or tester evaluate your worth in your own eyes. You must take ownership of your own learning and identity.

For others (possibly those reading this book), learning about the institution of schooling also can be eye opening and provide some important moments of insight. As Jonathan Mooney said, "Unfortunately, my mantra as a little kid was, 'You're stupid, crazy, and lazy.' This tape ran in my head constantly. In speaking with kids who have learning differences, and their parents, I find this is an almost universal mantra for kids who struggle in school. By high school I was able to repress that mantra, but it was still there lurking in the background. As I worked with my mom and teachers who understood my learning difference, a more positive foundation began to form. My mom and Mr. R., my third-grade teacher, told me, 'This isn't your problem, Jonathan. It's our problem. . . . You don't need to be fixed. We're looking at a broken educational system that needs to be fixed.' Mr. Starkey, my high school English teacher, always told me, 'You struggle with writing not because you're dumb, but because your mind moves quickly and in 3 or 4 dimensions, and text is only 2 dimensional.'"[6]

For Todd, Lauren, Jonathan, and Bernard, a burgeoning structural and political analysis of the institution of schooling brought moments of insight and allowed them to begin to break free. Jonathan Mooney described this in our interview. "Being labeled with learning differences [or having school troubles] is a whole system of values that breaks up coalitions and separates like-minded groups against each other so that no force can ever be exerted on the system to change it. My healing came through a political critique of my experiences. I began to see that we marginalize particular types of people." For Bernard, understanding that school was in some sense in the business of sorting and categorizing kids helped him see himself more clearly and helped move him to action to change school systems. "We need to stop [labeling children]. We are clearly hurting our children. What we are doing to our children is tantamount to giving them

A BREAK IN THE CLOUDS—
MOVING AWAY FROM SHAME AND DENIAL

- Moving to another school or classroom, where a student feels understood and appreciated—finally
- Having a teacher who really supported us, and experiencing what this feels like for the first time
- Talking with others about the institution and why we may not fit
- Studying the sociology of schooling, to understand that schools sometimes are designed to "wound"—that this is their purpose
- Having children and confronting our own school wounds honestly
- Becoming teachers and being healers to our students

drugs. Labeling them has the same effect. It dulls the mind and senses. They experience depression, confusion. It weakens their resolve. Their classroom instruction generally lacks stimulus. The flame is extinguished. Once extinguished, it is damn near impossible to ignite."

Stage Three: Anger and Sadness

Once we've accepted and recognized that we have some school wounds, we have to give ourselves time to work through our feelings. Without fully experiencing grief and anger about what has been lost, we cannot move on to the next phase—acceptance, reconciliation, and re-engagement. Todd Rose described what "comes up" when he looks back on what happened to him as a boy. He said, his eyes filling with tears, "I know none of what happened to me had to happen, or has to happen to any kids. Kids are trying so hard; they sometimes just don't know how to do better." I recall this experience myself, being lovingly mentored by a professor for the first time in graduate school, a teacher who seemed to expect and demand the best of me. What would it have been like if I had had this all through my schooling experiences? What work might I have been able to accomplish that I have not? How could I help create this feeling for my own children and students?

David Stoop, the grief counselor, describes this phase of the journey as a time of moving inward. "During the angry facet of grief, we are focused on the other person and how they hurt us. During the sadness facet, we become more focused on ourselves. We go through a period of self-evaluation, considering what has been lost to us. What is it that we will never experience again? What has been taken away that we can never regain? What has been our part in the process?"[7] Rather than resisting this as self-indulgent and solipsistic, we should see this is a critical part of the process of healing. As grief researchers Leick and Davidsen-Nielsen describe, "In our grief at what we risk losing lies the germ of joy at what we have. Through grief at what we have lost develops hope for what we may have in the future."[8]

During the grieving process it is normal to bounce back and forth between sadness and anger. Jonathan Mooney describes his sense of rage at the system that wounded and injured him, and the ways in which he tapped this anger to give him motivation to be successful. "Another motivating factor is anger. Anger can be quite energizing, although it tends to have diminishing returns. I admit that anger motivated me early in my college career. As a freshman I told one school official I wanted to major in English literature, which is my passion. After looking at my records and test scores, he smugly told me I should major in something 'less intellectual.' His attitude really angered me. I had a choice of what to do with that anger: either turn it inward and let it destroy my self-esteem, or take positive action. I chose the latter and promptly enrolled in four literature courses! I earned a 4.0 GPA that semester. The drawback of anger—of trying to prove others wrong—is that if you continue to run on anger long-term, you can lose yourself in the process."[9]

Simply being angry or sad (sometimes both at the same time) can have diminishing returns ultimately. At some point we have been in our feelings enough and are ready to move on. It often helps to have another person at our side, or a group of people, to help us recognize when it is appropriate to do this. With school wounds, however, given the cultural denial of them, many will be given insufficient time for grieving and will be rushed. It is important to resist this. Lauren described her moments of reconciliation, when she realized she was finished with her grief and anger for the time being, and was ready to begin to train for her own career as a teacher. "After getting recognition, and writing and talking extensively about my feelings [this semester], I think I am ready to move on."

Forgiveness for our school wounds, and moving beyond blame and the blame trap, is a final step toward re-engagement of our energies and (for many) becoming active in the reform of the institution of schooling. For Jonathan, this has involved an intense, extensive process of self-understanding and self-forgiveness, and redefinition of his restless energies and inventive mind. "I'm still in the same narrative, just a new phase. I always thought of myself as a striver. But now I'm searching rather than striving. There is a big difference."

After 18 years with the New York City school system, Bernard decided to return to school to get a doctorate in education so that his voice could be even more powerful and influential on the national reform stage. Bernard said recently, "There is so much work to do with changing schools. I am dedicated to continuing to fight the good fight for children."

Stage Four: Reconciliation and Re-Engagement/Activism for Change

Avoiding the "blame" trap for our school wounds, which actually makes us less personally effective and politically powerful, while still acknowledging the need for reform of our current educational system, requires emotional tending and self knowledge. For most, to get beyond blame, anger, and sadness, we need to collect ourselves, decide that we are ready to get on with it, and commit to re-engagement in our personal and professional lives. For almost every individual I interviewed, this has meant committing to the reform of the institution of education at some level, either as a teacher, administrator, political activist, or reformer. (This may be one of the reasons why educational reform is such a perennially popular political topic.)

For Todd, dedicating himself to producing neurocognitive research that will change the paradigms through which children with learning differences are treated in school has become a profound passion and life-long goal. For Lauren, becoming a teacher like the ones who supported and nurtured her, and making life better in classrooms for children like herself—and perhaps also publishing stories about her own learning history—is her specific professional vision. Jonathan has become a learning differences activist who has devoted his life to helping people "reconceptualize their value as human beings." Project Eye to Eye, a not-for-profit national organization founded by Jonathan and his coauthor David Cole, develops mentoring programs for students labeled learning disabled to empower them to celebrate their differences and to help envision successful futures.[10] Bernard has committed himself to becoming "a different kind of urban principal," going to graduate school to broaden the range and impact of his reform voice, and writing and speaking on behalf of young women and men like himself in urban schools.

Aspiring to make the world of schooling better, while also cultivating self-acceptance and peacefulness, has been a hard-fought place to reach. Jonathan says he understands now: "I have a nonstandardized mind. I have a restless energy and won't fit into a conventional work paradigm. But I'm feeling at peace now. I'm not going to be able to put myself in a box." No longer so tortured by the need for conventional acceptance and

~~~~~~

WHAT FOSTERS HEALING?

- Adult supporters (even one) who tell the individual he or she is worthy and has value, in the face of the many negative messages of school. For Jonathan Mooney, this was his mother, herself a wounded learner; for Todd Rose, his wife.
- School environments that tend not to label and categorize children
- School environments that provide challenges to unconventional learners; that honor and engage their unique learning gifts
- Constant reframing of experience in the most powerful positive light
- Critical consciousness about the institution of schooling

~~~~~~

success, Jonathan has found new energy for other projects, and discovered a new creativity and sense of freedom unlike what he has ever experienced. "I'm thinking about the next project," he says.

Exercises to Foster Healing

> When are we educated? When we know more or less which is the far-off planet that we desire, and when we do all that we can to set off for it. If adults are tough and sad, it is because they are disappointed. They do not listen well enough to the invitation to grace which is in them. They let their spaceship rust.
>
> —Jean-Francois Lyotard, *Spaceship*, 1995

We all want to connect more explicitly and consciously to pleasurable, spontaneous learning, yet many of us find this difficult as adults. The following exercises may help you explore your attitudes about learning and think about how your early experiences of learning affected you.

Exercise on Early School Memories

1. Close your eyes and think back to your earliest memory of school. When was it and what was happening? How did this experience imprint upon you some basic feelings about the process of education? What feelings come up from these early memories?
2. What are the components of a positive learning experience for you? (Can be a laundry list or a memory.) What makes a learning experience pleasurable for you?

3. How does what is in Question 1 compare with the material in Question 2?
4. What are you afraid of when you confront new learning experiences? (And in what contexts?)
5. If you could design a school that incorporated the elements of positive learning experiences, what would it be like?

Understanding Your Educational Values

1. What do you think the purpose of education is?
2. How should schools achieve this?
3. How central is the institution of school to achieving your life goals?

CHAPTER 6

Wounded Schools

Who is disabled? The learner or the school?
—David Rose, cofounder, Center for Applied Technology, 2008

Schools Are Wounded

As part of my school consulting, I recently visited a suburban public school that was struggling with a demoralized teacher culture and flattening test scores. Along with a team of my colleagues, I had been called into this school to try to help its leaders determine what was happening below the surface of the school's placid, seemingly unrippling waters—to help chart a course of improvement so that the school might better serve its students, address its morale problem, and push its leveling test scores upward.

Our school visits always involve visiting classrooms—as many as possible, hopefully every classroom in the building. I went from classroom to classroom, observing teachers and students interact. In the first classroom I entered on a snowy winter morning, 17 eleventh graders were being taught a lesson in graphing quadratic functions—graphing the vertex. The kids were genial and friendly—very willing to talk to me, an observer in the room, in part because they were looking for diversions from instruction that just didn't grab them. The class opened with the students getting computers off a computer cart, a noisy and distracting business that took about 6 minutes. "Eeew, this keyboard is disgusting!" one student called out. "Okay, get some hand sanitizer and a towel." "Oh my god, this one is awful, I can't use it," said another student emphatically, as classroom instructional time marched onward unproductively. The instructional purpose of the lesson was not described as the class finally got under way—the teacher said hurriedly to start things off, "You remember what we were doing yesterday," to which one student responded a mumbled, "Yup." The teacher then turned her attention toward the computer screen projected at the front of the classroom. In the semidarkened room, with the computer screen the center of her attention, the teacher stood and talked for a long, long time (12 minutes) about where to plug in the numbers for "a" to change the parabola, while students watched. She demonstrated. They watched. Again and again, quite slowly. Finally the instructor asked the students to enter an equation on the equation bar of their own computers, to which students said things like, "Ms. Smith, we don't know what we're doing." Two girls at the back of the room, who throughout much of the previous instruction had been discussing quietly how they might decorate their laptop covers, said about the parabola: "It's kind of pretty in its own ugly mathematical way."

Because I was at the back of the classroom, I could see how antsy kids were in their chairs, although they were genuinely trying to pay attention. During my observation of this lesson the teacher spoke about three quarters of the time, frequently asking questions to the whole group, to which no one answered (she then would answer the questions herself). A student at the very back of the room, an African American young man, was staring into space and spoke to no one during the entire period. The girls near me tried to amuse themselves by talking among themselves. When questioned after class, students said they did not know why they were learning about graphing quadratic equations—the big purpose or goal of the lesson was not apparent to them. The teacher had not addressed this (the context question—why learn this?), and the instruction moved ploddingly, with many fits and starts, while the teacher attempted to "show" what the lesson was about, rendering the students largely passive riders on the train of instruction. There was little chance for students to explore, interact with the concepts, try out their own ideas, or talk with one another about what was going on. Quietness in the classroom was prized, lack of movement was prized, following instructions was prized, and orderly conduct was prized.

The class ended with a whole-group, in-class "evaluation" of student performance, in which only a few kids participated. "Were you respectful and courteous when you spoke?" the teacher asked as she hurriedly moved through a school-instituted protocol. (Students were to offer a thumbs up or down.) "Did you contribute positively to the learning environment? Did you take responsibility for your school and personal appearance? Were you timely, prompt, and prepared?" While these may be important school goals overall, they had nothing to do with intellectual engagement, thinking, or instruction, and did not "remind" students that their purpose in the class was to engage their thinking or explore math. The girls at the back of the class who had befriended me said they "really didn't learn anything in this class" and it was "kind of a waste."

Next we went across the hallway into a very different classroom environment. There a teacher in her third year, who had come out of a teacher preparation program that emphasized the need for "backwards" curriculum planning, focused her instruction on the goals of the lesson and engaging students in deep ideas and thoughts. (She regarded this as central to all curriculum planning.) This kind of training also explicitly acknowledged that every human brain is wired differently, that not everyone learns in the same way, so there must be multiple ways of presenting information and participating in instruction. The students told me they "loved" this class. Why? "Because we do real things. We have to really think about hard questions and do our own work. Ms. Marquez really challenges us and forces us to read. We like her." In Ms. Marquez's humanities classroom, the walls were arrayed with students' previous work. A genocide unit and a pyramid of hate had prompted personal reflections and projects on acts of prejudice and prejudiced attitudes, many of which were on display. The class discussion began with a friendly conversation of leap year, and then Ms. Marquez described what would happen that day—they were working on a unit on war. There were choices. Some kids would finish their iMovies, some kids would finish watching *The Thin Red Line*, and some would continue in the voices of the war theater project or complete their poems about the war. A classroom aide, there to support students with learning differences, was employed to work one on one with students on their war poem, while Ms. Marquez would be a consultant to students on the iMovies kids were making about their reflections on war. The classroom was busy, almost immediately industrious, but not a quiet place: Students went right to their chosen activities, settled into groups, and began working. There was no off-task behavior, there was no correcting students for talking; students were profoundly engaged in what they were doing. No one wanted to talk to me.

As I moved throughout this school observing classrooms—sixth graders to seniors—mostly what I saw were classrooms like the geometry lesson. Teachers at this school were well meaning but very frequently ineffective, trying hard to offer instruction to kids whom they thought of as "disengaged and sometimes disrespectful." The instruction in most of the classes was teacher-centered lecturing (teacher at the front of the room), the teacher defining and calling out problems, kids going through the motions of learning—guessing the answer the teacher required. Kids were doing low-level cognitive tasks, rarely requiring them to do more than restate a procedure or recall information. In a sixth-grade classroom a teacher asked, "Are you doing the entry ticket?" and then began dully plodding through "Reader's Theater. " Almost no one in the class paid attention to the reader, the teacher included—she was busy trying to calm the boys in the back of the room who were passing notes and giggling. Increasingly irritated, the teacher occasionally would interrupt the child reading to correct someone who was off task. Snapping her fingers, she said, "Quit with the fresh. Fresh I don't need." It was very boring and slow, and had I been a student in the class, even as an adult, I might have had a hard time with my own behavior.

When I spoke with the teacher after class, she was bewildered. "This is the way I've always taught," she said. (She had been a teacher for about 10 years but was new to this school.) "The kids are so disrespectful here. I just don't get it. I think we have the wrong kind of kids in the building."

As described, while the instruction in this school overall was not effective or especially successful, it is not unusual, even in high-performing schools.[1] These unengaging, underperforming classrooms are like hundreds I have visited through the years—not better and certainly not worse than average—a modal kind of American instruction[2] that produces low test scores, low levels of student interest and engagement, frustration and burnout on the part of teachers, and—most important for wounded students—extinguishes entrepreneurial interest in learning. For pupils, the consequences of low-level instruction and lack of engagement are extremely significant: If a student has more than 1 year of ineffective instruction, it may take 2 years to catch up, and after 3 years of ineffective instruction, a student may never be able to recover.[3] In what school critic Roland Meighan calls a "stream of dominating and unwanted instruction,"[4] a great deal of how we teach today, evaluated simply on levels of student interest and long-term retention, is outmoded, undemanding to students, and frustrating to teachers. Schools themselves are wounded: organized in dysfunctional ways that separate adults from one another and discourage collaboration and talent sharing, crippled by old-fashioned ideas about the nature of learning and ability. Students' voices are undervalued and unheard, parents are kept at the margins, and schools' curricular and technology-challenged instructional environments make instruction uninteresting or inaccessible for many learners.

"Our curriculum is broken," says David Rose, developer of instructional designs that focus on making content accessible and engaging for all learners. "Schools are like Sturbridge Village [an early-19th-century historical village in Massachusetts], and most instruction is like learning how to drive a stagecoach, when kids need to operate a Ferrari."[5]

Learning to Change/Changing to Learn

In a video posted on YouTube recently[6] a variety of Australian, British, and American educators described the need for what the video calls "new narratives" for 21st-century learning. "For the last 100 years we've used an industrial narrative about order and control," says Greg Whitby, an Australian educator, in the video. That narrative—as this book and dozens of others suggest—no longer serves us well. It is not just the paradigms for understanding content and the nature of authority in learning that are outmoded, but the tools of the classroom. The education sector ranked lowest of any American enterprise in terms of information technology intensiveness, according to a U.S. Department of Commerce survey—below coal mining, notes Keith Krueger, head of the Consortium for School Networking in the United States and creator of the "Learning to Change/Changing to Learn" video. "Most children arrive at the typical school coming from a technologically advanced world full of interactivity and connectedness. Yet when they cross the classroom threshold, most technologies they find engaging are banned. If we want to prepare our students with skills to succeed, we need to rethink education. Technology has transformed every other industry sector. It is time we focus on how technology can personalize and transform learning."

This compelling video describes how kids exist in super-information-rich, technology-driven environments most of their lives—many students are great software developers and technology adaptors, and use a wired environment to think, reflect, research, retract, and connect. Students live in a world of the "nearly now," says Ken Kay, a British learning technology consultant and head of e-Luminate, a set of social environments in which they text and twitter and talk online, where they can experiment and posit with incredible flexibility. This "nearly now" is a wonderful place for learning, Kay notes. Yet "almost all these devices of connectivity are banned in school," says another educator in the video. Young Zhao of Michigan State University, observes that technology "is not really a choice . . . it has invented a whole new world." Students routinely experience their out-of-school lives as much richer places to learn than in school.

Once isolated critics, a chorus of voices is rising that describe the need for new ways to conceive of education in our country. With tools like the YouTube video, thought leaders seek to bring attention to the fact that a new world has come to students—if not to schools. Yet as the description that opened this chapter noted, we're stuck in a low-tech, bricks-and-mortar system of egg crate classrooms, and it seems very difficult for us to conceive of ways to get out. "We've got a classroom system where we could have a community system," noted one American educator, and this system doesn't produce the skills and knowledge we desire.

What skills do children need now? As described in Chapter 2, author Daniel Pink[7] says that in the new conceptual age, 21st-century literacy

TECHNOLOGICAL ILLITERACY: IS IT OKAY TO BE A TECHNOLOGICALLY ILLITERATE TEACHER?

If a teacher today is not technologically literate—and is unwilling to make the effort to learn more—it's equivalent to a teacher 30 years ago who didn't know how to read and write.

—The Fischbowl blog, September 11, 2007[8]

skills are the ability to find information, to validate it and synthesize it, to leverage it and communicate it. The capacity to understand context, to work in teams, and to be multilingual, multicultural, and multidisciplinary are critical competencies for successful new workers. "This is a totally different set of skills than those most adults now teaching in classrooms were raised with," reflects one educator in the YouTube video. Sounding very much like the school critics of the 1960s, Ken Kay notes that what we need now are "genius, collaborative, brave children. It's a very exciting time for learning. It's the death of education but the dawn of learning."

Teaching Is a Complex Technical Job

Yet teachers are poorly positioned to meet these new demands, given their current induction into the job and the structural and cultural surroundings of their work. Teaching is extremely demanding, complex work, requiring high levels of skill and knowledge about the subject matter taught, the range of learners in the classroom, and personal knowledge of one's students. (In the classroom I observed at the opening of this chapter, how did those sixth-grade students feel coming into humanities class that morning, when there were 8 inches of snow on the ground and "they should have had a snow day," as one boy told me? What could the teacher have done about the snow-day-ness of that morning?)

Additionally, teaching requires pedagogical knowledge and skills, a set of "tools in your toolbox" that allow instructors to plan and pace a lesson according to a specific group of students, to construct several types of learning situations (usually in one classroom, simultaneously), and to be able to read the energy and level of engagement of their students minute by minute. It also demands the suppleness to change those plans in midstream, requiring flexibility and firmness around instructional goals. It demands an acute diagnostic mind. The school in which I was observing instruction on the day I described had high numbers of students who had learning differences—students who do not respond well to traditional classroom instruction and who require innovative, creative strategies for delivering curriculum aimed at them particularly. Most teachers are not trained to do these things—to achieve these goals. Most principals are not trained to supervise teachers on instruction and in achieving these goals. Most teachers are involved in very little real-time mentoring, ongoing professional learning, or observation of their teaching practice after the first few years of teaching. Their opportunities for acquiring these complex skills, except based on their own initiative and in the privacy of their own practice, are few.

Good teaching also involves a certain gravitas, a sense of receptivity and taking students seriously and of being deeply interested in them, and an ability to communicate passion and excitement for what is being taught. It requires, paradoxically, the capacity to think big and small simultaneously: to have at the center the why of what students are learning, the heart of every classroom plan, and then an infinite number of small, well-executed plans to help everyone gain access to the big, important ideas. It requires hundreds and hundreds of small decisions minute by minute, often without the practitioner's knowledge that these decisions are being made. On top of all of these complexities, in the past decade we have added high-stakes accountability measures, which have imposed a new set of curriculum pressures and a push toward all learning being "measurable."

In a building of 30 classrooms at the school I observed at the opening of this chapter, no more than three or four classroom teachers were strong in all of the following: teaching technique, rigor (setting a high level of intellectual challenge in terms of the questions of instruction), and instructional engagement. Although the students at this school found their teachers "pretty nice, and caring," they weren't challenged intellectually in any serious ways except in the few classes noted. The school's test scores, the measure that now determines the fate of schools, were quite low, in spite of the teachers' 8-, 9-, and often 10-hour days and high levels of commitment to the school. There are thousands of schools like this in the country now—public, private, and charter schools that have not made adequate yearly progress and are likely to be highly scrutinized, reorganized, and reshuffled. But without the skills and knowledge to deliver instruction in new, different, and more effective ways, it isn't clear what effect a mere reorganization might have.

Because the world in which schooling is occurring has changed so dramatically, the ways in which we train and monitor teachers in terms of their induction and ongoing professional development are dramatically

mismatched.[9] We don't begin to have enough teachers or school administrators or school coaches who know how to deliver instruction in new
ways. Teachers have to invent a lot of their practice on their own[10] and
structurally are largely unsupported and too much alone in this work.
When my consulting team debriefed with teachers in the afternoon of the
day we visited the school that opens the chapter, after some discussion
of the levels of disengagement, off-task behavior in classes, and wasted
instructional time, teachers said, "We don't know how to do our work better"; "We don't know where to begin"; "We want to be more successful,
but we don't know how."

A Teacher Prepares

> One of the ironies of teaching is that it is one of the most
> social occupations, but it is also one of the most isolating
> professions. I remember my first year of teaching. The
> principal walked me to my classroom and wished me the
> best of luck. I'm not sure that he even came into the room
> with me. The generic cinderblock room was painted in
> an institutional off-white, the windows overlooked the
> playground and on one wall was a large chalkboard. There
> was a teacher's desk and roughly 35 desks for the fifth-grade
> children who were coming in the next few days. There was
> no real planning and, while a few other teachers said hello,
> I certainly did not have a mentor teacher. It really was like
> being dropped into the deep end of a swimming pool in
> order to learn how to swim.
>
> —Peter Cookson, *The Challenge of Isolation*, 2005[11]

A colleague, Tony Wagner, describes his path into teaching in his new book,
The Global Achievement Gap (2008). As a young man, Tony was interested
in teaching—not because he loved school but because he was interested
in seeing whether he could change some things about it he didn't like.
After completing an undergraduate degree, and with a couple of years of
teaching experience, he enrolled in a master's program in teaching at the
Harvard Graduate School of Education. He completed this degree, curi-
ously, with almost no real opportunities to teach or be observed in teaching. Then he moved to Washington, DC, to work in an alternative school
within a suburban high school. Although he had graduated from a prestigious graduate school, and had spent some years thinking and reading
about teaching, he had never been supervised in teaching and had never had another adult colleague or mentor consistently watch him teach.
In his first job, "I worked with the most disaffected students, trying to

understand what might motivate them to learn or even to stay in school. Because I spent much of my week working one-on-one with students, and in small groups with the at-risk students, I volunteered to teach a regular English class, so that I would better understand what teaching conventional classes was all about. I also wanted to be a part of a department and not to be working all alone. The head of the English department gave me a class of thirty-nine students, when most other English classes had only about twenty-five, and his AP English class had thirteen students. Did he want me to fail, I wondered?"

The intense aloneness of life in the classroom, the absence of adult mentors or colleagues, is a vivid part of Wagner's recollections. "I still remember the first time someone actually came into my class to observe me. It was the principal, and he was there to complete my annual evaluation. I tried not to look at him, and to focus on the kids, but it was hard. I felt naked—on display. Aside from having my master teacher in the classroom at Harvard pop in while I was teaching my five-day unit, no adult had ever actually watched me teach before. He sat in the back of the room for ten minutes, as we discussed a short story students had read for homework, and then quietly slipped out. We were to meet in his office a week later to discuss my evaluation. Though nervous, I found myself actually looking forward to the meeting. As the principal showed me into his office, he smiled and motioned me to a seat in front of his massive mahogany desk. Once I took a seat, he handed me a piece of paper, and said, 'Look this over.' Taking it from him, I remember my hand shaking slightly. Finally, someone was going to give me some feedback on my teaching. Looking down, I saw four pages of checklists with perhaps forty items grouped in five or six categories. There were only two columns running down the length of the pages, one labeled "Satisfactory" and the other "Needs Improvement." Quickly scanning the sheets in front of me, I saw that the Satisfactory box was checked for every single item."

Although the most cursory of evaluations, Wagner was told, "If you agree with this, then all you have to do is sign at the bottom." Although Wagner says he knows his teaching required much more scrutiny and development than he was receiving, "Who was I to argue and what questions would I ask? Besides, after most of a year, I still had no idea— other than sheer gut instinct which was mostly based on whether the kids seemed engaged—when I'd taught a good or bad class or even what were the elements of an effective lesson. I clearly wasn't going to get any feedback in this conference. I signed, picked up my copy, and left— the knot in my stomach was replaced by an empty ache. The conference lasted less than five minutes. A year later, the exact same scene played out—same principal, same checklist, same result. The same thing happened again in year three. But now, having completed the required three years of 'successful' teaching, I was not just certified—I was tenured! A teacher for life, if I chose to be."[12]

Wagner goes on to describe how after teaching at an elite private school, and becoming a high school principal and finally a college instructor, he continued to invent his teaching practice on his own, and to be largely unsupervised and to work alone. Although Wagner became a teacher long ago, this pattern is still quite typical, repeated thousands of times a year with thousands of new teachers, in spite of new efforts at teacher mentoring and creating conversations around the work of teaching for instructors in schools. As the former president of Teachers College, Arthur Levine noted in a devastating report on the quality of teacher education in the United States, teacher education is "a troubled [field] in which a majority of aspiring teachers are educated in low-quality programs that do not sufficiently prepare them for the classroom."[13] This lack of adequate preparation of teachers, lack of mentoring and opportunities for collaboration, and lack of opportunity for them to get better at their work in ways that matter lacerate schools and diminish experiences for all people in them.

One of the reasons that teachers find themselves alone and frequently burned out and overwhelmed in their jobs is that the traditional structure and cultural surroundings of the work in schools don't support learning for adults—and therefore aren't very powerful learning environments for children. In the words of John Medina, molecular biologist and director

HOW SCHOOLS ARE WOUNDED

- Structures and culture of schools generally are not designed to support complex, rigorous learning for students or adults. Because schools cannot deal effectively with the cognitive complexity of students, they try to "manage down" difference.
- Schools tend to be "technologically disabled" and are poorly positioned to take advantage of connectivity and collaboration in learning.
- New teachers are underprepared and undermentored, and experienced teachers are too alone in their work almost all the time.
- Our understanding of how humans learn becomes more differentiated and specific all the time; schools generally are poorly positioned to take advantage of this knowledge.

of the Brain Center for Applied Learning Research at Seattle Pacific University, "If you wanted to create an educational environment that was directly opposed to what the brain was good at doing you probably would design something like a classroom."[14] And as Tony Wagner's description of his induction into teaching describes, most teacher training and working conditions do not support ongoing learning and the ability to adapt classroom conditions to the needs of learners. Current school structures just don't create conditions for learning for teachers, and to change these patterns requires intensive effort—energy teachers often feel they don't really have. Add to this our understandings that human learning grows more complex and differentiated every day, increasingly adding to the mismatch between the batch processing model of learning we currently have in schools, and the research on the extraordinarily complex ways in which learning occurs in the human brain.

New Research on Brains

> If you are in education, you are in the business of brain development. If you are leading a modern corporation, you need to know how brains work.
>
> —John Medina, *Brain Rules*, 2008

In addition to the isolating conditions of teachers' work, and the ways schools are maladaptive technologically, new computer-driven technologies (PET scans, MRIs) are revolutionizing the way we understand learning. More and more we actually can see the brain as it learns. We know now, more than ever, that no two brains process information or store data in the same way.[15] With this neurobiological view increasingly available, we also are newly aware that the brain itself is an incredibly sophisticated, complex information processor, "easily the most sophisticated information transfer system on Earth."[16]

Recently I attended a conference on designing instruction based on new understandings of the brain, and an educator in the audience raised a question: Based on how the brain learns, does a whole-language (constructivist) or a phonics-based program better support literacy in young learners? The conference presenters paused and then said they couldn't answer the question because, they emphasized, brains are too complex to think about in this way—they learn neither top down or bottom up, but process information simultaneously from both directions—and no brains process information exactly the same way. A silence fell in the audience after this answer, as it underscored a central emphasis of the conference presentations—that one (or two) approaches to learning really don't meet the needs of students anymore, and that conceiving of learning as "top down or bottom up" also isn't really useful. In fact, as the question revealed, we don't even have accurate physical models or metaphors for imagining learning—we are hampered by the crudity of our conceptual models. The question and answer underscored the ways in which we have to reconceptualize how we conceive of learning based on how we are coming to understand the brain. As educators we are engaged in a revolution in how we think about learning, and we are only beginning to work out classroom and instructional technologies that respond to learner diversity.

While this is not primarily a book about the neurobiology of learning, some critical new findings are important for educators to understand, based on some of the work being done by individuals like Anne Meyer and David Rose, cognitive researchers and designers of learning principles and technologies that tap the capacities of new media to create more effective teaching and assessment practices in the classroom. In an early paper[17] Rose and Meyer, cofounders of the Center for Applied Special Technology in Wakefield, Massachusetts, outlined some fundamental neuropsychological principles educators need to be aware of as they plan curriculum and assessment.

- Learning in the brain is highly modularized. We learn about the color of an object in a different part of the brain than where we learn about its shape. The brain processes the word *cat* in a different region when the word is presented in print than when it is presented in speech, or when it is composing the word for speaking. The brain has lots of distributed modules that work in parallel, each with highly specialized learning functions.
- The pattern of activity varies depending on the task. When we listen to a speech, a different part of our brain is activated than when we listen to a symphony. The brain has a "signature" activity that corresponds to the task it is performing.
- The distribution for the task varies across individuals. Each individual has a particular "map" of activity: The brain activity of a person who has perfect pitch looks different from that of someone with normal pitch, or someone who is tone deaf. As John Medina says, "No two people's brains store the same information in the same way in the same place."[18]
- The maps change as we learn. Novices use their brains differently from experts. The size of individual processing modules can grow and shrink based on experience, even in adults, so the brain is constantly adapting and reconfiguring itself based on experience and environment.

Thus we know now that learning is not a generalized capacity, but lots of different modules, processes, and individual maps that change over time. Individual brains differ in many of their specific abilities, and these abilities change over time—our brains "sculpt" themselves in relation to the needs and demands of our environments in astonishingly complex ways.

From our increasingly sophisticated knowledge of the way the brain operates when it is learning, and the way it is changed by the act of learning, we also are beginning to understand that there is no one type of learner, but a great variety of learners. As Rose and Meyer point out, individuals who are "learning disabled" in a print-based environment may not be in a video- or audio-based environment. Making video- or audio-based learning opportunities more available allows educators to notice the unusual strengths of children: the visual memory of an autistic child or the capacity to recognize facial expressions among aphasics. "Given these data," says researcher John Medina, "Does it make any sense to have school systems that expect every brain to learn like every other? . . . The current system is founded on a series of expectations that certain learning goals should be achieved by a certain age. Yet there is no reason to suspect that the brain pays attention to those expectations. Students of the same age show a great deal of intellectual variability. . . . For example about 10 percent of students do not have brains sufficiently wired to read at the age at which we expect them to read. Lockstep models based simply on age are guaranteed to create a counterproductive mismatch to brain biology."[19]

These new data have powerful implications for how we should conceive of instruction and how we think about "disability" in learning. "Colocating" the disability of the learner with the environment is increasingly helpful in conceiving of how to meet the needs of individual learners—asking ourselves how the environment in which we are creating instruction can or cannot meet the needs of the learners in question (Is the learner disabled, or is it the school?). Thus it is clear that our whole system of conceiving of instruction and curriculum design requires dramatic paradigm shifts. While there is wonderful work afoot on this front,[20] most of it has emerged out of experiences with pupils traditionally labeled learning disabled. This new research is not necessarily translating very effectively into "regular" classroom instruction. Thus our wounded schools struggle along, trying to keep pace with new brain research and the increasingly sophisticated data on how learning occurs. Once again, as many of these new understandings of the brain are operationalized and more fully understood, it is not clear that the old-fashioned classroom model can accommodate these new ideas and knowledge. Again, John Medina notes that, "If you wanted to create an education environment that was directly opposed to what the brain was good at doing, you probably would design something like a classroom."

Implications for Productive Learning Environments

At the Center for Applied Technology (CAST) in Wakefield, Massachusetts, researchers and curriculum designers have been at work for over 2 decades on redesigning conventional instructional environments to make learning accessible for all students. "Schools are disabled by the poor tools and technologies they have access to. They have curriculum based disabilities," says David Rose, cofounder of CAST.[21] While Rose and his associates originally began designing assistive technology for learning-disabled children, as his work developed in relation to emerging brain science, he began to see that learning environments were disabling not just for some pupils with obvious differences in cognitive approach but that "kids with learning differences were like canaries in a coal mine. Gradually we came to see school as a caustic environment for lots of kids, not just those with learning differences. No one should be in these mines," notes Rose.[22]

Thus, according to David Rose and his network of colleagues, powerful learning environments provide:

1. Multiple means of representation. New instructional designs do not assume that there is a single "best way" to present a learning task or problem. Tasks should provide basic access for some students (Braille for the student who is blind), and multiple routes for all students (math concepts in text and graphically).
2. Evidence of learning can and should be communicated in multiple ways. There is no "one best way" to learn or to demonstrate emerging mastery. You can still write or type your essay, but you also may illustrate, create a video, or draw. The method of evaluation should suit the task, and may require some ingenuity and flexibility on the part of teachers and an opening up of definitions of mastery.
3. Instructional designs should provide multiple means of engagement. Depending on the disposition of the learner, learning experiences should grab and motivate in a variety of ways.

Concurrently, John Bransford, a researcher at the University of Washington in Seattle, is creating new kinds of assessments that dramatically reconceptualize our ideas about learning. "Contrary to popular belief," says Bransford, "learning basic facts is not a prerequisite for creative thinking and problem solving—it's the other way around. Once you grasp the big concepts around a subject, good thinking will lead you to the important facts."[23] Bransford and his colleagues are designing assessments that more directly measure the skills and knowledge useful in real life and in preparation for future learning. "What we want to assess is how well prepared people are to learn new things in a nonsequestered environment where they have access to technology tools and social networks. Compared to typical standardized tests, in which seeing outside information is considered cheating," Bransford and his colleagues are attempting to create assessments that model how we really tend to work in the world outside school. "This kind of assessment would be linked to curriculum. Rather than moving along the conveyor belt from one lesson to the next, students would spend time developing expertise in a subject. Through repeated challenges they'd build up strategies and resources over time, just as a worker would on the job."[24]

Vital Variety of Learners

> Our culture needs diversity and schools need to celebrate it.
> —David Rose, learning researcher,
> Center for Applied Technology, 2008

Most importantly, our views of learners in school also are changing based on brain research. When my children were little, we frequently visited the American Museum of Natural History in New York City—a great museums in a city filled with great museums. On a snowy day in February sometime in the 1990s, the museum was just installing a new exhibit on biodiversity—filling an immense Victorian exhibit space with fantastically exotic flowers, plants, and animals from the Amazon basin. There in the Great Hall, amid the Victorian pedimentia and colonizing sensibility that was at heart of the founding of this museum, was an exhibit on the vitality of variety—the concept that genetic and species diversity is central to a healthy, strong, and growing world.

One of the first presentations of what has now become a relatively common concept, the exhibit was designed to instruct viewers on the idea that ecosystems are strong to the degree that they are diverse—variety is vital. Without diversity, ecosystems are weakened on every dimension. They are much more subject to species extinction, climate dysfunction,

PRACTICAL IMPLICATIONS OF BRAIN RESEARCH

If you are an educator, you are increasingly going to have to know about how the brain processes, stores, and sculpts itself around new information. Instruction and conceptions of teaching will increasingly need to reflect the inclinations and brain wiring of individual learners.

Brain research offers some critical data on class size. "Students comprehend complex knowledge at different times and at different depths. Because a teacher can keep track of only so many minds, there must be a limit on the number of students in a class—the smaller the better," says John Medina. Batch-processing learners, delivering unimodal instruction, and moving learners along a chronologically driven instructional assembly line does not serve many well.

Learners themselves will have to become much more adept and knowledgeable about their own brains and learning inclinations and strengths, as teachers are no longer sourced as an exclusive seat of authority and knowledge in the classroom.

New media allow educational designs to move away from strictly "presentational" environments (books and lectures). New media allow for great customization, flexibility, and interactive learning experiences. New digital technologies allow us to move from strictly print-based learning (in most schools) to multiple representations of meaning.

disease, and crippling erosion. I was in graduate school at the same moment I was visiting this exhibit. In graduate school I was constantly realizing how much the diversity of my classmates—their many divergent points of view, their disparate styles of learning, their differences in expression, color, socioeconomic status, geographic background, and voice—added to my experience as a learner. Difference in my classes made my intellectual ecosphere stronger on every dimension. I was less subject to my own prejudices and too narrow points of view, less vulnerable to cognitive erosion, disease, and species extinction. I often think of the Great Hall, and this tremendously powerful realization about my own life as a learner, in relation to the kinds of paradigm shifts that I see occurring in the field of education.

Rather than cower under the specter of "radically individualized" practice that some teachers fear when they confront the implications of new brain research on learning differences, I believe new understandings of cognitive diversity will make us stronger and more coherent—more powerful as a learning culture, less willing to moralize and shame difference. New appreciation of vital variety will greatly enhance our ability to support and take advantage of the many talents of learners in classrooms. Many teachers and administrators have voiced their uneasiness in moving to a vision in which "all brains learn differently," where no two minds are the same. They are afraid this vision rejects the collective good of the classroom and the democratizing function of schooling, and they worry that learning will become atomized, individualized journeys of separate projects without comprehensible standards, shared values, or mutually supported outcomes. I believe the opposite will occur—that our new technologies, understandings of learners, and reconceptualization of curriculum will connect us more powerfully than we have been before, and move us out of an externally driven, competition-based model of learning. It seems genuinely possible that grades might diminish in importance as the pleasures of learning move to the forefront and better serve learners, wherever they are. I believe we will discover that variety makes us more vital, and appreciating and celebrating cognitive diversity makes us stronger, not weaker, in schools. As Tom Hehir, former director of the U.S. Department of Education's Office of Special Education, notes, in schools "change comes from the margins." By reconfiguring classrooms and schools to better meet the needs of diverse learners, schools "become better for all students. That's been our experience again and again."[25]

THE NEW BRAIN RULES: CREATING SCHOOLS THAT CELEBRATE COGNITIVE DIVERSITY

Bumper Stickers for a New Era

Practice random acts of cognitive tolerance

Rainbows of learning styles

Cognitive diversity makes us stronger

Schools of the Future: From Teaching to Learning

As the opening description of the school I observed with my colleagues indicated, we are now engaged in a profound paradigm shift in education—from an emphasis on teaching to one on learning. At a recent educational conference, Mary Dean Barringer, chief operating officer of All Kinds of Minds, discussed how education in the United States is transforming in relation to shifts in the economy. "There is a focus more on students now than on schools," explained Barringer. "Learning is the absolute central focus. We're moving from focusing on methods of teaching to how every student can learn well."[26] Not only technology, new ways of conceiving the work of teachers, and new neurocognitive understandings of the brain are bringing about this focus, but this shift is also fueled by a sense that students themselves will require something much more dynamic and interactive to help them achieve.

In 2007, the futurist Alvin Toffler was interviewed by *Edutopia Magazine* about the transformation of education, and how schools of today are wounded. Describing schools as designed for an earlier era and engineered to produce "industrial discipline," Toffler recommended shutting down the entire educational system. "We should be thinking from the ground up. . . . Teachers are wonderful, and there are hundreds of thousands of them who are creative and terrific, but they are operating in a system that is completely out of time. It is a system designed to produce industrial workers."[27]

According to Toffler, the schools of the future will look totally different from the ones we have today. In schools of the future:

- School will be in session 24 hours a day
- Schools will provide customized educational experiences
- Kids will arrive at different times
- Students will begin their formalized schooling at different ages
- Curriculum will be integrated across disciplines
- Nonteachers will work with teachers
- Teachers will alternate working in schools and in the business world
- Local businesses will have offices in the schools
- There will be increased numbers of charter schools to allow for greater choice of educational settings for learners and their parents

The 1960s school critics, whose words often presaged some of the educational reforms we are attempting to put into place now, noted that we ignore these visions of new schools and new ways of conceiving education at our peril. Our wounded schools cannot heal, and wounded teachers and students cannot perform and engage to their fullest, in the educational environments in which we currently subsist. As a group of architects involved in the physical planning of schools for the future say, "Planning for a long-term, and somewhat unknown future, requires an adjustment in thinking—futurist thinking."[28] To heal our wounded schools, we are required to fearlessly embrace futurist thinking.

CHAPTER 7

Parents
Who Heal

No one knows your kid like you do. Never give up, never give
up on your child, no matter how rough it gets in school.

—Parent in interview, 2008

School Is Difficult Terrain: It Was "Educational Malpractice"

Melody vividly remembers the dreams her daughter Claire had in third
grade of swimming through dark waters and being eaten by sharks. Claire
would wake up crying and frightened, moaning, "I want to go back to
kindergarten, Mommy, I want to go back to that grade." Concerned about
her sweet, sociable child, Melody was at her wit's end and frightened
about what had happened to her child in school. Where had their laughing, easy-going daughter gone, and did she make the right choices about
her school life?

A few years back, seeking the country, outdoors, and "a chance to be
more in touch with nature every day," Melody and her husband had moved
from New York City to Vermont, and had enrolled their two daughters in a
progressive school that placed strong emphasis on the individual development of children and attending to the learner's needs and learning proclivi-
ties. Melody's older daughter seemed to be thriving at this small, informal,
friendly school; she was deeply engaged in her schoolwork and had many
friends. But Claire, Melody's younger child, was floundering. Claire was
too active for the classroom, Melody was told; "Always up and out of her
seat," her teachers said. Claire had trouble focusing on activities for sustained periods, even if she had chosen them, and seemed to have trouble
paying attention. She was having difficulty learning to read, and this school
offered little structured intervention for emergent, less fluent readers. Although the school had a whole-child, accepting orientation toward differences among children, Claire's teachers were definitely frustrated with her.
Claire's older sister, who was in a classroom next door to Claire, said to her

mother, "I always hear them, all day long, saying 'Sit down, Claire. Pay attention, Claire.'" By third grade things had taken a serious downturn for Claire. "Here was this happy, lovely little girl whose light seemed to be going out in front of me. Homework was all tears, she had stomachaches, she wouldn't shake people's hands or look them in the eye. Mondays were awful, the worst day of the week. I was worried we were going to lose Claire—she was closing up on herself because she was so anxious about school."

In conference about what was "wrong" with her daughter, Claire's school discouraged a neuropsychological evaluation for Claire—"That's not the way they did it at this school." But Melody was determined to find out more about what was happening in her daughter's brain, and why she was struggling so much in school, especially since there was so much about this learning environment that she liked. As Claire's nightmares grew more intense, Claire's father insisted that they drive to Burlington and take Claire for a complete battery of tests to assess her learning needs and inclinations. The tests came as a huge relief, but also "they were the next wave of the tsunami."

Suggesting that in her first years of schooling Claire had been exposed to what amounted to "educational malpractice," the neurocognitive tests revealed significant developmental delays and differences in Claire's cognitive profile. These had gone undetected previously. Claire needed intensive speech and language therapy to help her catch up to grade-level language production, and highly structured, language-based learning interventions in small instructional settings. The clinician evaluating Claire noted that she was "desperate to read," but was unable to learn how to do so given her school environment. The assessor also observed that Claire's level of anxiety about her underperformance was akin to that of a child who had experienced war. "She had that level of stress," Melody recalled. Claire was almost incapacitated by her desire to do well and her inability to achieve what she wished. "The other kids were doing long division and Claire couldn't read, could hardly do addition."

To relieve some of the pressure on Claire, Melody and her husband decided that Melody would quit her job and homeschool Claire immediately. "Now here was a huge new learning situation for me: I had to find instructional programs to support my daughter—I am not an educator by background—and do it fast, because we were losing this kid." Melody described her frantic study of programs in literacy, Internet surfing through the night to try to understand her daughter's learning challenges, talking with experts and "any other parent who seemed to know something" to find resources and connections to others who were working with children with significant language-based developmental delays. She found a program designed by Lindamood Bell (http://www.lindamoodbell.com) that focused on integrating sensory information with highly structured literacy instruction, and "Claire began to respond. She learned how to read in fourth grade. It was a year of healing." Profoundly thoughtful while telling the story of her daughter, Melody pauses and says, "I'm so aware of the inequality in literacy instruction in this country. If I had not been able to quit my job and devote myself to Claire, where would she be now? What would have happened to her? The fact that we could afford for me to leave my job was huge for this child."

By age 9, Claire had learned to read and gained more solid mathematical skills. An animated, outgoing girl who always had a group of friends and who played soccer, she wanted to go back to school. This posed another significant challenge for the family. Claire's testing indicated that she would be legally classified as a special education student in a self-contained classroom, but when Melody went to visit the classrooms at the local school where Claire might be enrolled, she said, "Oh wow, I was overwhelmed by that. It was dark, dismal, filled with some kids who could not communicate at all with really severe disabilities and in wheelchairs. I thought, you're not going to dump her here." At this moment Melody's management and negotiation skills became essential. Melody went to school officials and described what she had been through at Claire's old school. She explained, "Claire has good social skills and lots of friends, she gets along well with her peers and can be a contribution to this class. Now, how can we work together to make this child's school life a success?" She convinced the school to create a Lindamood Bell, language-based instructional classroom within the school and to give Claire a classroom aide. Although Claire had to repeat fourth grade, she soared.

Now approaching the end of her eighth-grade year, the family is once again considering options for Claire in high school. "It's always been about keeping in mind what a wonderful child Claire is, in spite of her differences. One of the things that our original evaluator told us, which was great for Claire, is that we, her parents, could always envision a way for her to have a wonderful life. We weren't crushed by her differences and difficulties—we always saw her as a joy in our lives."

Melody has become highly knowledgeable about special education legislation, legal precedents that relate to Claire's funding and placements, and the language-based learning differences Claire will always have that make special learning supports necessary for her. "No one I encountered at Claire's school could deal with all the problems kids present with. I was told by one educator, 'Claire just needs to learn to write things down when she's told, and to tough it out.' Unless a parent takes these problems on, the child is hugely at risk. On the other hand, I was never angry or adversarial with school officials, because I knew that would not help either of us. I always approached this as, how can we get agreement on how to help her? I'm sure you can see that Claire is failing in this way, not succeeding. I know you want what is best for my child. You have to get beyond your own anger and say, 'Here are our circumstances. What are we going to do about this?' I think this is what she needs. I'm sure you agree."

Although Claire has continued to have some struggles, Melody and her husband hope that she may one day go to college if she can pass the Vermont high school graduation exams. "My dreams for my child?" Melody says, "I'm following her lead. She will tell us what she wants. She's coming out a happy, healthy, sociable, well-liked young woman who is a great babysitter, a strong soccer player, and a reader. She says to me all the time, 'Mom, I'm a reader!' Philosophically what I believe is, Claire came with a gift, just as we all do, and I've always felt that in many ways she is here to teach us unconditional love. Her father and I have both always known that she has her own destiny, and supporting her in uncovering that destiny is what has become most important to us. Despite all the fear and worry, we've been able to believe that she has her own path to honor."

Melody now advises other parents in finding schools for their children with learning differences, and is involved in a national advocacy effort for children in poverty with language-based learning differences. After our interview I urged Melody to write about her family's experiences with Claire. Melody said, "If there is a book there, or the opportunity to support other parents in some way, than that opportunity might just come someday!"

I hope Melody pursues this. Her daughter's story exemplifies many of the tenets of the healing, nurturing stance parents must adopt around their children's school wounds: the capacity to learn and keep an open mind about the nature of their child's difficulties or school-supplied labels, unrelenting support and positive encouragement for the child, an optimistic belief that the child can and will find his or her own special destiny and honoring their path, and interacting positively and knowledgeably with school personnel. Like so many stances described in this book, this is not an easy balance to find.

Whether children have diagnosed learning differences or not, or have been labeled "average" (as so many wounded learners have been), millions of parents wonder how to advocate effectively for their children in an institution where their influence is fluctuating and where they often feel they have little real control. How do we empower our children to work effectively on their own behalf without being labeled troublemakers or misfits? How can we help children see what school can do for them, and what it cannot? How do we help school personnel preserve their necessary

PARENTS WHO HEAL

- Believe in the importance of effort, not fixed ability.
- Praise their children for specific efforts, not for generalized abilities or talents. For instance, they don't say, "You're so smart." They say, "I really appreciate the way you stuck with figuring out that difficult math problem."
- Are knowledgeable about learning and support their children in demystifying their own ways of learning.
- Talk openly about how school may not support their child's learning; do not see this as undermining school's authority.
- Support critical inquiry on their child's part about why school is the way it is: Why are kids placed in fixed math groups? Does this help children as learners? Why or why not?
- Unrelentingly reframe mistakes, failures, and disappointments positively for their child—as opportunities to learn. What did you learn from that? What would you do differently in the future? What can we do to figure this out?
- Acknowledge that "it's just school." Melody and her husband took Claire's difficulties in school very seriously, and also told Claire frequently—it's only school. They emphasized the importance of Claire having a balanced view of life: enjoying her friends, her babysitting skills, her athletic talents. "As hard as things have gotten sometimes, we try to keep it in perspective for her."
- Encourage their child to advocate for their own instructional needs, while also honoring—not discounting—the needs of other students.

and desired authority, and also take care of our children? Through years of interviews with parents, and my experiences attempting to guide my own children through school, it has become apparent that first we must start with our own biographies. We must deal with our own ghosts in the classroom.

Parents' Own Ghosts

In her book about parent–teacher conferences, educational researcher Sara Lawrence-Lightfoot describes the delicate terrain between parents and teachers around schooling. There is no more terrifying moment for parents, says Lawrence-Lightfoot, than the parent–teacher conference, when parents are attempting to express their hopes and dreams for their child, and teachers are trying to offer feedback on performance. Although parents and teachers ought to be allies, "more often than not parents and teachers feel estranged from and suspicious of each other."[1] Parents and teachers are sometimes "natural enemies,"[2] reflecting a fundamental tension between the two most important arenas of acculturation in society: school and home. As Melody's advocacy for her daughter Claire demonstrated, while productive engagement with teachers and administrators is essential for a child's learning and growth, a parent's primal passions and deepest vulnerabilities are almost always aroused when advocating for a child in school. Rather than a fruitful collaboration, the school–home negotiation can feel like "a bloody battle, with parents, children and teachers shaken and vulnerable in every encounter," Lawrence-Lightfoot observes.

My investigation of school wounding suggests that in order to be effective, balanced advocates for their children in school, parents first must engage in some archeological exploration of their own school wounds. (See the exercises in Chapter 5.) To effectively support our children and the people we love in school, we must get into a healing and wise stance with ourselves, and understand our own educational values clearly before we are able to help someone else. Some of this work may be simply allowing ourselves to revisit and remember clearly some of our own experiences of schooling—recollecting first memories of school, important turning points in our educational lives, and attitudes about academic achievement that were especially influential to us that we may not be consciously aware of. As the story of Marcus in Chapter 1 illustrates, many parents have had the experience of being almost out of body, or "off the leash," when they encounter their own intense anger, hurt, or resentment about their children's treatment in school. It is important for us as parents to consider the roots of these intense feelings and take responsibility for them. As Henri Nouwen, the Christian healer and priest, observed, "As long as our wounds are open and bleeding, we scare others away. But after someone has carefully tended to our wounds, they no longer frighten us or others."[3]

Once we've begun to understand and heal our own wounds, we can be more effective advocates for our children in school, encouraging children in a variety of healing stances—ways of thinking about and understanding their experiences in school—that can help them feel more resilient, more powerful, and more in control as they face the many challenges and hurdles of schooling.

No Bake Sale: Schools Are Designed to Keep Parents Out

Many of the old-fashioned cultural norms and structures of school— teacher as sole source of knowledge and authority, "privacy" around instructional practices[4]—have functioned to keep parents out of important educational matters. School administrators often function as barriers to parents and "protectors" of teachers, "doing their job" when they keep parents from intruding into the classroom or the instructional workings of the school.[5] Educational researcher Don Moore writes about an incident in a Chicago public school where an enterprising young principal recruited more than 120 parents to a kickoff breakfast at the school designed to encourage kids to read more and for families to read together. Rather than being lauded for her efforts, however, the young principal was criticized for "losing control of her school," because there were too many parents in the building.[6]

While claiming to welcome parental involvement and to value parental input, in fact many schools often find parents threatening and overwhelming. Although hundreds of research studies describe the critical importance of parental involvement in children's academic lives for school success,[7] schools often function subtly and implicitly to protect themselves from parental involvement and remove parents from activities that go "beyond the bake sale," in the words of one researcher. For instance, a group of parents from two Manhattan elementary schools discovered by accident that their children had been chosen to participate in field tests to help the state's testing company vet questions for future tests. In the parents' view, their children were already significantly overtested under the laws of No Child Left Behind (children in New York City take as many as six diagnostic tests a year in Grades 3–8). Parents found about the field testing by accident when a PTO mother overheard teachers talking it. "Everything seems so secretive," the mother commented.[8] Parents organized a boycott of the "extra" testing, while the mayor of New York responded that he was sure educators would use the diagnostic testing to improve education. "As parents of children enrolled in the public school system, it seems that we're informed about issues that affect our children in one of three ways. Too late, too little, or not at all," commented Tonya Gray, the editor of the Public School Parent's Network website. "It's as if there is an unspoken, unwritten code of silence keeping us at arms' length from being true participants in our children's education."[9]

As many parents also have experienced, schools usually claim special authority over learning matters, sometimes without demonstrated expertise—think of Melody and Claire and Claire's teachers lacking the expertise to teach her to read, or to diagnose her learning difficulties. Pediatrician and learning specialist Mel Levine's many books on "all kinds of minds" demonstrate again and again the need for diagnostic skills and more nuanced and detailed understandings of the variation in human learning—more than many schools demonstrate. As one mother explained, "We were told by our son's second-grade teacher, whom we loved, that our son might have dyslexia. Fortunately we talked with one of our friends who teaches at a local college about dyslexia and how to diagnose it. Right away we eliminated that as a possibility, but we could have gone down that road and wasted a lot of time with a misdiagnosis of our son. It was chance and luck that we didn't." Parents need to understand that many school leaders and teachers, well meaning and benevolently intentioned, were not trained in an era that offered them clinical-level diagnostic skills in understanding learning. Yet the authority of schools, and the cultural and social structures that surround teachers and administrators, make it difficult and awkward for parents to question this.

Parental Involvement Influenced by Class and Culture

Parents themselves often see appropriate involvement with their children's schooling very differently based on their social class, cultural background, and their own educational experiences.[10]

For lower-income families, parents with interrupted schooling themselves, or new immigrant families who may not be familiar with the norms and expectations of American schools, schools can be daunting places. In many traditional cultures, teachers and school administrators are authorities whom parents turn their children over to, so the idea that parents should interact proactively with school personnel is a new cultural norm for which parents feel unprepared. Parents working in full-time jobs and struggling for economic survival also have a hard time attending events at school and finding time to volunteer, or giving money for school events. Finally, some parents may feel disapproval for their lifestyles or values at school—schools are generally middle-class institutions and those who are not living middle-class lives may feel subtly or explicitly excluded.[11]

So while schools may "welcome" parents into their midst, and parents may feel it is their duty to be involved in their children's school lives and knowledgeable about their instructional experiences, this involvement is not without conflicts and mixed messages. Aware that parental involvement in a pupil's education is immensely helpful to supporting the child's well-being in school, parents also may be subtly or explicitly repelled by interactions around instructional matters or issues of school culture. By middle school or high school, most parents have gotten the message to keep out. As a mother of four children, I have experienced this frequently myself: My children's schools welcomed my volunteer efforts on behalf of fundraising or school promotion, but generally were much less

PARENTS:
GETTING YOUR OWN HEAD STRAIGHT

- Allow yourself to unmask some of the myths of schooling: that the educational system always has your child's best interests in mind, that teachers are always adequately trained to analyze and judge your child's performance, that assessments actually test what they are intended to measure, or that there is sufficient knowledge in the system to reach the stated instructional goals of the educational entity. While knowledge about educational practice is improving, it is unlikely that all of these conditions are true.

- Speak to your child frankly about your educational values, and how they may (or may not) contrast with the school's. Assume that your child is sophisticated enough to handle these complexities.

- Encourage (and support) your child's academic performance, even if you do not believe in all the values of the institution. This attitude was brilliantly summarized in the movie *The Great Debaters*, when James Farmer, Jr., was asked about his homework by his father. "What do you need to do now?" James Farmer, Sr., asks his son. His son answers, "We need to do what we have to do so we can do what we want to do."

- Help your child develop real strategies for advocating for him- or herself: how to talk to teachers about his or her learning needs in ways that are effective, and to make suggestions about what could be done to improve the learning environment, without making the teacher hostile or angry.

- Recognize what is a good fight, and one you are likely to lose, and help your child understand which is which. Decide together when you are going to do battle with the school. Model that social justice and caring for others is an important life value.

- Be realistic: You cannot completely shield your child from wounding experiences, but you can help balance the negative influences or experiences of school.

- Try to model joy and enjoyment of learning in your own life. The best way to reset the thermostat of curiosity in your child's life is to be a curious, adventurous learner in your own life.

- Believe that your child is tough and wise.

- Never give up on your child. No matter what school may have communicated to him or her, or how wounded and angry he or she may be, you have special insights into the beauty and wisdom of your child. Nurture these traits and help your child see them in him- or herself.

willing or openly hostile to discussions of the school's instructional core or pupils' curricular experiences. The fragility of knowledge around the instructional core of schooling, or a system's lack of capacity to adapt to differences in students' learning profiles, may be a part of this hostility and keeping parents away. Unfortunately, however, it is around students' instructional experiences or their learning issues that children are most frequently wounded. Parents need to give themselves permission to believe that these conflicting messages are real, and that these interactions with school personnel really are difficult.

Effort Versus Ability: "Look Smart, Don't Look Dumb"

> Achievement consists of never giving up . . .
> If there is no dark and dogged will, there will be no shining
> accomplishment; if there is no dull and determined effort,
> there will be no brilliant achievement.
>
> —Hsun Tzu, Chinese philosopher

Once parents have confronted some of their own educational ghosts, gotten more clear on their educational values, and acknowledged the reality that schools may give very conflicting messages to parents about how, where, and when they should be involved in their children's education, how can parents most effectively support their child in school? How can we help kids to not be wounded, or to heal from wounds they may already have sustained?

First and perhaps most important, parents can become effort theorists rather than ability theorists when interacting with their children. As described in Chapter 3, we have cripplingly limited views of human ability instantiated in our educational systems, beginning as early as kindergarten. Unfortunately, in many American public schools we tend to believe, and act on the belief, that human beings are born with certain fixed abilities that do not change over time and are not subject to experience or environmental influence. Historically, schools have tended to be intensely preoccupied with sorting and tracking pupils based on their purported inborn abilities.[12] Not only is this inborn-ability view contradicted by a huge new body of neurocognitive research and evidence, but it also tends to dramatically limit the talents and skills we develop and reward in schools. This body of evidence points us more and more to the view that human ability is emergent, plastic, and changeable over time. Ability is not fixed at birth; it develops over the lifespan, has many dimensions that current intelligence tests cannot measure, and can "grow" based on persistence and effort. Schools are tremendously hobbled by not adopting this view.

WHAT TO DO

I vividly remember a car ride with my Dad. We were talking about what I wanted to do when I grow up and where I thought I would go to college. I remember a lump rising in my throat as he repeated everything I already knew: "You will have to make sure you get your grades up and do well on your SATs. I think you can work a little harder in school, you know." I think he must have noticed my eyes filling with tears because he cut himself off and said, "But, you know, whatever you want to do in your life, you will find a way to achieve it, because that is the kind of person you are." What a cheesy moment this was, looking back on it now, but it was exactly what I needed to hear.

—College student, 2007

So are parents. As parenting advocate Kerby Alvy frequently informs groups of educators and parents, "There is no one in the world who can influence the life and future of your children like you can."[13] And with regard to a child's view of his or her "ability" in school, and the relationship between effort and outcome, no one has greater influence than the child's parents or family. It is important for parents to develop what educational psychologist and researcher Carol Dweck calls "a growth mindset"[14] in regard to their children's school careers—to encourage children to think of their mistakes as learning opportunities, and testing events as information-gathering moments that do not reflect final judgments of their ability or capacity.

For the past 30 years Dweck has intently studied the relationship among praise, motivation, and effort. She and her fellow researchers have formulated two startling, somewhat counterintuitive conclusions about school wounding and parenting. First, parental praise for students' "innate" ability (telling kids they are "smart" or "gifted") actually lowers children's motivation to work harder because with this kind of praise students become mistake avoidant and less persistent in the face of difficulty. They aren't convinced that effort matters. Second, the view children adopt of themselves and their abilities (based on what their parents tell them) has huge implications for their wellness in school. Looking first at her own biography, Dweck explains that how we understand the reasons for our successes (or lack thereof) is central to school performance and school wounding. "Some of us are trained in this [fixed] mindset from an early age," Dweck says, reflecting on her own school experiences. "Even as a child, I was focused on being smart, but the fixed mindset was really stamped in by Mrs. Wilson, my sixth grade teacher. . . . She believed that people's IQ scores told the whole story of who they were. We were seated around the room in IQ order, and only the highest-IQ students could be trusted to carry the flag, clap the erasers, or take a note to the principal. Aside from the daily stomachaches she provoked with her judgmental stance, she was creating a mindset in which everyone in the class had one consuming goal—look smart, don't look dumb. Who cared about or enjoyed learning when our whole being was at stake every time she gave us a test or called on us in class?"[15]

In other words, to what you attribute your successes or failures—your theories about ability—matters immensely in terms of how you approach a learning task. As educational researchers Harold Stevenson and James Stigler noted in their years of comparative study of Asian attribution models of achievement in relation to American ones, "The relative importance people assign to factors beyond their control, like ability, compared to factors they can control, like effort, can strongly influence the way they approach learning. Ability models subvert learning through the effects they have on the goals that parents and teachers set for children and children's motivation to work hard. . . . Effort models offer a more hopeful alternative by providing a simple but constructive formula for ensuring gradual change and improvement: work hard and persist."[16] Stevenson and Stigler also found that effort-based teachers do not "adjust" the curriculum according to a student's perceived ease of learning or ability, but emphasize that slower students need to exert extra effort to keep up.

In another confirmation of the importance of becoming an effort-based parent, in a fascinating study of what she calls "grit," cognitive psychologist Angela Lee Duckworth examined the components of academic success among a broad group of research subjects. She found that contrary to popular belief, ambition, persistence, and self-discipline were the major components of academic and professional success—in other words, the capacity to persist in the face of daunting obstacles and to learn from one's mistakes is what really matters in achievement—and that "innate" ability accounted for less than 50% of human outcomes.[17] This echoes Carol Dweck's advice for parents: Don't try to shield your child from failure, and don't offer global praise to your child for his or her "intelligence" or talents. If you praise them too much for being "smart," rather than focusing on the effort that is required to achieve their goals, children actually will become challenge averse (they aren't willing to risk showing that they aren't smart) and perhaps may set lower goals for themselves. They will be less gritty when it counts.

Effort-based, or growth-mindset, parenting tends to view achievement as gradual, incremental, and occurring slowly over time—and errors as a natural part of learning. Growth-mindset parents do not believe that some students just "get it," that errors show lack of ability, or that their child will be overwhelmed by too much challenge in school. Instead, they focus consistently on the progress children have made in overcoming obstacles, breaking difficult learning challenges into smaller, doable pieces or chunks, supporting their children in acquiring the skills and knowledge they need to be successful, and not overgeneralizing the meaning of mistakes and setbacks. "Mistakes just mean you didn't get it this time, you have to try harder," one parent told me as she moved to an effort-based model of parenting with her own children. "What can you learn from what didn't work here? Is there anything I can do to help you improve?"

After reading Dweck's book *Mindset*, one New York City father reflected on his own withdrawal from praising his 5-year-old unconditionally and globally, and coming to understand that, paradoxically, unconditional praise for his child's intelligence and accomplishments could make him more averse to embracing challenges. Right after withdrawing global praise, this parent noticed positive changes in his son's behavior. The problem, it turned out, was not with his son but with himself. "Truth be told, while my son was getting along fine under the new praise regime, it was I who was suffering. It turns out that I was the real praise junkie in the family. Praising [my son] for just a particular skill or task felt like I left other parts of him ignored and unappreciated. I recognized that praising him with the universal, 'You're great—I'm proud of you' was a way I expressed unconditional love. Offering praise had become a sort of panacea for the anxieties of modern parenting. Out of our children's lives from breakfast to dinner, we turn it up a notch when we get home. In those few hours together, we want them to hear the things we can't say during the day—we are in your corner, we are here for you, we believe in you. In a similar way, we put our children in high-pressure environments, seeking out the best schools we can find, then we use the constant praise to soften the intensity of those environments. We expect so much of them, but we hide our expectations behind constant glowing praise. The duplicity became glaring to me. Eventually, in my final stage of praise withdrawal, I realized that not telling my son he was smart meant I was leaving it to him to make his own conclusion about his intelligence. Jumping in with praise is like jumping in too soon with the answer to a homework problem—it robs him of the chance to make the deduction himself. This morning I tested him on the way to school: 'What happens to your brain . . . when it gets to think about something hard?' 'It gets bigger, like a muscle,' he responded."[18] Learning to be an effort theorist, or moving to growth-model parenting about our children's abilities, is a major avenue to healing and supporting them—keeping them safe and engaged in themselves as they navigate the tricky waters of school.

Demystifying Learning

Given the somewhat antiquated state of practice around learning in many American schools, and the overemphasis on innate ability and compliance in many instructional settings, parents need to bridge the gap between their child's learning profile and the teaching and testing practices embedded in school. While this may not be a fair or glorious state of affairs for parents, it is the reality. Parents (and other adults) must talk to their children about the nature of learning, the pathways of learning, and their own learning styles, because students cannot work on their learning problems or manage their school lives if they do not understand how their minds function, organize, and process information. An expert on assessment and learning says, "Demystification is the process of taking the mystery out of learning"[19]—and everyone deserves to be demystified. Because many schools still aren't very good at teaching students metacognitive skills—thinking about their thinking—parents need to become knowledgeable themselves so that they can help their kids understand their own learning strengths and weaknesses.

My college students, especially those with learning differences, reinforce the importance of learner self-knowledge every semester, in every class I teach. In a class presentation, one of my students said that through the process of demystification—receiving a neurocognitive evaluation, reading a great deal about his learning differences, becoming a peer mentor for other kids who have learning differences—"I have come to understand my own mind—all the ways it works—much better. I know I'm good at grasping big concepts and creatively putting things together, seeing things in new ways. I'm not good at writing traditional expository essays, and lots of details and organizational tasks are challenges. But I've learned to use the tools at my disposal—text readers, books on tape, things like that. This way of understanding my mind allowed me to advocate for myself—it's why I'm here at college. I go to my professors the first day of class and explain to them what my learning needs are, and talk about how they can be accommodated in class."

For students without identified learning differences, it is also incredibly valuable to know how one's mind tends to process information. If we like to look at big comprehensive ideas or whole concepts first using pictures, a flip chart, or graphic materials, we may be visual learners. If we like to learn primarily by engaging in demonstrations and activities, with chances to practice, we may be primarily kinesthetic learners. Robert Fried, in his book *The Passionate Learner*,[20] describes five affective "types" of learners:

- The *cautious* learner, someone who likes to proceed slowly around new learning experiences before jumping in and trying to do something new
- The *impulsive* learner, who likes to plunge into new learning situations, muck around, and then try to analyze what happened
- The *analytic* learner, who wants and needs to ask a lot of questions and get a lot of background information before engaging in a learning task
- The *social* learner, who learns most from interactions with other people and in collaborative, conversation-oriented situations
- The *visual* learner, who finds it very helpful to have a picture or a visual map of the task before beginning

Fried notes, "Most schools don't allow these differing modes to operate freely."[21] Additionally, most schools don't encourage self-reflection and self-knowledge about learning on the part of students. (This is changing, but change is occurring slowly.) For parents the point is not to judge one cognitive style as better than another, but to support self-understanding in our children. If a child comprehends his or her own mind better, and feels it is a worthy lifelong project to engage in investigation of it, he or she is much less likely to be wounded in school interactions.

For parents, becoming a learning demystifier means doing some research and reading oneself, understanding ways in which learning processes are identified and measured, and also being acquainted with how educational settings regard various kinds of learning differences. This is a significant commitment on a parent's part but, just like reading this book, is critical in understanding your child's experiences in school. As one mother I interviewed put it, "I had three children who were totally different in their learning styles. Each one had their own separate struggles in school. I had to learn as much as possible about each one of them to help them stay grounded as they got a lot of negative feedback on what they weren't good at in school." As Melody demonstrated in the opening story of this chapter, becoming knowledgeable about learning and literacy instruction allowed her to advocate successfully and positively for her child.

In a more ideal school world, all children would be demystified in school. As one parent wrote in a blog post, "I definitely believe that all students in a classroom should go through the process of demystification. Just think how it would bring the parent, child, and teacher relationship in sync, with the purpose of enabling the child to maximize

~~~~~~

RESOURCES ON LEARNING FOR PARENTS

Mel Levine, *A Mind at a Time* (2002),
    and the All Kinds of Minds website
Carol Dewck, *Mindset* (2006)
Daniel Pink, *A Whole New Mind* (2005)
John Medina, *Brain Rules* (2008)
Jonathan Mooney and David Cole, *Learning Outside the Lines* (2000)
Lynn Meltzer, *Executive Function in Education* (2007)
Robert Fried, *The Passionate Learner* (2001) and
    The Game of School (2005)

~~~~~~

his/her learning potential. Demystifying each student would provide the students with an understanding of the constructs, and a base for teaching the construct strategies. Through learning the constructs, and each child applying strategies that pertained to his/her learning needs, class discussions could be started on how these strategies are working in the individual child's learning, bringing about a community of learners. One major reason for demystification of all students would be the teacher's ability and understanding to effectively introduce new content in the students' different learning styles. I realize that this demystification of all students would be an awesome task, but doing profiles on those students with the greatest needs first, then gradually demystifying the rest, might be the answer to creating successful, lifelong learners.[22] Unfortunately, however, we are far from capacity in the demystification of every student in school. Teachers themselves are often un-demystified—unclear about their own learning styles and pathways—and for many, demystifying students is outside of the realm of their training.

The All Kinds of Minds website, with its special section for parents, is full of helpful vignettes, anecdotes, and expert advice about what demystification is and how parents can support their children's learning. It also advises parents on appreciating and understanding the differences among learners, and ways parents can help to meet individual learners' challenges. While a parent may feel overwhelmed venturing into this territory (I understand!) given all the demands of modern parenting, if one's child is in danger of being wounded in school, it is imperative to be armed with knowledge and a sense of the current state of research around learning interventions. Without that, the child is wholly subject to the institution, and therefore profoundly vulnerable to school wounding.

Unmasking the Myths of Schooling

> I was brought up to believe that the school system always had the best interests of its students in mind. I was so shocked and angry when I repeatedly encountered a system that ignored and outright denied the needs of my child. Before my eyes my son became an unhappy, withdrawn child. The boy who was reading before he entered first grade now, I was told, was "below grade level."
>
> I confess I fell into collusion with the school in urging, pressuring, even punishing him to do better. When I began seeing that the school really wasn't going to protect my child, I felt like he'd gone to church and been molested. That was my level of disbelief.
>
> —Letter from a parent to the author, 2007

Most of us have been brought up to believe that school systems are benevolent and have the well-being of our children in mind. In order to support our children, however, we may need to deepen and become more nuanced in our view of the system of education that has custodial power over our children for many hours each day. While I do not recommend an openly adversarial stance toward the educational institutions our children attend—think of Melody at the opening of this chapter—as the hundreds of school wounding stories that are the basis of this book attest, we cannot assume that school is a necessarily compassionate, well-informed institution.

Therefore, parents should not presume that the school system is always "fair" or right or that it always has the best interests of their children in mind. Your child's teacher, while undoubtedly well intentioned and working very hard, is under accountability pressure in terms of testing and is responsible for a wide variety of children and learning situations—often without sufficient training, time, or extra support. As already described, teachers often are unable to provide for all children's learning needs, and parents need to compensate. Additionally, if a child feels that an assignment, grade, or teacher's remark or comment is unfair or hurtful, parents need to listen carefully to the child. They need to ask questions about what actually happened, and talk through with the child what the teacher might have meant or been trying to do. If parents are still unclear or have questions, they may need to speak with the teacher or an administrator directly.

Your educational values and the school's also may be in conflict. Parents must allow themselves to consider this possibility as well. As one parent said to me in an interview, "The school was really focused on producing kids who were going to perform well on standardized tests and succeed conventionally. It wasn't that I thought that wasn't important, but that wasn't all I was interested in. I thought my daughter was getting turned off to learning." This parent withdrew her child from the school and found a small charter school with an emphasis on experiential learning that suited her educational philosophy better. On the other hand, Ron Ferguson, a lecturer at the Kennedy School of Government and head of the achievement gap initiative at Harvard, has different goals for his three teenage sons. "I want my boys to be able to ace the SAT." As a matter of equity for his three African American sons, Ferguson has chosen an academic environment that will prepare them to succeed in this way. Parents need to be clear on what their own educational values are, and to find environments and institutions that are congruent with them. Schools have very different cultures and values, whether they are explicit about them or not, and instruction and outcomes tend to reflect those values. Parents need to exercise self-awareness and discernment when selecting a school, and choose carefully.

Supporting Critical Inquiry

Encouraging students to notice how school works—to stand apart and observe its rituals, customs, taboos, and myths—is an important step in guarding them against wounding (and possibly, in building a profile for social action later on in life). Learning how to negotiate institutional situations in which one is vulnerable and dependent, and to not be wounded and become "school sick," is one of the most important gifts a parent can give a child. Parents need to be able to look dispassionately at the institution and their own school experiences, without mythmaking, in order to help a child. Parents can encourage critical inquiry in relation to a child's school experiences, to unpack some of the wounds of school, with these "stances":

- *The Anthropologist.* I encourage children and young adults to become ethnographic observers of the practices of schooling— as if they were gazing at a strange new culture for the first time. What customs and rituals do they observe? What kinds of behaviors are rewarded, and what is punished? How are roles assigned in school?

    I also invite children to talk about the basic functions of school and ask them to talk about what they think schooling *ought* to do. I describe what schools are designed to do: to teach skills, knowledge, and some new ways of thinking, but also to sort and track individuals based on their perceived value as assessed by the institution. I say to my own children that this is not always a thoughtful, fair, or complete process. There will be instances where our children are treated unfairly, superficially, are disrespected or underchallenged by educational situations and structures. This hurts. But on the other hand, we cannot accept these conditions as life determining, fixed, or "natural." Learning to "see" how school operates is powerful in staying well, and children quickly become good observers of this. My children frequently report ways in which "good" students are favored and given the benefit of the doubt in school, for instance, and the ways in which teachers often penalize those who are "not good" students. For instance, one of my children noticed how children who get As are frequently allowed to turn in their homework late, whereas students who are poor performers are chastised and punished for the same behavior. Why does this matter? What system of values and assumptions does this reflect?

- *The Change Agent.* I encourage my own children to act on their observations and perceptions of the ways in which schooling is unfair, to the degree that their positions as students allow. My 13-year-old son recently described an incident at his school that he wanted to discuss with us. My son and another student were talking in class during a groupwork time. The two kids were talking about the basketball game on the previous day—one in which the other student was a star player—and my son and this student became loud and disruptive. Suddenly the teacher's attention was on them. The teacher called the other pupil, who is African American and not a strong pupil (but a star basketball player), to her desk to speak with her about her behavior, while not saying a word to my son (who is White and generally a strong student). My son felt this injustice. At the end of the week, he went to his teacher to discuss this. Awareness of his privilege as a middle-class White boy, and trying to do something positive about this, was an important step in his being well. Teaching our children to speak up and to notice the ways in which school may be caustic and unfair helps keep them strong and active, and places students squarely in the project of reforming schools. I think this is where they belong.

- *The Conscientious Objector.* Increasingly, many parents are deciding that traditional schooling isn't for them or their children. (The nonreligious homeschooling movement grows by hundreds of thousands every year and has been tremendously

enlivened and strengthen through networks on the Internet.)
Abundant resources are now available to anyone who wishes
to become a "conscientious objector" to traditional schooling,
which is how I think of many homeschoolers. Even if you feel
certain you will never become a homeschooler, it is animating
and empowering to dip into this literature—blogs, discussion
groups, wikis, books, lectures, films, Internet lessons, and online
learning collaboratives, all of which challenge conventional
academic constructions of knowledge, ability, and performance.
One of homeschoolers' most powerful voices is Grace Llewellyn,
who wrote *The Teenage Liberation Handbook*[23] and cowrote
*Guerrilla Learning: How to Give Your Kids a Real Education with
or Without School.*[24] Among hundreds of powerful suggestions
for refiring a love of learning and exploration in your child,
Llewellyn suggests that you can go to college without going
to high school, and that "intellectual fervor is for everyone."
("I recognize June by the flowers now. I used to know it by
review tests, and restlessness," writes an unschooled teenager
in Llewellyn's book.) Llewellyn's basic point is that life is "the
flash of a firefly in the night," and that schooling is a terrible
waste of time. Her books are popular among many who are
uncomfortable with aspects of traditional schooling, and useful
to middle and high school students in thinking about ways to
stay well in our contemporary educational system.

Many parents also conscientiously object to aspects of school from
within the system. They try to negotiate with schools about allowing their
children to opt out of some homework, support their children in refusing to take some standardized tests, and talk with school administrators
and teachers about what might constitute meaningful learning exercises
for their children. Part of a healthy, healing stance for parents is to advocate for intellectual environments that are fair and meaningful for their
children, and to speak up and object when school seems to be hurting
their child or other children. Increasingly, there are resources that help
parents thoughtfully object; for instance, the website Child Advocate con-
tains some good suggestions for conscientiously objecting to some school
practices (http://www.childadvocate.org/3_home.htm), with questions
like, "Is homework a waste of your time?" or discussions about the differences between discipline and punishment. These resources, and parents
connecting with one another to form networks to thoughtfully work to
reform systems of schooling, are some of the most hopeful signs of the
revolution that needs to occur in American schools.

One mother who had been engaged in difficult advocating for her children in school for many years told me, "When I start to tap into my feelings about this stuff, I am overwhelmed, flooded with memories, can see faces of adults who said and did terrible things to my kids and to me, administrators who flat-out lied in meeting after meeting, figuring that they would wear me down eventually. When I think about the encounters or allow conversations to bubble up out of the bank of memories I feel empty, I feel sick. The manipulation. The humiliation. The power plays. And even with all of these awful feelings that won't go away after all these years, I wouldn't change anything I did or said. I am proud of myself for refusing to back down. In every case, I started out 'nice,' trying to appease and placate. It never worked. Not once. That makes me sad. I'm not a mean person. But I learned the hard way that I had to stop caring about being liked. If I hadn't been willing to fight for my kids, they'd have gotten worse than no help. They'd have gotten an education in how to feel stupid, not an education. And that would simply have been unacceptable. The thing that keeps me from getting bitter is that I can see the work I've put in making a difference. The kids have blossomed."

I asked this mother what advice she'd offer other parents. She said pithily, "No one knows your child the way you do. If you sense that your child is not thriving academically or socially at school, trust your instincts and find out why. Once you have answers that are consistent with the child you know and love, do not let up until the school is meeting your child's needs and is helping your child learn how to learn. The goal is always for your child to have a chance to know her- or himself and then to understand what she or he needs and loves. If your child learns differently, make sure they have plenty of opportunities to master compensatory strategies. Maybe these won't come easily or quickly, but, in the long run, they'll make all the difference. If you aren't willing to stand up for your kid, who will? Don't let anyone shame you into silence or passivity."

"Drawing a Fuller Portrait": Advocating for and Supporting Your Child

On precisely this note of wise advocacy and critical persistence, a mother described a letter she had written to her child's teacher after a parent conference. It concerned her second-grade child. "I left our parent–teacher conference with a heavy heart, feeling somewhat overwhelmed by the discouraging tone we concluded on. It seemed to me that by the end of our meeting, the view of Martin had been clouded by an emphasis on

~~~~~~

WHAT ELEMENTARY
SCHOOL STUDENTS NEED TO SURVIVE SCHOOL

- Supportive, positive parents or guardians who rebalance negative messages from school
- Parents who reframe mistakes and school failures as opportunities to learn, who emphasize the importance of effort
- Parents who demonstrate a love of learning in their own lives
- Friends who encourage one another and have positive attitudes about school achievement
- Knowledgeable supporters who can help demystify learning and the tasks of school
- Adult supporters who will advocate effectively for children in school when necessary

~~~~~~

his vulnerabilities, his trouble with 'timing' in class discussions, and his difficulties fitting into the social scene on the playground. . . . I am sure all these concerns are valid, but after several days of feeling haunted by the tone of our conference . . . I have felt the need to write to you, as a mother wanting to redraw a fuller portrait of Martin."[25] As parents, we serve a critical function in rebalancing the picture our children present in school.

Jonathan Mooney's mother (in Chapter 4) also supported her son consistently through his dire school troubles, assuring Jonathan that he was of value, that he was a wonderful person and learner, no matter how many negative messages Jonathan was getting at school. Someone who had had school trouble herself, Jonathan's mother frequently critiqued the system with Jonathan (this did not lessen Jonathan's desire to be successful) and tried to accommodate his emotional needs while staying present in her responsibilities as mother. (She and Jonathan frequently took time out to go to the zoo on school days during elementary and middle school; she also made Jonathan complete assignments and other schoolwork.) Jonathan's mother consistently told him that he was a good and worthwhile person. Wounded kids are often desperate for a parent or adult supporter to counteract and balance the negative messages of school, and providing this kind of positive mirroring is a central piece of parenting for those of us who seek to keep our kids well in school.

In the game of schooling, even though they make mistakes, take shortcuts, "forget" assignments, and don't quite tell us the complete truth about many school situations (for which they need to experience

WHAT MIDDLE SCHOOL
STUDENTS NEED TO SURVIVE SCHOOL

- Attentive adult supporters who balance negative peer messages students may get about school
- Opportunities to experience the self in positive situations outside of school: musically, athletically, in volunteer work, in politics
- Lots of opportunities for complex, self-directed, pleasurable learning
- Intellectual challenges and a sense of mastery gained from them
- Frequent opportunities to consider the lives of others, to rebalance focus on self
- Opportunities to complexify thinking, to take responsibility, to organize, and to administer

the consequences) in the larger scheme we need to communicate to our children, "I am on your side. Let's figure this out together." Too often when our children experience difficulty in school, we side with educators because we believe this is our "appropriate" role as a parent. First and foremost, a supportive parent listens when his or her child speaks about school. The parent listens without interrupting, without rushing to judgment, with a view toward simply understanding what the child is saying. "What is the teacher expecting you to do?" "Do you think the assignment is challenging?" "What do you need to do better?" "Could you ask the teacher?" If children genuinely feel that you will listen without judgment, and that you are willing to see things from many points of view (theirs, the school's, yours), they are learning to think through, by themselves, the difficult problems school presents. Through your example, they also are learning to listen to themselves. This is perhaps the most crucial step in being well: learning to value one's own opinions and beliefs while considering the beliefs of others.

Reframing Positively

Ned Hallowell, the ebullient physician and coauthor of *Driven to Distraction*[26] and *Positively A.D.D.*,[27] recently gave a graduation speech at the Eagle Hill School in Massachusetts, a high school for students with various kinds of learning differences. As someone who has ADHD and who positively embraces the many and wondrous gifts of being cognitively different and not fitting the mold of "normal," Hallowell has long spoken of his own struggles with conventional schooling, the way he has come to understand his own mind, and his process of self-acceptance and patience with his own way of doing things. He is a very skillful and superbly positive reframer. As an advocate and doctor for individuals with learning differences, in his graduation speech Hallowell told seniors at Eagle Hill to embrace their differences and to revel in them, because the world depends on them to change the world. "You are beautifully, magnificently, and so very variously talented. You do not fit the mold, thank God. In fact, God depends upon you to keep changing the mold. Others in this world, the ones who plod ordinarily along, living with attention surplus disorder or the other disabilities of normalcy, sometimes don't understand you. Sometimes they place misleading labels on you, like LD or ADD. But believe me, they rely on you. The world relies on you."[28] Hallowell told the graduating seniors that they were part of a group of the "magnificently minded," those whose gifts give them extraordinary talents and abilities if they can learn how to appreciate and use them. This is a powerful message for parents to give to their children, no matter what their learning profile.

Research and anecdotal evidence describe the critical importance of interpretation of difficulties and setbacks in a positive light to avoid school wounding. A 2002 study in Britain looked at 41 mothers of children with "intellectual disabilities"—those with some kind of significant learning difference—measuring the influence of mothers' attitudes toward the child in terms of family happiness and overall student outcome. (The mothers filled out questionnaires on their perceptions of the child and their ideas about how the child affected the rest of the family.) The study overwhelmingly concluded that mothers' positive perception of the child, in terms of seeing the child as a source of happiness and fulfillment and a wellspring of strength and family closeness, was associated with overall family well-being and better adjustment for the child.[29]

Cognitive psychologists have looked closely at the idea of explanatory style: the reasons we use to explain another person's behavior and our own. A parent who is intent on guiding a child through school without laceration, or is dealing with a child who is already wounded, must be an inveterate and practiced positive reframer, able to interpret the child's behavior in a positive light and recast it for the child. In a wonderful book about the gifts of children who have ADHD, clinical psychologist Lara Hanos-Webb describes ways in which parents can constantly "reframe" negative events in school, looking for positive motives in their children's behavior and appreciating their unique gifts. She offers some helpful hints for parents about positive reframing.[30]

- When a child behaves in school in ways that are counterproductive—like calling out in class and annoying the teacher and other classmates—instead of thinking of the behavior as defiant and antisocial, ask your son or daughter why she was doing what she was doing. She may explain that she was trying to make the classroom livelier. Your child actually may be trying to add vitality to the learning environment, or make people laugh.
- Encourage your child's reflection on his or her own actions. Listen attentively (and without judgment) when he or she offers reasons for the behavior.
- Notice and praise your child's creativity. It may be that calling out something funny was a unique way of dealing with what he or she perceived to be a dull classroom, and it is important for parents to notice and support these qualities as they may not easily find expression at school.

Whether a child has diagnosed learning differences or not, given the likelihood of negative and discouraging feedback for students in school, parents need to be flexible and muscular in positively reframing, adopting optimistic and strength-seeking explanatory styles. "Keep their good qualities in mind even when you want to strangle them," says Ned Hallowell—good advice generally for any parent in any circumstance.

"It's Just School"

> Each of our sons had to find within himself the motivation to be a true learner and not merely an obedient student.
> —Robert Fried, *The Passionate Learner*, 2001

As Melody demonstrated at the beginning of this chapter, while honoring the seriousness of school and the importance of effort (persistence, self-discipline, and ambition), parents also need to keep school performance in perspective for their children. Although school increasingly occupies more and more of a child's existence, with longer school days and mounting burdens of homework, it is critical that children have other experiences besides school, and develop other competencies beyond school, that fan the flame of passionate, pleasureful learning. Robert Fried, the author of *The Passionate Learner*, offered this reflection on his own sons' struggles with school:

Having lived through the K–12 experiences of two boys who had their ups and downs with public schooling, I have the luxury of some perspective. Among the experiences we went through during these years, were battles with a third grade teacher over disciplinary practices; the refusal of one son, during grades seven through nine, to allow himself to excel in any school activity; the social life of another son that threatened, at times, to overwhelm all other concerns; the studious avoidance of all high school advanced placement courses by one; the other's lack of desire to push himself to achieve ivy league eligibility scholastically. Neither tried to be a star athlete or a class officer or a prizewinner, academically or otherwise. . . . Both boys graduated from high school. . . . Both were accepted by a very good college, despite not having a stellar school record, and both have very positive feelings about their college experiences. One has since graduated; the other is enjoying the intellectual adventure at college that seemed to have eluded him in high school. . . . Each of our sons had to find within himself the motivation to be a true learner and not merely an obedient student. It was there despite just okay SATs and few extracurricular embellishments. I think now that it is this independence that has made their college experience more than a stepping-stone to a career or a four-year holiday from home. Each in his own way brought to college a quiet determination to be his own person, as a learner—to explore subjects he had no previous experience with; to take chances in signing up for courses that seemed especially challenging; to change majors several times without panicking. I am very proud of them for that, and it has reaffirmed for me the value of a parent's backing off and waiting for the child's own sense of self, as a learner, to emerge. Backing off is rarely an easy choice.[31]

For parents, constantly balancing the influence of school; providing children with a place to reflect on their academic experiences without judgment or critique, and to experience noncompetitive and choiceful, self-directed learning; and emphasizing that while they are very important, elementary, middle, and high school are not the decisive experiences of one's life, are all critical messages parents need to give their children. Remembering a child's early joy at learning and exploration—the way a child learning to walk persists and experiences pleasure in newfound abilities, the ways in which young children dive into art projects and imaginary play—will help parents support their children through the difficult years of less choiceful schooling. Preserving the flame of pleasure in learning, guarding and fanning it, can help children pass over the shoals of schooling without being shipwrecked.

KEEPING IT IN PERSPECTIVE

Jen, who just turned 7, gets off the bus from school with tears in her eyes. A second grader, she got back her first marked paper with a large "-1" at the top. "I'm no good," she says. "I'm less than nothing!" As children come home from school with some of their first marked papers and worksheets of the year, concerned parents may wonder how to support their children's academic competence and empower them for the many years of school to come. First, we have to face a bit of reality. As parents we need to understand that our children are, in all likelihood, going to be tested more often than we were in school, and more time will be spent preparing for and taking standardized tests during the school year—in particular, those mandated by No Child Left Behind and others required by the state and district. Additionally, our children's learning environments often are dominated by curriculum designed around the demands of a test. With this extensive prepping, testing, and marking, keeping a child interested and engaged in school, is an important issue parents must attend to.

Help your child keep grades and standardized test scores in perspective. All parents want their children to do well in school, but grades and test scores really don't provide a full range of information about your child. Your child has many strengths and abilities that a report card or a test score can't communicate. You need to keep these things in mind—and let your child know how much you value him or her. Laying the groundwork for this view of testing and marking will become even more important as your child faces high school SATs, AP exams, and minutely calibrated grade point averages. While you don't want to communicate a laissez-faire attitude about tests and grades, you need to tell your child how much other things about them matter.

Know that standardized tests are fallible and do not always provide accurate information. Lots of research shows that test scores can vary from day to day, and it is wrong for a school system to make judgments about a child's placement or "ability" based on a single test or grade. Furthermore, that a child actually has had a chance to study the material tested on state and federally mandated test is not always a given. The kinds of tests that most children take are useful for judging how whole groups of kids in schools are doing, but not as useful in determining the progress of an individual child. You are entitled to information about how a test was prepared for, what the results mean, and how the school intends to use the scores. Teachers and administrators should be able to tell you this in clear, nondefensive language.

Stay in dialog with your child's teacher and school. This can't be
emphasized enough. Not only will your child benefit greatly from
your parental involvement in the school or classroom, but every
time you set foot in your child's school you will learn more about
his or her experiences and the goals and style of the teacher.
Volunteer to go on class field trips or help with enrichment nights,
if it is not possible for you to be at school during the day. Teachers
and administrators positively notice parents who are involved with
the school, and this helps your child feel recognized and seen at
school.

Speak to your child about your educational values. What is really
important to you about your child's educational experience? It's
critical you do a little soul-searching about *your* most meaningful
school experiences and tell your child about them. If your most
powerful learning experiences came in art class and not geometry,
tell your child why. Explain what you'd like for your child and how
you think this might happen. This helps kids gain perspective on
the many tasks and kinds of learning they must demonstrate in
school, and feel that they have choices and can shape their own
way.

*Provide your child with alternative environments in which to learn, be
creative, and demonstrate mastery.* As learning advocates Grace
Llewellyn and Amy Silver note in their book *Guerrilla Learning*,
powerful learning involves being able to choose what you are
learning, being interested in the topic, and having freedom to
explore and make mistakes. You will need to set aside time in your
week to give kids "free space" to think about what interests them,
and support them in pursuing it. If this means a messy art corner
with cut-up magazines and spilled paints, this is part of supporting
your learner. I know of a 7-year-old who became fascinated with
opera after finding an old LP at a tag sale. Now he's becoming an
accomplished musician and routinely makes his family dress up and
act out parts of operas.

Believe in your child's strengths and help him or her to see them. You are
the strongest and most articulate advocate for your child, and
always will be—especially during your child's school years. Going
to school is more demanding and filled with more hurdles than
it was in the past, and children need lots of support and specific
encouragement in getting through their experiences whole and
well. If a child needs academic support, help him or her find it. If
your child does poorly on a test or has a bad year, help him or her
see what didn't work and how he or she might be able to change

things. Emphasize that each new year is a chance to start again and to work to meet his or her own goals. Helping your child strategize about how to overcome the inevitable mistakes and obstacles of 12, 16, or even 20 years of schooling is an important life skill. As a parent you are always a mirror in which your child sees him- or herself. You need to reflect back positive, hopeful, forward-looking messages.

Demonstrate a love of learning in your own life. As school becomes more oriented toward performance on tests and other measures, it's important that you show your child how you continue to love learning outside of school. What engages you and makes you feel curious and eager to know more? How do you pursue these interests? Talk to your child about this and let him or her see you passionately engaged in your own learning, so the fires of his or her interests continue to grow.

CHAPTER 8

Teachers
Who Heal

Nearly 32 years ago, while serving an 18-month sentence in a New York State Division for Youth detention facility, I met a teacher who taught math in a way I could understand. Before I met him, I was totally turned off to math. My teachers did not explain it in a way I could understand, so I shut down. Here's what I remember about this teacher. He wore his hair in a ponytail. He wore jeans and a t-shirt. He cared about us. He made us feel special. He took some of us fishing. He was nice. He was cool. He was patient. I never forgot his impact on my learning experience. . . .

As a New York City educator for over 20 years, I have been in the presence of greatness. Many teachers are worth their weight in gold. I have seen teachers perform what many may describe as miracles. A teacher touches individual students. A teacher teaches individuals, not classes. A teacher sees the possibilities in her students. A teacher gives hope. A teacher gives voice. A teacher navigates. A teacher explores. A teacher is patient. A teacher learns with his or her students. A teacher discovers. A teacher is a parent. A teacher accepts children as they are, not as he or she would like them to be.

—Bernard Gassaway, superintendent of alternative schools
in New York City and doctoral student at Teachers College[1]

"A Teacher Accepts Children as They Are,
Not as He or She Would Like Them to Be": Two Recollections

Teachers matter enormously in the wounding and unwounding of students. As the stories in this book describe, teachers have immense power to lacerate students with small, careless comments; through aggressive acts of institutionally sanctioned cruelty; or by ignoring silent, disengaged, or undisruptive learners. They can label children "average" or not gifted, and expect far too little of them; they can create instructional environments where students have no idea of their own intellectual or moral capacities. On the other hand, teachers also have the power to transform lives and create meaning and connection in ways that few professions offer. My undergraduate students, when given an opportunity to express why they are interested in education, write passionate and beautiful essays about some of the extraordinary teachers in their lives who "saved" them, who believed in them, who communicated to them that they were of value when they felt unvalued in the system, or who saw unusual capacity in them and challenged them to reach for it. These teachers, my students say, inspired them to become teachers themselves.

To open this chapter on teachers who heal wounds, the following are two recollections from my undergraduates, of teachers who touched their lives in ways that they have not forgotten—in ways that healed and inspired them. The first is from a student who recalled an especially thoughtful elementary school teacher.

Recollection 1: "Take Your Time"

"My eyes follow Mrs. Schmidt as she makes her way over to her desk and picks up a pile of papers. 'These should not take you long,' she says as she walks around the U-shaped semicircle of desks, licking her thumb and pointer finger as she separates the slippery pages. The other children eagerly grab the single sheet of paper and hastily begin to scribble their answers, tongues sticking out the corners of their mouths, light-up sneaker feet wrapped tight around the legs of their miniature chairs. Perfect concentration. As she approaches me, I extend my small hand out to meet the flimsy page that is now waving delicately in the air, mocking me, taunting me, 'you'll never get it.' Once on my desk, the problems are staring me straight in the face. Blinking, I'm lost. Another deep breath and let's try this again.

"But now the boy to my left is pushing back his chair and the screech of the metal against the linoleum floor hurts my ears. I try to shake the outside noises from my head but it seems as though everyone is talking, screaming. Every inch of air in this small third-grade classroom is filled with the excited squeals of kids who have just finished their multiplication quiz and now are free to go to recess early. My hands are now clenched into fists and my throat becomes hot with tears. I dig my fingernails hard into the sides of my temples, deep enough to leave a mark. Don't cry, don't cry.

"And then, as if I had spoken the words out loud, I feel the touch of a hand on my back. 'Take your time.' My eyes turn up to see Miss

Alvarez, the black-haired, brown-eyed intern whom I first became fond of because she said we looked alike. Now those kind, familiar eyes are focused on mine. Her calmness covers me like a blanket and my breathing slows. The classroom is empty now but I don't care. Miss Alvarez says I have all the time in the world.

"When I reflect on why I want to become a teacher, this memory will forever come to mind. Had it not been for Miss Alvarez, I am not sure I would have made it through third grade alive. Looking back now, I am able to see how Miss Alvarez recognized my frustrations and dealt with them in a way that was kind and soothing. She was able to understand me on a level that no other teacher had before. I wish I could tell Miss Alvarez how much of a difference she made that year."

—Sherry, college student, age 20

In this second recollection, a student ponders the differences between the classroom environments of two teachers in her senior year of high school. How can two instructional spaces be so different in tone and feel? she wonders.

Recollection 2: "A Reciprocation of Glances"

"I sit and stare blankly at the clock as the seconds pass as hours, the monotone lesson in the background as I look down and realize I have signed my name over and over and over again, filling an entire sheet of paper. Another question asked and no response. Heads bob and notes are passed. Cell phones buzz and muffled laughter is hidden. Blank glances are visible all over the room, the front row empty. As I look up to catch Mrs. Coates's attention, as if to show I am making some effort to listen, she stares at the floor, never looking up, completely unaware of the circus her classroom has become. Numbers scrambled on the board and half-erased formulas. Unopened books and new crisp notebooks, free from notes, other doodles, or notes to fellow classmates. My mind wanders as I wish I were anywhere but here. I used to like math—I'm not the only one who can't stand it now. No one is listening, no one cares to listen, and listening seems painful. The second hand creeps along until the long-awaited bell tolls. Papers fly, and chairs screech, gossip is spoken and assignments and announcements are ignored. I feel guilty, yes, but how could I listen when I can barely stay awake? Would this really last a whole year? Was I the only one who cared?

"The bell rings and I move to the next class. Unbelievably, the teacher shakes our hands as we enter room 316. I realize this has never happened before. Our handshake frees me from intimidation, as if we are on the same level. I mention my name and the teacher, Mr. Wilson, immediately recognizes me as having attended a basketball camp he coached over 4 years ago. Casual conversation with a teacher? It did exist. I could get used to this. International Relations? I think to myself. Who expected this?

"I had never experienced a class like this before. Would everyone think I was dumb? Did everyone know what we'd be learning already? Smiling faces fill the room as the class period opened with a few hilarious jokes about current events. I can see myself enjoying this class—is that possible? I find myself intrigued by every aspect of Mr. Wilson's first lesson. His passion for this subject is apparent in each statement he makes. His enthusiasm spreads around the room like wildfire as he shares his plans for the semester with us. Interactive lessons, presentations, field trips, movies, guest speakers, what more could anyone ask for? 'I want you to remember this class, as corny as I may sound, forever,' he emphasizes. Heads nod and notebooks are cracked open as students begin to take copious notes. 'I deal with homework a little differently than most teachers,' he explains. 'I'm a big fan of response writing and reflection on the day's class, and I always want you to be keeping up on current events. Tests, yes, we do have them, but I'm not going to fool you, I'm very fair, I want you to have fun. I'm never going to talk at you, I can promise you that much. If you ever catch me talking for more than 10 minutes without class interaction, please stop me.' A wave of relief passes over the room, as Senior International Relations becomes a favorite class. The bell rings and no one moves. The discussion continues until he urges us to leave and enjoy our weekend.

"I might want to be a teacher in order to do everything Mr. Wilson, my International Relations teacher, did for me (and for others), and everything Mrs. Coates did not do for me, for others. My International Relations class was a true inspirational experience that will stick in my mind forever as the first moment I considered teaching. I constantly found myself thinking that I could see myself in his position, I could be like that. I might want to be a teacher because I would love to look out onto an array of faces and based on the reciprocation of their glances, know that I am making a difference in their lives. I might be a teacher in order to make up for and amend the bad experiences I had to go through. I want to be a figure of inspiration, a source of knowledge for eager and developing minds, a helping hand, a friend. I might want to be a teacher because I can see it as something I would love, something I would be good at. I might want to be a teacher because someday I could be the memory mentioned as someone else's source of inspiration."

—Jacinta, age 21

The New Professional

> The new professional is a person who is not only competent in his or her discipline but has the skill and the will to deal with the institutional pathologies that threaten the profession's highest standards.
>
> —Parker J. Palmer, *A New Professional*, 2007[2]

In a powerful recent essay, author and social activist Parker J. Palmer writes about the original meaning of the word *professional*. A professional, in its centuries-old meaning, says Palmer, was not someone who merely possessed technical skills and was highly knowledgeable in his or her area of expertise, but who made a "profession of faith in the midst of a disheartening world," who embodied (and acted on) the passions and commitments that took him or her into the work, who was animated by a sense of calling in his or her day-to-day life. How do we stay close to the ideals that originally drew us to teaching, Palmer asks, when so much of what we know about the profession of teaching is discouraging and alienating? How do we keep ourselves powerful and active—"challenging myself, my colleagues, and my institution to keep faith with [my] profession's deepest values?"[3] Citing losses of "healing heart" in the medical, legal, and education field, Palmer calls for a new kind of professional education for teachers—one that places a high priority on the moral purposes of the work of teaching and other helping professions. Palmer wishes to create individuals who are able to actively voice objections to the "institutional inhumanity" of the settings in which they work.

From the students whose recollections open this chapter, we know that teachers are the critical component of students' affective experiences of school—more than the school building, more than the attitudes of the principal, more than the instructional goals of the lesson, more than the falling of snowflakes outside the window of the classroom, or the fight between the pupil and his father before school. The live connection between two human beings in the instructional environment—the emotional experience of this interaction—is the soul of educative practice. Yet we also know that the conditions of teaching make it increasingly difficult for many instructors to achieve their goals and dreams for their profession— they themselves are wounded teachers—denuded of their delight in this intensely challenging work. Many teachers feel powerless to take action against the forces that make their work overwhelming and difficult to do well—teachers describe themselves frequently as "cogs in the machine," or unheard, and fall into wounding behavior toward themselves and their students. "We professionals . . . have a bad habit of telling ourselves victim stories to excuse unprofessional behavior. . . . The hidden curriculum of our culture portrays institutions as powers other than us, over which we have marginal control. . . . But while we may find ourselves marginalized or dismissed for calling institutions into account, they are neither other than us or alien to us: institutions are us. The shadows that institutions cast over our lives are external expressions of our own inner shadows," says Palmer, cautioning against passivity or acclimation to the wounding conditions of many instructors' lives.[4]

Healing teachers, three of whom are profiled in this chapter, have recognized the need to act against some of the violating cultural norms of the schools in which they work, and to establish communities of caring, recognition, and personal challenge in educational environments they (too often) find caustic, alienating, and anti-intellectual. This chapter celebrates these professionals—teachers who recognize and act on student wounding and seek to create "spaces of shelter, islands of comfort in a hostile school climate," as Eve puts it. Some of the commonalities of their experiences—their sense of aloneness in their work, their need to find community around their beliefs about teaching and relationships with students and instruction, and their efforts to exert change on an institutional system that frequently seems overwhelming—are part of the heroic (but still too individualistic) work of healing teachers. We need to join together to form movements of teachers who object to the institutional conditions of our work, and who create community and momentum for changing those conditions from within.

What qualities are most important in teachers, from a student's point of view? In one broad-ranging research study, *preservice teachers* were asked to identify and rank the most important characteristics associated with excellent teachers.[5] Six themes emerged (ranked in order of importance): student centeredness, enthusiasm for teaching, ethicalness, classroom and behavior management, teaching methodology, and knowledge of subject. Another study reviewed the literature on teachers who "had made a difference" in students' lives and concluded that teacher knowledge of the subject, enthusiasm for the subject, the tone of class discussions, the quality of a teacher's voice, and the ability of a teacher to inspire students to think deeply were the qualities most valued by students.[6]

As a participant in a professional development workshop that I recently conducted said, "The good news is—teachers matter. The bad news? Teachers matter." Without the skills and knowledge to construct meaningful lessons, and lacking a commitment to student unwounding,

WHAT MAKES AN EXCELLENT TEACHER?

Research-based investigations of "teacher as professional" provide ample evidence of the importance of teacher knowledge and skill to student outcomes. We know that teachers account for 30–50% of the variance between students in what is learned year by year, and that focusing on teacher knowledge and skill is the most effective way to improve student achievement.[7]

In a fascinating study, researcher Brian Rowan looked at the degree to which teachers regarded their work as a complex set of "non-routine" activities.[8] Not surprisingly, he found that how teachers see their work—and how they think about the complexity of the acts of teaching and learning—has a dramatic effect on how they approach their work and perform tasks in classrooms. Rowan found that most teachers in his study viewed teaching either as a set of routine tasks or "expert" tasks, and that even teachers who had quite complex views of knowledge and learning tended to regard many of their teaching tasks as routine.

> English teachers, more than all others, endorsed a constructivist view of teaching, seeing knowledge in their subject area as dynamic and emphasizing creative classroom discussion and student-directed learning. In contrast, mathematics teachers saw knowledge as relatively cut and dried, felt a strong need to cover fixed curriculum, and endorsed the idea that knowledge was best learned in small chunks organized in a sequence from basic to higher order skills. . . . Teachers who viewed school knowledge as relatively fixed, sequenced and standardized also viewed the task of teaching as relatively routine. . . . By contrast, teachers who viewed school knowledge as more fluid, relative and learner-constructed tended to report higher levels of task variety and uncertainty.[9]

But this study makes a critical dilemma for teachers more clear. Teachers who saw the act of learning as highly complex and non-routine experienced *more uncertainty* as they approached their teaching tasks than teachers who saw learning as relatively straightforward. "As teachers come to endorse constructivist beliefs about teaching, they have fewer established procedures to rely on as they teach, move away from understandable sequences of steps to guide their actions, and are thus faced with higher levels of task uncertainty. This conflicts with current views of teaching as an expert task."[10]

For teachers like Eve, Abby, and Ennis—as portrayed later in this chapter—coming to view one's work as increasingly uncertain, non-routine, and full of dilemmas and unknown complexities, in many school settings, is directly in conflict with accountability measures that emphasize the predictability of results and teacher knowledge as concretized, readily sequenced, and delivered. In many school settings, to be an expert teacher is to be certain, and to have a routinized set of teaching moves—whereas Rowan's research suggests that precisely the opposite is true.

teachers have much power to harm. But with their moral and intellectual powers rightly aligned, as shown in the stories of Eve, Abby, and Ennis, they also have power to inspire and transform.

Eve: Creating an Island of Acceptance in a Harsh School Climate

Eve is a high school art teacher in a suburb outside of Houston. She has been a teacher for 25 years, working briefly in advertising early on in her career, but missing the passion and energy of high school students too much, she returned to school. Born and raised in the midwest, Eve opens our interview by telling me she grew up on a farm—animals were everywhere, and her parents, her central role models, were self-reliant, independent-thinking people who were "always in touch with beauty and practicality. Those tenets make up the fabric of my personality—this is deeply a part of me and why the arts are so important to me in education, at every level. I have learned that I will fight for what I think is right in my profession." Last year, due to steady budget cuts and accountability pressures in a No Child Left Behind testing climate, Eve's school district threatened to do away with any arts requirements for high school gradua-tion. This meant, in effect, that all district funding for the arts was in jeop-ardy at every grade level. Eve said, "I learned a long time ago not to be someone who just lies down and takes it." She organized a district-wide protest among teachers, presented research to the school board on the im-portance of arts instruction to the curriculum, and penned a few "well-timed" newspaper pieces describing the disastrous nature of the funding cuts. Ultimately, arts funding was restored. "Part of my self-image, my biography, is to question. That doesn't necessarily make me very popular with my administrators or every colleague. I get my motivation from my students. Where would they be in their lives if the curriculum had no arts? What were they thinking?"

In addition to her scrappy, upstart persona, a few years ago Eve also became the first national board-certified art teacher in her region[11]—a long and arduous process—and the only female in her entire district with a doctorate. (She says she got this degree so that she could continue her own learning, but also make her voice more prominently heard in a male-dominated school administration.) Although she is passionately devoted to her work, and believes that she makes a difference in some students' lives, Eve chafes under the current leadership of her school. "I teach in a very restricted, standardized environment of a suburban high school. The principal is a driven, controlling person who can never be pleased with his staff or students. In this atmosphere, I strive to create a safe haven for my creative arts students and the teachers and students in my department. My curriculum values imagination, human relationships and the exchange of ideas, somatic knowledge, and open-ended learning. In the art studio, we learn through experimentation, processing, and embracing ambiguity." Eve's art studio at school is a huge open space at the far end of her building, a geographic island in the school with windows on three sides that look onto a stand of trees. Student art projects cover the walls, hang from the ceilings, and crowd every corner. Art Tatum plays on a boom box in the corner of the studio, and when I visit, a student has just heated a tray of muffins in the microwave oven in the "kitchen" of the classroom for everyone to share. "Eating is allowed here," Eve says. "We are a family."

Eve reflects on her own school wounds that prompted her to become a teacher and to continue to work in an institutional environment she sometimes finds hostile or uncongenial. "I endured 9 years of Catholic school and was deprived of my passion—art—so I've seen school wounding up close. I guess I realized in first grade that I was an oppositional person, that I was going to be in the margins at school. I didn't fit. During a lesson in first grade I started drawing, and the nun humiliated me, said I was lazy to be drawing when I should have been writing." She told Eve she was going to hell. Eve was mortified and terrified. She went home and told her mother, a non-Catholic and an artist herself. Eve's mother laughed and defended her daughter. "My mom is really cool. She said, 'Adults are often wrong. You need to question stuff, Eve, don't believe everything you are told.' I've become a very critical thinker."

Sketching her own pathway into teaching, Eve immediately describes her mother, herself a wonderfully inspiring teacher. "She is an incredibly creative woman who is straight out of John Dewey. She was so good at making and doing, always creating something beautiful. She is a renowned local artist, and she fostered this sense of imagination in me. She told me I should be an artist." Now as an adult Eve keeps watercolors and an easel set up in her kitchen, so that between moments of cooking and taking care of her family she can sit down and do a quick painting. "That's what it's all about: incorporating our love for the visual, and our imagination, into our work and lives."

Eve tries to make her own classroom like her kitchen, a haven for creative expression, practicality, and inspiration. "I build a safe place in my classroom. You can be weird in my classes and you're fine. We celebrate everyone's birthdays, and we know each other's histories. Last week a girl told the class, through a family history art journal project, about her family's bitter divorce, and another student told about finding his dad drunk behind the bowling alley."

One of the most touching stories Eve recounts is of a young male student who, in ninth grade, came out about his sexuality in her class. His family was unaccepting of his sexual orientation and he struggled during his next 2 years of high school. Early in his junior year he was arrested for a minor drug offense while hanging out with a group of kids. He spent 3 months in a juvenile detention facility. Eve says, "The way the class came together around this young man was remarkable. We all stayed in touch constantly. We were his lifesavers. We were all worried about him getting abused in jail and we sent him messages about our concerns and hopes for him. After he was released, he came back to class on a Monday and we had a huge party! It was the highlight of the year. This troubled young man brought the class together in a community that isn't very tolerant of alternative sexual identities."

I ask Eve about the isolation she sometimes experiences in her work—whether there are other teachers in the building who share her philosophy and who seek to create similar relationships with students. Eve says this has been a struggle, one of the reasons she became a department chair, so that she could hire teachers who would "create a center of gravity" in the fine arts department. "The band director, the chorus teacher, and the theater teacher, who are all grouped together in my wing of the building, are all of the same mind—that our first priority is to build relationships with students, to create a safe haven, and to create opportunities for them to be the best they can be in the arts. Although we are generally well liked among the faculty, we fine arts teachers have all had disagreements with the academic teachers at times. We've had words over issues such as keeping students out of our classes to make up academic tests, using the band and chorus rooms for meetings without asking permission, and leaving these rooms a mess. There are also many demands that must be limited, such as the idea that the art students and our supplies should be available at the drop of a hat to make banners and signs for every schoolwide event. The underlying issue is lack of respect for the arts, and our lack of parity with academic subjects." Eve says that she's been fighting these battles since she became a teacher. "I don't teach in a wealthy district, and I don't teach rich kids. The role of the arts isn't always well understood here."

Describing her teaching philosophy, and talking about the way in which creation is central to the act of teaching, Eve describes some of the influences on her instructional philosophy. "Imagination is at the heart of my curriculum. An art project can communicate the features of an adventure: the excitement of beginning, the enjoyment of the process, and the intrigue of not knowing the precise outcome. The unpredictable and indeterminate aspects of curriculum encourage transformative learning. My curriculum framework draws on the work of John Dewey, Maxine Greene, and Elliot Eisner."

Sounding like the district reformer that she has fashioned herself to be, Eve goes further in illuminating the ideas that undergird her teaching philosophy. "No change can happen unless we first imagine it. That's what [educational philosopher] Maxine Greene believed. Greene defined imagination as a means through which we can assemble a coherent alternate world . . . something that permits us to give credence to alternative realities. Like Dewey, Greene saw imagination as a unifying force, but she rejected closed-end purposes for imagination." Pointing to a laminated quote Eve has hung on her studio classroom wall, she references Maxine Greene again: "The role of imagination is not to resolve, not to point the way, not to improve. It is to awaken, to disclose the ordinarily unseen, unheard, and unexpected." Eve says that for her, participating in this kind of "unresolved" creation is at the heart of a satisfying life, and that's what she tries to encourage in her classroom with students. "The imagination and its attendant aesthetic experiences are not complete without the full sensory stimulation that comes with creating in the physical world." Eve says she wishes she could spend more time in the transformative creative process, but the demands of school simply don't allow this.

In spite of her many successes and her passionate connection to the work of teaching the arts, Eve is considering leaving the profession. "This career has been uplifting until I came to this school 4 years ago. It is now draining most of the time. This is because too much of my creative energy is sapped by nonteaching duties such as paperwork and department chair meetings—they are very stressful and make me feel powerless. The greatest loss is that I no longer have time to make samples of artworks for our projects. Teacher-made samples have long been a staple in my motivation when introducing a new project, and the student work is never as high quality or as expansive without the samples to energize the introduction."

After speaking with me for this interview, however, and revisiting some of the roots of her love of teaching, Eve phones me back to talk a little more. "I just did a workshop on creative thinking for high school students. It showed me how much I adore working with adolescent artists. There's nothing like their creative energy! I realized I can't give this work up, no matter how tough it gets. It is what feeds me, and what allows students to express things they cannot in other places in their life. We are mutual healers in the classroom. That is my vision. We all need that, Kirsten," Eve explains.

Abby: Teaching in a Democratic Environment

Working in a large comprehensive high school outside of Boston, Abigail (Abby) Erdmann teaches in one of the few remaining democratically organized high school programs in Massachusetts. Philosophically rooted in the educational movements of the 1960s, School Within a School (SWS) was founded in 1970 by a group of teacher leaders to provide a democratic education for high school students who chose, by lottery application, to enter this alternative program in their sophomore year of high school. With its philosophical roots still evident and frequently discussed—society is oppressive and technocratic, and school is a possible agent of liberation—students in SWS must take at least two SWS courses each semester (generally more) and attend the weekly SWS Town Meeting, a representative decision-making body run by students.

Today, unlike so many other educational experiments that sprang from the 1960s, the program is a thriving democratic community, serving 115 sophomores, juniors, and seniors, with over a dozen full- and part-time teachers. Dramatically oversubscribed and popular—this past year more than a fifth of the freshman class applied for admission to SWS for 40 spaces—"SWS has become the place where kids who really care about their education want to be," one junior remarked. "It used to be considered alternative—not in a good way alternative, at least by some kids. Now it's considered alternative—good. It's viewed as the place where actively thinking, engaged students want to be." In Abby's program, all major decisions are made collectively in the weekly, mandatory democratic-style Town Meeting or in subcommittees, including course choices for the coming year; policies on discipline, attendance, and grading; and the hiring of new staff members. Participation in community activities, committees, and the classroom is in some sense mandatory—students sign a contract at the point of enrollment agreeing to take responsibility for their own education and for the community. SWS teachers emphasize the development of student identity and voice, cooperative learning styles, and social action as a part of engaged learning. A founding member of SWS and one of its pillars, philosophically and interpersonally, Abby has been teaching in SWS for over 35 years. "Many of us [staff members] have been at the school longer than we've been with our families. This is part of who we are, this is our fabric. We have all grown up and transformed together."

Philosophically, democratic education tends to view learning as "a natural part of growing up." Abby says she believes that, in most circumstances, human beings can be trusted to learn. "Fundamentally, students are motivated by interesting things," Abby observes in an interview. "If

~~~~~~

WHAT ARE DEMOCRATIC SCHOOLS?

Schools that are entirely managed by adults do not teach democracy, and do not enable young people to experience or practice meaningful participation in the social institutions with which they are most intimately involved.

—Ron Miller, *What Is Democratic Education?*, 2007[12]

- Democratic education is rooted philosophically in some of the radical educational movements of the 1960s.
- Society was viewed as oppressive and technocratic, and school need to be constructed as an agent of liberating individuals from it.
- Learning was viewed as a natural part of growing up, and the human impulse to learn was regarded with great trust, while the institutions of society were often mistrusted.
- Democratic schools generally practice participatory democracy, based on the Deweyan notion that "all those who are affected by social institutions must have a share in producing and managing them." In democratically organized schools the belief is that students ought to have the same power and responsibility in school, where they spend so much of their lives, as adults have. "When individuals are bound by limitations, expectations, or rules they had no part in establishing, then they cannot be said to live in a democratic environment."[13]

For more information on democratic education and schools around the world that practice it, see the Online Directory of Democratic Education.[14]

~~~~~~

we teach well, we don't have to mangle and twist students to comply. Good learning, in some sense, is voluntary and self-motivated."

For Abby, making the transition from a traditional, hierarchical, grade-driven educational environment of her own student days to SWS "was not immediate." A radical war protester and 1960s activist, Abby graduated from Smith College in the 1960s and loved English—she loved reading books, talking and writing about books, and thinking about writing. She said to herself, "If I can do this as my job, and spend the rest of my life with great authors, that's a good life." After teaching at several much more traditional school programs in the Boston area, and wanting to "live my ideals" as an activist more explicitly, Abby heard through the teacher grapevine that SWS was being started at a high school in the Boston area. "I was fortunate to get that job. We really were all just putting things together at the beginning, feeling our way. We had a lot of help from educators who were philosophically and practically more experienced than we were," and even so, she says, as a teacher she still had a lot to learn. "We were all working on moving from our own traditional educations in the first years of teaching to establishing SWS, where there was a different model of the teacher. It is not, of course, the teacher in charge. With students, we are carrying something together, but we had to learn how to do this. In a democratic teaching environment, it's not just my classroom, it's ours. If there is an overall strand or theme in my teaching through the decades, it has been about giving up control," Abby reflects. An intensive yoga practitioner starting in her 40s, Abby notes that the physical discipline and philosophy of yoga have influenced how she teaches. "Doing yoga myself was a big help in changing the way I thought about teaching: do the pose and think about what's in your life. Bring that into your teaching. I teach from myself."

Abby is considered by many of her students to be "the best English teacher they've ever had," and her scores of ongoing relationships with former students speak to her influence on the individuals with whom she comes in contact as a teacher. (When I am interviewing her, she gets a call from a former student, and is going to meet a student for dinner at the end of her day.) When a group of students present SWS's program to the parent body of the main high school on an open house night, one effervescent junior talks about the intelligence, skill, and commitment of the teachers in SWS. He says, "This is really the best of the best kind of education—an opportunity to grow and stretch ourselves as thinkers and writers." Then, in conclusion, he exclaims, "I want to be Abby when I grow up." (Many of SWS's students do go on to become teachers.)

At the heart of Abby's connection to kids, and in her stance as an unwounding teacher, she says, is her emphasis on relationships. "It starts when you walk through the door of school. You look at every kid in the face. You assess what's going on. You have a whole-child model—you know kids, you know their families, their siblings, what's happening in their lives. You have to be available to kids, to meet with them, and sometimes you have to initiate contact even if they don't seek it out. At our school you can bump into 40 kids a day just by being in our community. I am in constant communication with teachers, parents, students, with our alums. I talk with someone I've taught every week." For Abby, the practice of being a healing teacher involves "seeing students as completely as possible." "I am a demanding teacher, I ask for a lot. But I really do try to know my students, to know when I've pushed too far, to be honest about what is going on with me and how that might affect our interactions. I think I'm good at raising the expectations. I just said to a kid who was doing B+ level work, 'I'd like you to take this up a notch to an A,' and he said, 'I was just thinking the same thing.'"

Abby notes that her pupils have changed through her decades of teaching. "Kids have become much more driven academically through the years. At first they were much less focused, a bit more creative. The kids used to be like wayward horses out at pasture. You'd have to grab a handful of oats, go out into the field with a halter, and bring them into the barn to get them ready to learn. Now, they come into class all groomed and tacked—they are ready to go. It's a big change." Not always sure that this new intensity of academic focus produces the best work, Abby says she has to do more modeling of the kind of classroom interactions she is looking for, the fact that she is not going to "tell kids how to do it." All her classes are conduced in a seminar style, with desks in a circle, and with the establishment of classroom norms and collective caring for diverse points of view "pretty much the first thing that is up." Describing a brand-new course she recently designed (and students approved)—The Literature of War—Abby describes how she opened the class on the first day. "I told them that I had been waiting 40 years to teach this course, that in the 1960s I was a war protester and had been violently against the Vietnam War. I had been unfair in my judgments about the soldiers who had to fight— black and white and judgmental. This course was a chance for me to make amends, to understand more deeply the conflicts and sacrifices of fighting for one's country as a soldier." This honest expression of "where she was" prompted equally honest and powerful commitments to learning from her students, who also shared on the first day why they had decided to take the course.

Abby says she learned how to do this kind of teaching collaboratively and informally, with other teachers she paired up with through the years. "When I was a young teacher, one of my best collaborations was with another teacher. We'd call each other up every night after we'd put our own kids to bed and talk to each other. What worked today? What didn't go well today? Why? What are the important questions we need to ask tomorrow? This kind of training is something anyone can do, to team with a teacher who knows something you want to know." In a theme repeated by most of the deeply committed teachers interviewed for this book, Abby tells me, "Teachers need to do more of it. That's central to getting better at your practice, to be thinking about it in a critical way."

"A lot of my teaching is recovery from Brearley," Abby says, describing the highly competitive, socially prominent all-girls school she attended in Manhattan as a girl. "The way writing excellence was modeled at Brearley," she recalls, "was that the teacher kept one 'perfect' paper to read to the rest of the class, while everyone else sat holding their graded, 'nonperfect paper.'" Abby decided at some point in her own teaching that she was going to turn that model on its head. As part of the structure of her classes (literature or writing) every student reads their papers aloud to small groups of the class, and their final papers to the entire class. The final paper-reading events are usually held at a student's house, and everyone brings food and contributes to the celebration. In the final reading, every paper has been through at least a couple of drafts, edited by fellow students and Abby. "Everyone produces amazing work," Abby says—"it is a focal point of the community fabric of the classroom," and a powerful message about learning as nonprivate, collective, and shared by all. A senior in SWS concurs, describing how much she learned from the paper-editing and reading-aloud process. "At first, as a sophomore, I was intimidated by all the great writers in the class. But I learned so much from everyone. That was where I really got better as a writer—from Abby and from other students. It's one of the most amazing learning experiences I've had."

Now with retirement age approaching, Abby actively considers teaching for as long as possible. "Although it may be easier for some students to approach a younger teacher, I still think I'm pretty accessible. I'm still learning as a teacher, which means I think I still have something to add. For me, teaching is an oasis. I'm always up for it. In the 40 years I've been coming to school, I've never had a bad year. When I'm standing outside ready to come into the building, there is never a place I'd rather be."

Ennis: Living the Questions

The unwounding teacher's life is full of conflicts, nowhere so strongly demonstrated as in the work and biography of Ennis, a teacher in his early 30s I met at a well-to-do suburban high school in Cincinnati. Eager, self-deferential, and hesitant about telling his learning and teaching story, Ennis was the child of somewhat hippyish 1970s parents who sent him to an alternative elementary school that focused on noncompetitive relationships and learning by doing. Although "the work was too easy for me," Ennis said, he loved this school and attended it until sixth grade. At that point his parents divorced and he was transferred to the local elementary school, where he was immediately bullied and picked on. "I was small, I was kind of shy, and the public school was competitive and hierarchical. I was teased on the playground, made fun of. I foolishly went to my teachers to try to get them to intervene, and they completely failed. They called my tormenters into the office with me and said, 'Ennis says you did this.' Like that really helped!" he said shaking his head.

Although Ennis found middle school academic work boring and was "always a misfit in some ways," by high school he was on more stable ground socially and began to find his "sea legs" in school. He had grown physically, had made friends, and had begun to know more "what I wanted to do and what I was interested in." Even so, Ennis told me, "I was really wounded in middle school, and I haven't forgotten."

In high school Ennis mostly coasted. "It was the 1990s, a somewhat more rebellious, alternative time then, and it was possible to get away with more things. I basically didn't do any homework in subjects I wasn't interested in, that I thought were pointless. I was a slacker, and not really engaged intellectually, although I always did a lot of reading outside of high school." He remembers high school without fondness—he says there were no teachers in school who really captivated him or stood out in any special way. "But I had a girlfriend and friends and so I was okay." After high school graduation, "by some miracle of connections," he modestly says, he was admitted to the Massachusetts Institute of Technology and became an English major there—again coasting along the margins at a school dominated by its math, science, and engineering programs. Ennis says his teachers were kind to him at MIT. "Everyone was very supportive because there weren't that many of us English majors and our professors gave us a lot of attention and freedom." It wasn't until he graduated, and actually was out on his own, however, that Ennis became engaged in reading and learning. "When I was 22 I basically put myself into a classical reading program. I designed a set of readings for myself—the canon—and read everything I thought was important. I was driven by that." After his reading program came his own writing—he wrote a novel that was accepted for publication and published to "good but minor reviews."

Now a novelist, Ennis also had to find some daily means to support himself that would allow him to be with his girlfriend (now his wife), who was completing her own graduate degree at the University of Chicago. "I heard from one of my old friends that my old high school, my dear old high school, was looking for a substitute teacher—teaching American literature to juniors in an honors class. And again because I had connections— someone in the English department liked me—I got a job as a substitute. The next year I applied for a full-time position, and I've been here ever since." Ennis has been teaching for almost 10 years, an irony not lost on him.

Someone whom school "never really suited," and never really "fit" his intellectual style—and who, like some school critics, describes high school as a "benevolent minimum security prison," Ennis is back at his old school, "representing the administration many times a day," while teaching creative writing.

"The first years it didn't really feel good," he reflects. "I felt like an imposter—how could I be doing this? It just wasn't a feeling of legitimacy, and I didn't want to become legitimate, because that would mean I was embracing all those attitudes and ideas that had turned me off to classrooms myself." He was in a serious dilemma. Like Abby in the earlier portrait, Ennis observed that most of his students at his highly competitive upper-middle-class high school are very interested in achievement, in grades, and in engaging in activities that will help them get into college. "They accept authority much more than I did and they aren't as interested in thinking on their own." At first Ennis had to really struggle with how to engage them. He compares himself to a popular and well-known AP history teacher at the school, "who kind of has almost a stand-up comic routine when he teaches. He lectures nonstop for the entire period, he often doesn't even learn his students' names, but the kids love him. He's really entertaining and they just have to sit there. In fact, he sometimes gets bothered when they ask questions because it breaks his stride, his routine. He's been teaching this way for 30 years. That's not me at all. How was I going to be successful with these students?"

Slowly, cautiously, Ennis began to find his way as a teacher, "to be who I am and also be in school." In contrast to the popular AP teacher, says Ennis, he does very little lecturing in class. Although he's had to insert a little more structure in his classes than he did in his first years of teaching, "when there would be long, awkward gaps in the period every day because kids were expecting me to do the talking and I wouldn't—they had to," Ennis says he's grown much more clear and confident about his style of teaching. "I am not going to tell kids how to think or to entertain them. The first principle of teaching, I think, should be, do no harm to students. Thinking for them will harm them. I want them to be subversive, and to teach them, allow them, to be subversive." Although he is now a popular and sought-out English teacher, he also describes feeling isolated and lonely at this school. "I don't know if I really have colleagues who believe the same things I do. I feel I am alone a lot in the classroom, doing what I think the right thing is. I can feel the isolation."

Like Eve and Abby, Ennis says he also had to "learn and unlearn" a lot of lessons about teaching—mostly on his own. At first as a teacher, Ennis says he was not well organized. "I assumed that kids would just put things together a lot more than they were able to, because that's how I learned about writing and reading. I have an apprentice model in teaching writing. We read some great writers: Hemingway, Faulkner, Cather, and then students try to imitate them. These writers are the 'authorities' in the classroom—what do they have to tell us, to teach us? Gradually I've learned to add a little more structure, to have a little more authority as a teacher." Much of what his English department would like teachers to do he considers bad for students, not helpful in their thinking or writing. "That literary analysis essay we're supposed to teach them, it's crazy, awful to get students to do this. Students can produce brilliant work in their own voice and then we ask them to write these pseudoprofessorial analysis essays that are terrible. Why do we do that? And then we have to grade them. Grades are such a nightmare, useful only for the administrative function of education. They have nothing to do with writing and reading well."

What kind of learning community is Ennis trying to create, I ask him—where did he find models for his classroom since he was such a misfit himself in school? "One that does not violate learners," he says. "While I don't believe the classroom necessarily has to be violating to learners, you have to set it up very carefully to address learners' needs. The most powerful group of learners I've seen is skateboarders. I advise the skateboarding club at school, and there is a huge range of abilities in that group: Some kids are almost national-level competitors and others are just starting out. But the more experienced kids help out the less experienced ones, they teach one another skills and practice together, and everyone encourages everyone else. There is no judgment about making mistakes. Everyone learns there, and everyone encourages everyone else. When I was just starting to teach, I used to go from the skateboarding club to my classroom and think, they are so much better at teaching than I am. How can I make my literature classes like the skateboarding club?" Ennis says this question is at the center of his teaching now. "The point is with writing, there is not a 'best.' I try to make my classroom like the skateboarding club—a noncompetitive place." Sometimes, he says, he is even successful by his own standards. "When things are going well, my classroom is really a dynamic place to be. My students let me know how powerful the environment can be for them."

Ennis isn't sure he's going to stay in teaching, he says, and now the father of a child himself, he and his wife struggle with their son's education. "I don't really like school, and I don't think it's a great place to learn. Should we subject my son to the boredom and alienation that I experienced? What will the consequences of that be? So far, school hasn't been good for him. It is making him a bully."

Ennis lives at the nexus of the conflicts of the unwounding teacher: passionately committed to the act of teaching and to creating a classroom community that is communal, nonhierarchical, and a place where students are initiators, not passive recipients of instruction—but also cauterized by feeling too much alone in his professional life. Ennis says, "It is a lonely life.

Thank god my wife is also a teacher and understands the dilemmas." Ennis remarks, in closing our interview, that he would like to be in a teacher community like the skateboarding club at high school. "There's a model: teachers getting together to hang out at our school, to try out moves for each other and then to talk about what worked and what didn't. People of all different abilities and levels of experience helping each other." I ask Ennis, would you be willing to try to establish that kind of teacher collective in your city, with other like-minded teachers? He says, "If I knew they were out there, meet me on the steps. Bring your board."

FLICKR AS A MODEL LEARNING COMMUNITY?

Ennis's comments about the instructional environments he is trying to create in his classroom echo other interviews with teachers and students about the liberatory qualities of participation in new, online learning communities. In an interview, a university professor of education who became very interested in photography described his experiences of becoming a learning participant in Flickr, an online photo-sharing and photo management community on the Web. In contrast to his own 30 years of teaching at a research university, he described the differences between the atmosphere and climate of the Flickr community and an academic environment.

"I joined Flickr because I got interested in photography. But what I began to notice right away was the learning environment. It's all voluntary, you only participate because you want to, it's all about compassionate critique. People never go off on each other, no question is too simple, there are hugely varying levels of expertise (that's okay), very few restrictions on content, and most of the quality and appropriateness of presentation of material is by individual decision—it is self-monitoring." How different this is from university-level teaching and colleaguing, he notes, where participation is allowed only based on expertise; expressions of not knowing are shameful and professionally disadvantageous; and external, authorizing bodies decide what is of value. "On Flickr, no one tells you what you can be the authority on, what you can specialize in." Specialization is the central focus in academic life, but on Flickr, he noted, "It's all self-determined. Voluntary groups form around special interests. There is no limit on the number of groups or the numbers you can affiliate with, and these specialized learning communities are driven by the learners' interests."

Is this a model for a new kind of learning community? I ask. "I have found this new world incredibly liberating. It has served my learning needs so well. It's incredibly accessible because you can get an answer to any question you have because there are so many people involved. It's dynamic and self-correcting: You get to see thousands of examples of others' work, with lots of technical information available." Imagine if we had this for teaching? he concluded.

UNWOUNDING TEACHERS

- Establish noncompetitive learning environments, where internal motivation for learning is emphasized
- Honor and welcome difference in race, in social class, in gender, and in sexual orientation
- Put the student at the center—the student is the "author" of instruction
- Build and create experiential learning models, where students can learn by doing
- Emphasize multiple avenues of content presentation, reflection, and assessment
- Make communities of caring central to every learning situation
- Honor "personal" knowledge: what the student already knows or may intuitively feel is of value in creating new learning
- Accept many types of students and consciously value diversity of backgrounds and experiences in the classroom
- Acknowledge self-doubt and lack of knowledge as part of teaching
- Are playful and experimental in instructional design: "Mistakes are my best teachers."

In concluding his essay on the "new" professional, Parker J. Palmer urges educators to take their students' emotions as seriously as they take their intellects. While not without conflicts or difficulties, Eve, Abby, and Ennis, as teaching professionals, are actively involved in taking their own emotions about their work as seriously as they regard its intellectual demands. Their greatest difficulty has been finding other colleagues, other adult professionals, with whom to expand and explore their visions. One of the lessons of these unwounding teachers' practice is that they have formulated their craft knowledge mostly on their own, without a network of colleagues whom they could consistently call on and be in reflective practice with. "One of the great problems with teaching is that we are still doing everything too much by ourselves," Ennis said. "I'm a part of this myself. I don't seek out other teachers as much as I should," which means that Ennis's craft knowledge will be lost. "The lack of sustainability of these kinds of explorations, the way we don't pass things on, is one of the real problems of our profession," I once heard an innovative school starter say. So the call to walk next door, to engage one's neighbor in conversation about the work of teaching, to form a collaborative learning group or a book talk community, is strong. Millions of teachers are out in their isolated classrooms, waiting for colleagues to initiate these conversations. All that is required is raising one's hand and knocking on one's neighbor's door.

CHAPTER 9

Students Healing One Another

"I am bored 99 percent of the time."

"Engage us more."

"Don't just stand in front and tell."

"They don't let us do things—they just talk to us."

—Students describing how they feel about school[1]

A recent, broad-ranging, and authoritative survey of American high school students reports that two out of three students are bored in class every day. Moreover, 17% of students say they are bored in *every* class, and 31% of high school respondents report having virtually no interaction with teachers day to day in school.[2] These figures, from the High School Survey of Student Engagement (HSSSE), the largest national survey of high school students' attitudes toward their education,[3] indicate that a vast majority of high school students dislike their course material and have inadequate interactions with teachers, and a third of students sit in classrooms every day in which they feel completely unseen and unengaged—or, in the words of one of my interviewees, "like we were just passing through, marking time, no one even knew we were there." In the HSSSE survey, only 2% of students said they were "never bored" in high school; 60% of the survey's respondents said they didn't see the value of the work they were being asked to do. The HSSSE survey also showed that, except for a small percentage of high-performing students, 43% also spent almost no time on homework—less than 1 hour a week. Many students now find that when they enroll in college, they are underprepared academically and must take remedial classes to begin to reach adequate levels of undergraduate performance. Do students need to wait around until adults "fix" the educational system they exist in? What can students do on their own to take action in a school system that compels them to attend, diminishes their experiences of learning, and devalues or domesticates their energies for changing their educational environments?

From the many stories in this book it is clear that the educational system in America is at a critical juncture, and in a time of intense dysfunction and critique—roiled by new conceptions of learning and ability, challenged by technologically rich environments outside of school, and poorly adapted to supporting students in developing the kinds of skills they need once they graduate. Yet during this time of transition, millions of students must continue to go to school every day. While those nominally in charge of creating and maintaining this institution (adults) consider how schools might be reconfigured to become more functional, less wasteful, and less wounding of the individuals within them—what should students do?

In this chapter I examine some student efforts to identify and objectify—to make real—some of the ways in which school wounds and disheartens them, and to do something about it in their own lives. One of the ways school wounds us is by teaching us that we must wait passively until someone else does something about the conditions of our lives that make us unhappy—many schools reward quiescence and compliance with institutional expectations and punish iconoclastic, reform energy. The students profiled in this chapter, however, have decided that they can't wait until the system gets better. They have to do something about the conditions of their lives in school now. From the story of Emma Abby, a nonconformist who decided to find her way to graduate school on her own schedule and by following her own path; to a group of students who started a cross-institutional consciousness-raising group about school norms; to a student with learning differences who taught himself how to advocate for himself and now encourages others to do the same— these students are models of authoritative action to change and reform schools and student lives within educational institutions. The individuals profiled here discovered that students can aid and heal one another, by banding together, by making clear what the objectionable aspects of the system are, by not internalizing those wounds as their own private failures, and by becoming active to name and change them. To paraphrase the great school reformer John Holt, schools are institutions that are run on fear and shame. Students can work actively to change the conditions of their wounding by not being afraid, by joining with other students to identify the conditions of their educational lives that do not work well for them, and ultimately by acting as reformers of them.

A Nonconformist's Educational Journey

At age 14, Emma Abby, a real, "regular" teenager from suburban Massachusetts, decided that conventional, suburban high school was simply not right for her. For Emma, it was clear from the first days of ninth grade that conventional high school just wasn't going to be a congenial culture for her. Always an academically successful and outgoing elementary school student, at age 12 Emma and her family moved from rural Massachusetts to suburban Boston, a transition in which Emma was uprooted from her childhood friends and schoolmates at a time when "your peer group of girls" matter almost more than anything else. "Immediately I started struggling academically," she says. "My old school had been more working class, more diverse, more blue collar. Suddenly I was going to school with a lot of upper-middle-class, rich White kids. I had never been exposed to that before." She also was forced for the first time to take the Massachusetts state accountability tests in eighth grade. "I didn't believe in them," she said. She wrote protest essays and tried to boycott them. "People were bewildered."

I met Emma Abby after a *Boston Globe* profile told her story of being awarded a prestigious Fulbright Scholarship at age 20, after completing her undergraduate college degree with a 4.0 average and never having completed high school in a conventional sense. "I've always had an idea of what I wanted, even if it didn't fit the stereotype of most overachievers," she says modestly. Emma dropped out of high school in ninth grade because it was a "waste of time," and realized she was ready for college-level work at age 16. "I'm a hard worker, I'm ambitious, and I hate doing things that I think are stupid and don't make sense." Emma had to find her own unconventional path in education, even though it caused her parents "a lot of sleepless nights," and her siblings and friends thought she was "a screwup. My sister called me a 'dodgeball student.' Things have worked out pretty well, though" she noted.

Entering a new high school in a new district in ninth grade, Emma said, was "a nightmare." There were a lot of mean-girl issues, she said, and she felt lost and alienated in the huge high school building, walking around anonymously day after day. "Upper-class boys would deliberately try to be intimidating, I wasn't doing well academically, I felt I was wasting my time taking things that didn't mean anything to me. I sat there in class not doing anything, not doing my homework," protesting in her own mute way, she explained. The second week of high school, "9/11 happened. That was the extreme tipping point for me. The teacher in our class that morning was called out, and we knew something really bad had happened. We were afraid. We asked if we could turn on the TV in the classroom and find out what was going on. The teacher refused to allow us to turn on the TV. That was too much." Not just denial of critical information and control of students' lives bothered Emma, but little things that "were so trivial, like they'd punish you if you needed to go to the bathroom at the wrong time, or for chewing gum. I think I can be trusted to dispose of my gum properly. Every step of the way little rights were taken away," Emma says. It just felt wrong to her.

Instead of passively accepting her situation, however, Emma decided to get active. She refused to go to school, in spite of her parents' frantic efforts to convince her otherwise. Emma said she would find herself another school and set about arranging visits to all kinds of educational institutions. Finally, Emma found an alternative school (called the Sudbury Valley School) relatively close by, a school founded on free-school principles and one of the oldest consistently operating alternative schools in the country. Emma went for a visiting week there and realized, "I wasn't going anywhere else."

At Sudbury Valley, like other progressivist democratic schools described in Chapter 7, students are afforded much more choice about their learning than in conventional schools. Teachers act as guides rather than task assigners and behavior controllers. "It was small, it was real, I needed it to recover," Emma said. "My old high school felt so fake in every way. If I had stayed at my old high school I might have become someone who cared about the latest fashions and hairstyles. It's hard not to try to fit in." At Sudbury Valley Emma met students she clicked with (including her boyfriend—now her husband) and recouped from her old high school. Eventually, after about a year and a half, she decided to get serious about school and to prove herself to everyone. "I wanted to show everyone what I could do. In my own way I am a competitive student." Emma's boyfriend, Kurt, was enrolled at a local community college and was taking several courses, and she took a look at his assignments and realized, "I could do that." She determined she would take her GED so she could enroll in community college, bought herself a GED study guide book, studied for 2 months, and passed every section.

With Sudbury Valley's blessing, she enrolled in community college full time. She did very well, receiving all As and winning praise and notice from her professors. Ultimately, she and her boyfriend transferred to a state college to complete 4-year degrees. Emma considered applying to an elite private college but decided she didn't want to borrow huge amounts of money to pay for a brand-name school. "I'm cheap," she said. "I think you can get a perfectly good education at a public college." In college Emma became fascinated by environmental studies and decided she was interested in environmental sustainability as her career. Unable to find a graduate program that directly suited her needs in the United States, she looked abroad and found one in Sweden. Her professors helped her apply and also urged her to consider a Fulbright—something she'd never heard of. She applied, although, she says, "I considered it an extreme long shot." She won, allowing her and her husband to live in Sweden for a year with full tuition and a small stipend for living expenses. "We were pretty psyched," Emma said.

When I ask Emma about her dreams for the future, she says she has a lot of plans. "I want to help Americans change. I want to help normal people live in the natural environment without destroying it, in a sustainable way. I want to be a part of the paradigm shift that has to happen in this country that will help people think about how to live their lives in more connected and less wasteful ways." She says she might want to get a doctorate someday, if it would help her in her work, "but first we'll get our master's degrees and live in Sweden." For Emma, following a conventional path will never be what is most compelling—what feels inevitable. "People always told me I was doing the wrong thing. There has been lots of crying and fighting about my educational choices. My advice to other students is: Listen to your own instincts. Don't allow the people around you to change your mind. No one can tell you what is right for you. If you're a student, you need to make change happen and make your voice heard."

Emma says that she does not recall a single teacher at her old comprehensive high school who had a positive impact on her. "I'm not sure what would have happened to me if I had stayed there for 4 years. I'm not sure where I'd be." Inspired by Emma's optimism and hard work, I recently described her journey to another high school student "trapped" in his own conventional setting. "Maybe I should try to do what that girl did," he told me. Only in her early 20s, Emma is already a role model for other students who don't fit.

Critical Inquiry About School:
Starting a Consciousness-Raising Group

> Admitting the problem is half the battle.
>
> —Saying from the women's
> consciousness-raising movement of the 1960s and 1970s.

Carlos and Susan are sitting together talking about their junior years of high school, a time of intense stress for many high school students who are intent on attending competitive colleges. They are describing the range of issues they've confronted: AP classes that demand immense amounts of memorization and coverage, but offer little intellectual flexibility or creativity; four to five hours of homework a night; weekends consumed by hyperdemanding sports schedules and academic projects, homework, and studying for exams; all of which feel "pretty much like the norm." Add that to increasingly intense pressure from parents, peers, and administrators to work on college admissions portfolios, including studying for SATs, SAT IIs, ACTs, and AP exams, and both students are overwhelmed by a sense that not a minute should be spared—literally—in the quest for the holy grail of college admission. This quest includes academic excellence in every subject; meaningful, targeted extracurriculars that express something unique and powerful about them as individuals; volunteer work; perhaps some travel to a distressed area of the world. They feel exhausted and burnt out—even though they know that they should be grateful that they're at the top of the heap of an academic pyramid that has allowed them to compete for a place at a selective college—a goal they've quietly begun to question in their own minds.

Across town in the same city, Delia and Shandrel, also high school juniors, are considering their course options for their senior year at their large, comprehensive urban high school. Bored at school, even their part-time jobs (one at a gas station, one at a coffee and doughnut chain) seem more real than the schoolwork they are asked to do in regular education classes. Both have considered dropping out of high school but have promised their families that they will not. Both have significant family commitments outside of school—Delia to babysitting for her younger brother after school and Shandrel to paying a portion of his mom's apartment rent. Yet they constantly are told by school officials that they are not keeping up with their schoolwork and are letting themselves and others down. They are hanging on with C averages, and without much enthusiasm for the coming school year. Delia and Shandrel experience little success, excitement, or engagement in school; what holds them there is their social lives and the sense that their parents would be furious with them if they dropped out—a threat whose impact they increasingly question. In terms of the institution of schooling, and the ways that it does not serve the needs of adolescents today, all four students are oppressed by an educational system that is dysfunctional, byzantine in terms of its testing and grading requirements, frequently irrelevant in its curricular offerings, and deeply unsupportive of engaged and self-directed learning.[4]

Getting perspective on the institution of schooling, becoming anthropologists of the system of education that they are in, is something students can do immediately to make their lives more coherent and less painful. Activist Susan Brownmiller, a central actor in the women's liberation movement of the 1960s, recalled, "In the Old Left, they used to say that the workers don't know they're oppressed, so we have to raise their consciousness. One night at a meeting I said, 'Would everybody please give me an example from their own life of how they experienced oppression as a woman? I need to hear it to raise my own consciousness.' Kathie [one of Brownmiller's political collaborators] was sitting behind me and the words rang in her mind. From then on she sort of made it an institution and called it consciousness-raising."[5] Starting consciousness-raising groups is exactly, in effect, what an organization called Stressed Out Students, founded by Denise Clark Pope of Stanford University, is encouraging students (and their parents) to do.

Denise Clark Pope is the author of *"Doing School": How We Are Creating a Generation of Stressed Out, Materialistic, and Miseducated Students.*[6] In it, Clark Pope profiles the lives of five students at a high-achieving high school in California as these students negotiate the codes of behavior and patterns of complicity (and duplicity) that are required of students to be "successful." Based on reception of the book, Clark Pope formed the organization Stressed Out Students, designed to help middle school and high school pupils and their parents understand the ways in which school can be dysfunctional and wounding for students.

"What would happen to a corporation that made it a conscious policy to devote all of its energy and resources to its top 10 percent of employees, while basically ignoring the rest of the organization? How about a company that rated its managers only on the basis of how their top 10 percent of workers performed?" Clark Pope wondered in an interview. "Yet those are precisely the perverse incentive systems that drive most high schools today. From a very early age, students are relentlessly 'tracked' to separate out the academically gifted from the 'rank and file.' The achievers are driven to the point of physical and mental breakdown, while the majority of others are branded as 'losers' of whom little is expected and who, in turn, expect little of themselves," Clark Pope said. (Think of the homework data from the high school engagement survey at the beginning of this chapter.)

The whole way in which learning is conceived in middle and high school, Clark Pope says, wounds students. "The basis of learning organizations is on solving concrete problems, with people in different areas and disciplines working together. That's exactly the opposite of the way the curriculum is being presented to students, as a series of discrete, disconnected subjects where everybody is supposed to be learning exactly the same thing at the same time to come up with the same answers. In the outside world, the premium is on the ability to think in new ways, to cultivate strong interpersonal relationships, and to be willing to sometimes risk (and experience) failure in order to learn. In all those ways, the schools are failing miserably to prepare these kids."[7] Clark Pope notes that if nothing else this system dampens initiative among students by focusing attention on the top 10% while training the other 90% to be average or, in some cases, less than average.

What if Carlos, Susan, Delia, and Shandrel got together to talk about their experiences of schooling? In my own life as a school consultant, this has begun to happen. At an urban school where I work, I help facilitate a student group that creates a space for students to talk about their

experiences of schooling, which for many of these students has been profoundly negative. Many students have received almost constant messages
about academic failure, lack of interpersonal compliance, and threats
about behaviors and attitudes. This student group decided to visit a high
school in a wealthier part of the city, where we met students Carlos and
Susan, who were enrolled in a high school course that examined the role
of institutions in individual life. Informally, these two groups began to
talk about the things they found productive and unproductive in their
schooling lives. "This helped us get perspective on the fact that this wasn't
just our individual experience, but many kids were having this. It made
me feel less crazy," one participant said. When the personal becomes political, to adopt the language of the Old Left, students can begin to make
small, micromovements toward objectifying their experiences and not being overwhelmed by them—this allows us to "stop normalizing dysfunction," as one activist framed it. Susan and Carlos eventually decided to
become peer mentors to younger high school students who also wanted to
form consciousness-raising and support groups around school wounding,
and Delia and Shandrel are going to spearhead a discussion and exchange
program between the two schools for next year, a school-based project
they are enthusiastically engaged in.

THE PERSONAL IS POLITICAL: CONSCIOUSNESS-RAISING GROUPS FOR WOUNDED STUDENTS

How can students get a consciousness-raising group started? As the Chicago Women's Liberation Union from 1971[8] instructs, the first work of a
consciousness-raising group is to engage in dialog and sharing of experiences. This might begin with simple questions like:

- How does school make you feel about learning?
- Are you bored in school?
- What kinds of behaviors are most rewarded in school? Is this the
  same kind of behavior that is valued in the outside world?
- What is the point of grades?
- What are standardized tests for?
- What are course "levels" for?
- When do you feel most engaged in learning?
- When do you experience pleasure in learning?

Most consciousness-raising groups, after some period of dialog and analysis,
feel the need to begin an action or reform project. Students decide what to do:
What actions can be taken in their own lives to heal one another around school
wounding? (See some suggestions later in the chapter.)

Becoming Metacognitive About Learning

> I understand my strengths and weaknesses a lot more than
> other people my age from all the struggling and tutoring; it is
> kind of like survival skills.
>
> —Tom Skiba,
> *Understanding Students with Dyslexia in Higher Education,* 2008

Another way students can become healers of themselves (and others) is to learn about their own learning—to become metacognitive specialists of the way they think. A few years ago I had the pleasure of instructing Tom Skiba,[9] an outstanding student at Wheaton College. Tom's journey of learning about his own learning was initally prompted by his own very rocky school experiences, feeling so devalued and unseen that the anger and pain were sometimes overwhelming. Told throughout his elementary and high school years that he wasn't trying hard enough, that he was lazy, that if he would just apply himself he would do better, Tom was not diagnosed with dyslexia until he was in high school. He talks feelingfully about his experiences of being pulled out of classes, of being tracked into "dumb" classes, of his parents' bewilderment about his extremely unpredictable, up-and-down school performances. In high school Tom's family realized that he was suffering emotionally and intellectually in the school system he was enrolled in, and found a way to juggle resources to place him in a much smaller private school, where he received some of the first intellectual encouragement and understanding of his life.

A brilliant, insightful, straightforwardly honest college student, Tom takes pride in the fact that he can describe in considerable detail how he learns, how he grasps concepts best, and what specific interventions he will need for particular assignments to be a successful student. On the first day of class with me, Tom told me we needed to meet in private so that he could talk to me about his learning needs, the areas in which he might need flexibility in assignments, and how he might be able to contribute best to class. Tom was the consummate communicator in my classes, describing to me in considerable detail what aspects of my course design were not helpful to him, and how these might be redesigned to better suit a range of learners. In a moving, hour-long presentation to the class without using notes, Tom described his experiences as a "special education" student throughout his school career and how he had had to learn, largely on his own, how to deal with his learning needs. (He detailed, for instance, his use of a digital text reader in the basement of his college library to get through the required reading for his Russian literature course in his junior year. He loved the course, but to deal with the hundreds of pages of reading a week, he had to learn to use assistive technology. Unfortunately, he said, not enough kids were doing that—either they didn't know about the technology or felt stigmatized about using it.) As the capstone of a very successful college career, Tom completed a research-based honors thesis investigating the experiences of students with dyslexia in higher education.[10] He was awarded highest academic honors at his undergraduate institution.

In his thesis, Tom described the importance of self-knowledge and self-advocacy for students with learning differences in higher education. "In college, I have come to believe that the education standards for performance discourage students with learning differences and do not provide them equal access to education or postgraduate success. As a student with dyslexia, I must work significantly harder than most other students in order to achieve similar grades. I do not believe that the majority of students, professors, and administrators without learning differences understand the experience of dyslexia."

Using his own story as a guide in one part of his research, he continued, "I was diagnosed with dyslexia the summer before my junior year of high school. It was very relieving for me to hear that I was not stupid and that I had potential to succeed. I did not receive any additional academic support from my diagnosis while in high school, but I did work harder because I believed I could succeed. I ended my high school experience with high honors and gained admission to a competitive four-year college.

"I identify positive and negative characteristics to my experience with dyslexia. Before college, I went through the majority of my education without formal assistance or a diagnosis of dyslexia. This had several negative effects on my confidence as a learner. Beginning in first grade, I had negative experiences with teachers labeling me as lazy and unintelligent. Due to the lack of support I received when I was a child, I was unable to read at grade level and did not comprehend the story of a book until my freshman year of high school. In order to get through school I developed many coping strategies to counteract my inability to read. From this experience I have adopted a very negative perspective on the United States educational system as well as most teachers."

Tom described his experience helping students learn to negotiate some of the hurdles of college-level work when he was an intern to the dean for academic services. "During my junior and senior years I have worked as the dean's Intern for Academic Advising and Special Needs. Through this job I have been exposed to the experiences of other students with learning differences and learned how LD [learning disabled] issues are treated by the campus administration. I have taken on the job of advocating for students with learning differences by teaching seminars for academic tutors, professors and administrators. In addition to advocacy, I work with individual students with learning differences to help them with solutions for success. Through my work I have learned about many struggles students with learning differences endure and I have been exposed to many different types of students with learning differences."[11]

As an advocate for students with learning differences, Tom came to see two distinctly different stances toward learning and disability among students—those who became "citizens" of their disability, meaning they lived in a universe constructed around their learning differences, and expected schools to accommodate to them in ways that were often unrealistic[12]—and those who were effective self-advocates, knowledgeable about the system of education and their own learning patterns, but also realistic about what they needed to do to help themselves survive and thrive in it. The differences in these stances, Tom's research revealed, were critical to their outcomes.

Tom found that Citizens of Dyslexia had a harder time asking for help, felt more disengaged from their professors, and ironically had more difficulty accessing the accommodations they needed. On the other hand, effective self-advocates actively engaged the institution in setting up accommodations for themselves, developed the skills to speak with professors about their learning issues, and had fewer expectations that administrators would help them secure what they needed in order to learn effectively. Self-advocates focused less on getting help and accommodations from the administrative deans, and more on their own responsibility for dealing with their learning situations. For Tom, learning how to take care of oneself and "knowing your own mind—literally" were his guiding principles and ultimately the ones that created greatest opportunities for success. Tom emphasized again and again that learning about his own mind—understanding how his brain functioned—was a vital and ongoing project for him. "I know how I think really well," he said. His experiences suggest that this is information that should be available to, and pursued and cultivated by, all students.

I draw attention to Tom's thesis—his learning experiences, and his journey of marginalization, self-education, and advocacy—because I think his case and research represent a vision of students healing themselves, through self-analysis and self-study at an exceptionally high level. Starting in eleventh grade of high school, Tom began to engage in critical inquiry about the system of education he was in. He began learning about his intellectual "difference" and how the educational system he was in was designed to label, from both a legal and cultural point of view, those who do not fit a conventional learning mold. This process allowed him to gain some perspective on his own difficult experiences and to start to locate the sources of his unhappiness and negative labeling as something external to himself. But as he grew more sophisticated in his views of education and more knowledgeable about himself, he also did not become more reliant on the system to take care of him, but more determined than ever to advocate for himself. Now doing clinical research at a large university, Tom also wants to engage in advocating for individuals with learning differences on a regional and national level—he is in the activism and re-engagement phase of wounding and healing.

As Tom described his own experiences, he said, "As a person's identification with dyslexia becomes more complex and abstract the emphasis of the label moves away from a diagnostic category of disability defined by the education system. The person begins to understand the label as a description regarding their unique set of skills and perceptions, which *offer them privileged insights into the world*. The process of personalization of the label involves external awareness of why the label was originally negative and deep introspection regarding one's thinking process."[13] Tom, along with many other individuals I met while writing this book, convinced me of the immense gifts of those with (what our education system calls) learning differences, and, as a teacher, to welcome those who learn differently for the richness and depth they bring to the classroom.

Students Becoming Active to Change Schools

Beyond the examples of iconoclastic Emma Abby, starting consciousness-raising groups, or Tom Skiba's research project on difference, self-efficacy, and disability in school, other recent student activism projects reveal the power of students to change their environments and relationships with school simply by engaging in critical inquiry and investigation. Because learning in schools traditionally has been dominated and controlled by adults, students seldom make decisions about their own learning. In the examples outlined below—an ever-growing number immensely aided by the Internet—several student projects upend the traditional paradigms of schooling and critically examine some aspects of school that are often considered sacrosanct or too big and overwhelming to tackle. In these student research and activism projects, students are passive no more.

In 2004, students at Brighton High School in Boston looked at data on graduation rates and resource differentials at their urban high school in relation to several wealthier suburban neighborhoods that surrounded them. Digging into these data was eye opening—students at Brighton High were shocked and baffled when they realized that their school's graduation rates were much lower than those of surrounding schools, and that "the education here at Brighton High is not very high for minority students." Students decided to figure out exactly where the inequities lay. In a 21-minute, near-professional-quality video they created, *The Problem We All Live With* (available on the What Kids Can Do Web site),[14] these students looked across several domains (resources, courses, discipline styles, teaching expectations) at the differences between Brighton High School and surrounding suburban Boston schools, using footage shot at their urban high school and at suburban high schools. Cross-cutting between interviews with students, teachers, and administrators at Brighton High School and students at suburban high schools, suburban students describe the incredible array of high school course offerings and resources at their institutions (literature of war, media studies, Arabic; dance studios, pools, springy running tracks), while the video shows pictures of Brighton High School's decrepit ceilings, collapsing doors, and crumbling gymnasium. "What I didn't realize is how much our school looks like a prison," said a student on the video. Teachers talk about what they expect from kids. At Brighton High, students will "get a job, join the military after graduation," says an administrator, whereas at suburban high schools teachers simply assume all students will go to college. The cross-cut interviews and footage are stark and illuminating and, in their simplicity, are a call to social action. "Going to other schools really made me realize what other opportunities I'm not getting," said one Brighton High School student researcher. The video, which won several national awards, makes suggestions for improving the state of urban education and now is used in other urban high schools as a conscious-raising group centerpiece.

On the other side of the country, the organization South Central Youth Empowered thru Action (SCYEA) has also been actively organizing urban youth for critical, positive social action for several years. The youth component of a larger community empowerment and political action committee (Community Coalition in South Los Angeles), SCYEA comprises "Black and brown high school students that work together to improve social and economic conditions in the their schools and community." I first heard about SCYEA at an educational research conference, when a prominent educational equity researcher noted with approval that kids in south L.A. were bringing to national attention data on systemic marginalization of students of color in school in ways that her 2 decades of tracking data never had. SCYEA forms high school organizing committees within big urban Los Angeles schools: Washington Preparatory, Fremont, Dorsey, Manual Arts, Crenshaw, and Locke. With support from local activists at each high school, SCYEA facilitates meetings and organizes committees to "inform students about their power to improve the quality of their education and the conditions in their schools." These committees help students physically organize and also "enforce the belief that not only can student voices be heard, their voices should be heard." These committees also act as the political and campaign center on each of the respective high school campuses; they meet once a week and host 15–20 students per meeting. With two big "wins" in recent years—one to bring more equitable funding to impoverished and overlooked high schools in south LA,[15] and one at a local high school that demanded transparency in course scheduling and greater equity in course enrollment to align with state university admission requirements[16]— scyea's organizing model has received national-level attention and has had dramatic impact on the Los Angeles United School District's administration. Currently scyea is engaged in a multi-high school campaign to examine the tracking of students of color into vocational classes like cosmetology and auto mechanics.[17] (See Box on facing page)

A Web-based organization run by teenagers called DoSomething.org allows students to design, publicize, and organize social activism projects directly online. The DoSomething.org site sponsors political action programs in dozens of areas and is especially active in education. Supporters can subscribe to the site or an individual project, get guidance on starting projects, or volunteer directly for existing projects that interest them. In education, more than 12 education projects are currently up and running. Here are reports on two recent DoSomething education projects.

- When students in the government classes at Poughkeepsie High School discovered the very real consequences school budget decisions had made in their lives, they were determined to inject their voice into the funding debate. Students wrote, distributed, and collected data from a 57-question survey that solicited opinions from their peers on what should be included in the next year's school district budget. They subsequently submitted to the Poughkeepsie Board of Education, the school district superintendent, and the business manager a 149-page budget report documenting their findings and suggestions. (Poughkeepsie Students Submit Budget Recommendations, http://www.dosomething.org)
- Ariela Rothstein, a senior at Lexington High School in Massachusetts, founded the Best Practices Club. The organization aims to foster dialog between students and teachers about successful teaching methods. The nuts-and-bolts of the club are fairly simple: Individual members of the club visit individual classrooms. They sit in the back and quietly observe the teacher's actions and the responses of their peers as a class unfolds. They look for moments of engagement, and methods that create the most learning. If they see problems, they try to

IS SCHOOL PREPARING YOU
TO WORK AT McDONALD'S?

This blog post, by a 19-year-old SCYEA Los Angeles school activist, is linked to the SCYEA Web site. It urges urban high school students to get political about school tracking.

Don't want to be another Los Angeles Unified School
District (LAUSD) youth who ends up working at McDonald's?

Many students don't know that LAUSD has only been providing students with just enough of an education to get a low wage labor job like working at McDonald's. Students have been taking classes like woodshop and cosmetology, because classes like Algebra and Chemistry either aren't offered or are full. The result is that LAUSD kids graduate with options of pursuing low wage labor jobs that don't provide a living wage, or going into the underground economy like selling drugs or food on the street.

Why is this? Students haven't met eligibility requirements to apply to college through the University of California or California State systems. These requirements, known as the A-G classes, haven't been required or even available to all students. Other areas of Los Angeles and most schools in the country make these classes a part of graduation requirements, because they are so essential to students' basic learning. However, LAUSD students have been denied these same privileges under the assumption that our students can't learn and can't go to college. Luckily, there's now hope! I was a part of a big campaign that recently went on in Los Angeles to improve our schools. I worked with South Central Youth Empowered Thru Action (SCYEA) to inform students about the lack of A-G classes being offered and help them understand why the classes are so important.

Although the campaign really took several years, I worked hard core for months making phone calls to students and parents, and inviting them to attend rallies. In the schools we passed out fliers and made presentations, so people could become aware. In June of 2005, all our efforts paid off. In response to our efforts and the sea of passionate students and parents that flooded downtown in protest, the Los Angeles Unified School Board passed a resolution to provide all students with A-G classes and eventually make A-G classes part of graduation requirements. Good news huh? But will they actually follow through? We'll keep you updated, but you do the same—If you're not sure if you've taken your A-G classes, go ask your school counselor and get enrolled.

If they can't or won't enroll you, then hopefully you know that it is your RIGHT to have them. I mean hey, you don't want to be just another LAUSD youth who ends up working at McDonald's do ya?[18]

come up with solutions to suggest. Then, they sit down with the teacher to get an understanding of the motivations behind teaching decisions. The student club meets as a group to discuss their observations. Finally, the observing student writes up an analysis and offers it to the teacher, along with a conversation about the learning he or she saw taking place. Students created the club as an outlet for providing positive feedback on teaching and learning. (http://www.dosomething.org)

For other student activism projects from all around the country, readers also might visit the Web site What Kids Can Do: Voices from the Next Generation (www.whatkidscando.org). Founded in 2001 and based in Providence, RI, What Kids Can Do is an activist group that promotes the idea that young people—students currently enrolled in schools—can and should be seen as "valued resources, not problems." Focused especially on students who are marginalized due to race, poverty, and language, the organization sponsors, supports, and publicizes dozens of education reform projects initiated by students for students and their schools. For a complete list (and how to apply for research grants), go to http://www.whatkidscando.org/specialcollections/student_research_action/index.html. Web-based communication is central to student activism projects in education, and, like the design of learning itself, promises to be a central tool of the education revolution.

Opting Out of the System: Homeschooling

> School is not for learning.
> —Grace Llewellyn, *The Teenage Liberation Handbook*, 1998

One of my college students, who was homeschooled for several years, recently completed a research project on the viability of homeschooling and the increasingly wide acceptance of homeschooling as a legitimate option to public and private K–12 education. Much to her surprise, her research revealed that not only are homeschooled students ever more actively desired by colleges, due to their intellectual curiosity, self-sufficiency, and independence, but many more mainstream, middle-class American parents and students themselves are beginning to see homeschooling as a way of conscientiously objecting to the wounding culture of schools. More and more people are opting out of school, and finding the alternatives viable, attractive, and very rich socially, academically, and economically.

At the center of my student's research project and her curiosity about the viability of homeschooling were her reflections on her own homeschooling experiences. "I was homeschooled in 3rd and 4th grade. The decision to homeschool came entirely from me. When I was in 1st grade my family and I moved after I had only been in elementary school for 3 months. We relocated. Two years later, my family and I took a vote and decided to move back to our house in our old area. I was more than happy to do this because I missed my best friends. What I did not want to do was go back to the elementary school I had spent so little time in. My best friends were homeschooled by their parents. This gave me the idea to homeschool because I was determined not to go back to my old school that I hardly knew. Somehow I convinced my mom to homeschool me. This allowed me to be in my own home and focus on things that I loved, while still being able to see my friends and often do group activities with them.

"Homeschooling allowed me to move at my own pace, and I was soon working at a more advanced level than other students my age. I can remember working in math books that were two and sometimes three grade levels ahead of mine. I loved the independence that came with homeschooling, but after 2 years of it, I wanted to go back to public school because I missed being in a classroom environment with my peers.

"I enrolled in 5th grade. I was thrilled to be back in school, but I remember being surprised at how easy it was. I was placed in a special reading program by myself because no other student had reached my level of reading capability. I remember this transition was particularly difficult for me at times because my classmates would tell me I was really smart, but I would wonder why they could not be as smart as me. Eventually, I became too adjusted to public school, and did not try to overachieve as much as I had when I was homeschooled," my student reflected at age 22.

A recent report from the *Chronicle of Higher Education* observed that colleges and universities like Stanford, and other competitive Ivy League institutions, increasingly seek out highly qualified homeschooled pupils due to their "inquisitive, self-directed learning style—an educational model that often gets lost in the highly structured, problem-set oriented environment of traditional high school."[19] Homeschooling networks, advice, and support groups are increasingly available on the Web, so that the social isolation of homeschooling, once thought to be a problem, has lessened greatly. For high school students, it is also important to consult Grace Llwellyn's wonderful book, *The Teenage Liberation Handbook: How to Quit School and Get a Real Life and Education.*[20] In it, Llewellyn unpacks almost every aspect of the mythology around the "essential" nature of high school, and describes how if one is truly devoted to learning and becoming well educated, departure from high school to self-educate may be one of the most responsible decisions a student can make.

When my college students read Grace Llewellyn's book—for the most part my students have been conventionally schooled, and conventional

SURIVIVING HIGH SCHOOL: WHAT HELPS

- Take care of yourself. In all probability, the institution you are enrolled in unfortunately allows only a certain number of kids to be successful in particular ways. Find ways to balance the negative messages high school gives most kids.
- Take on the project of learning about how you learn. What are your unique patterns of learning? What helps you learn? You must become a metacognitive minder of yourself.
- Find support. Find a peer mentor to whom you can talk about school, who will not just tell you to work harder or be more disciplined, but can talk about the institution of school as well.
- Start a consciousness-raising group about the system of education. This also will help you find group support.
- Take social action in school. Decide on a school policy you want to try to change. Get others to join you. Speak out about injustice and unfairness.
- Engage in pleasurable learning every day.

*   *   *

"Listen!" said the White Spirit. "Once you were a child. Once you knew what inquiry was for. There was a time when you asked questions because you wanted answers, and were glad when you had found them. Become that child again: even now."

—C. S. Lewis, *The Great Divorce*, 1945

schooling teaches us to look askance at other options for education—they are initially disdainful and wary, and not at all sure that high school students could be trusted to think carefully about their own learning or to construct their own social lives and activities. For some adolescents, I am sure they are correct. But eventually some of my students also begin to question whether high school, as it currently is designed, really was necessary for them in order to enter college, and what, as an institution, it contributed to their lives. As one wrote, "In America there is an ingrained acceptance that the only way to go about a 'proper' education is through a public or private institution. However, the 20th-century movement labeled homeschooling has grown increasingly popular among American families. Parents, often with student approval, are now taking their children out of the public school system and are teaching them at home in hopes of offering them better, fuller educations. As a controversial practice in education, homeschooling does not follow the conventional schooling route. This raises a series of questions: what is the best way for children to be educated, and is homeschooling worth it?" Evidence suggests that not only are homeschooling networks becoming increasingly sophisticated and self-sustaining, but the qualities of intellectual independence, initiative, learner self-knowledge, and persistence are attractive attributes in the workplace of the future.

Changes in Thinking About the Nature of Education

> A radical change is going to be needed to get a learning system fit for a democracy. It needs to get away from domination and its endless stream of uninvited teaching. It needs to recognize that, in a democracy, learning by compulsion means indoctrination and that only learning by invitation and choice is education.
> —Roland Meighan, "An Education Fit for a Democracy," 2006

A radical visionary who echoes many of the deschooling critics of the 1960s, British academic Roland Meighan describes why our system of education is no longer suitable or just for raising empowered young adults. We live in an information-rich society that increasingly obviates the need for conventional schooling as we have known it, particularly for adolescents. Meighan writes, "Adolescence used to be thought of as a time when people have the free time to work and play with their peers. What I find is students so absorbed in passing tests that they are emotionally and intellectually unconnected to their friends. Even so-called extracurricular activities have less to do with group play or learning, or even with genuine interests like hobbies or avocations, than with pleasing adults by making the moves to have on their record." Meighan compares institutionalized schooling to 19th-century workhouses. "[Workhouses] were an accepted part of the social landscape for centuries, [but] they now seem impossibly inhumane and counterproductive. One day, school will be seen like that—a transient phenomenon, destined to fade gracefully away."[21]

LEARNING BY INVITATION RATHER THAN INDOCTRINATION

- Schooling needs to be reorganized for participation rather than imposition.
- Procedures for monitoring education must celebrate learning rather than incessant and stultifying testing.
- Schools must adopt a learner-directed, learner-centered approach to all education.

—Roland Meighan, "An Education Fit for a Democracy," 2006[22]

I hope Meighan is right. He is not the first to call for the complete reinvention of institutionalized schooling. I wrote my dissertation on a group of radical school critics from the 1960s who eloquently called for the reinvention and reimagination of American institutions of education. Fundamentally, these critics believed that educators, parents, and students needed to regard the act of learning as something more sacred, spiritual, and powerful than the current shrink-wrapped, compliance-oriented understandings of performance in school allowed. While these critics' voices were powerful and compelling in their time, they made their claims based on emotional and psychic grounds. Today, with equal fervor, mainstream business leaders are engaged in talk about the necessity of transforming schools, no longer simply following a test-and-punish model of educational reform and improvement. They, too, are calling for more creativity, initiative, and cognitive self-regulation from students, young people whom they might one day hire. Only within the past few years, Bill Gates, former chairman of Microsoft, called for the complete reinvention of the American high school, saying that "America's high schools are obsolete."[23]

What is different about this time of educational critique and disruption in relation to the 1960s, I believe, is that so many business, cultural, and intellectual voices surrounding school also are demanding radical change of the institution, not just school critics. These surrounding cultural and capitalist voices are saying that schools don't produce the kinds of skills, knowledge, and learning habits students need to be successful in the world—and this matters. This gives me hope that schools are not being critiqued exclusively on moral and spiritual grounds, as they were in the 1960s, but that their very structural foundations and reason for existence are being called into question by a broad coalition of social forces, particularly students—because the world around these institutions is changing dramatically.

As this book expresses, I believe that it is incumbent on every person who has been wounded by schools to take account of his or her wounding and to honor it, to not be ashamed of it, and to work to change the conditions of schooling that lacerate. By making this commitment to disruptive change, we may be able, once and for all, to help give birth to institutions of education that truly serve us better. "The world needs America to get public education right," says Kyle Dodson, an urban public school teacher in the student-produced video *The Problem We All Live With*. He is right.

WHAT IS OLD SCHOOL CULTURE?

Old School Culture is a set of old-fashioned ideas and attitudes in school that construct teaching as hierarchical, learning as passive, and the bureaucratic structures of school as about serving adults, not kids. Old School Culture also says: "We can't change school, that's just the way it is," or "It's too hard to change school, it's too complicated, this isn't the right moment. Just wait."

Students can lead the way in standing up to Old School Culture because often they're the least committed to it but are the ones most victimized by it. Students often see Old School Culture the most clearly.

HOW DO I STAND UP?

We all have to start by actually noticing, in a clear and relatively objective way, the things that are dysfunctional about school: how it's organized, how it makes learners feel day to day, how it achieves its "results," and whether those results are the ones we actually want and intend. Lots of us involved with school—teachers, students, parents, policymakers—complain about educational systems, but don't take action or join together with others to actually do something about them. The first step in standing up is forming groups to begin talking to others about school practices that don't work—groups that help us understand why schools are as they are, and what we can do about them. Standing up often involves starting with small acts of protest—asking hard questions, supporting others in objecting, refusing to accept "because that's the way we do it" answers. Seemingly insignificant, little changes can lead to big transformations. It's a matter of getting started.

Notes

Introduction

1. Homeschooling was not an option for our family, for many reasons.

2. Olson Lanier, K. (2000). Artisan and Virtuoso Learners. Unpublished paper, Harvard Graduate School of Education, Cambridge, MA.

3. Csikszentmihalyi, M. (1996). *Creativity: Flow and the Psychology of Discovery and Invention.* New York: HarperCollins, p. 173.

4. From a poem about the "average" child, first presented at the 1979 National PTA Convention by Michael Buscemi, Quest International.

Chapter 1

1. Vann, A. S. (1997, January). Average Kids: Round Pegs in Round Holes. *The School Administrator*, p. 1. Available at http://www.aasa.org/publications/saarticledetail.cfm?ItemNumber=4897&snItemNumber=&tnItemNumber=

2. Ibid., p. 1.

3. Holt, J. (1970). *What Do I Do Monday?* Portsmouth, NH: Boynton/Cook.

4. Inskeep, S. (2008, January 28). Latino Vote Marked by Generation Gap, quoting Luis Clemens of Candidato USA. *NPR Morning Edition* (program aired on National Public Radio). Available at www.npr.org/template/story/story.php?story/d=18468236

5. Although it is impossible to discuss school wounding without diagnostic language, many researchers and writers are beginning to cover this territory admirably: Mel Levine and associates, Carol Dweck and associates, and Robert Sternberg and associates, to name only a few.

Chapter 2

1. Compton, R. A. (2008). *Two Million Minutes: A Global Examination* [Documentary film]. Available at http://www.2mminutes.com/index.html

2. Dennison, G. (1969). *The Lives of Children: The Story of the First Street School.* New York: Random House, p. 75.

3. Fried, R. l. (2001). *The Passionate Learner.* Boston: Beacon Press, p. 243, emphasis in original.

4. Csikszentmihalyi, M. (1996). *Creativity: Flow and the Psychology of Discovery and Invention.* New York: HarperCollins.

5. Olson Lanier, K. (2000). *Artisan and Virtuoso Learners.* Unpublished paper, Harvard Graduate School of Education, Cambridge, MA.

6. See, for instance, Maria Montessori's definition of learning, also used by Piaget: "We discovered that education is not something which the teacher does, but that it is a natural process which develops spontaneously in the human being. It is not acquired

by listening to words, but in virtue of experiences in which the child acts on his environment. The teacher's task is not to talk, but to prepare and arrange a series of motives for cultural activity in a special environment made for the child."

7. Scarry, E. (2001). *On Beauty and Being Just*. Princeton, NJ: Princeton University Press, p. 7.

8. Holt, J. (1980, July/August). Plowboy Interview. *The Mother Earth News*, pp. 11–16 [emphasis added]. Available at http://www.bloomington.in.us/~learn/Holt.htm

9. Weil, S. (1951). Reflections on the Right Use of School Studies with a View to the Love of God. In *Waiting for God*. New York: Harper Colophon, p. 110.

10. Schroeder, T. (2004). *Three Faces of Desire*. New York: Oxford University Press.

11. Kim, in blog post, "Perseverance or Why We Are Not Unschoolers." (March 29, 2008). Available at http://starryskyranch.typepad.com/starry_sky_ranch/2008/03/perseverance-or.html

12. Duckworth, A.L., Peterson, C., Matthews, M. D., & Kelly, D. R. (2007). Grit: Perseverance and Passion for Long Term Goals. *Journal of Personality and Social Psychology, 92*(6), 1087–1101.

13. Goleman, D., Kaufman, P., & Ray, M. (1992). *The Creative Spirit*. New York: Penguin.

14. Sternberg, R. J. (2006, February 22). Creativity Is a Habit. *Education Week*. See www.edweek.org

15. Pink, D. H. (2005). *A Whole New Mind: Moving from the Information Age to the Conceptual Age*. New York: Riverhead Books.

16. Sarton, M. (1961). *The Small Room*. New York: Norton.

17. From collected writings of Eric Margolis. Excerpt from online student reflections of educational experiences, Sociology of Education course. Available at http://coursed.ed.asu.edu/margolis

18. Delpit, L. (1995). *Other People's Children: Cultural Conflict in the Classroom*. New York: New Press, p. 19.

19. Page, B. (2006). *At-risk Students: Feeling Their Pain, Understanding Their Plight, Accepting Their Defensive Ploys*. Nashville, TN: Education Dynamics Publications, p. 9.

20. Ibid., p. 9.

21. Fried, R. L. (2005). *The Game of School*. San Francisco: Jossey-Bass, p. xv.

22. Resnick, A. M. (2007, March 7). Educatocracy. *Education Week, 26*(26), 26–27. See http://www.edweek.org/ew/articles/2007/03/06/26resnick.h26.html?qs=educatocrac

23. Colucci, K. (2000). Negative Pedagogy. In J. L. Paul & K. Colucci (Eds.), *Stories Out of School: Memories and Reflections on Care and Cruelty in the Classroom*. Stamford, CT: Ablex, pp. 31–32.

24. Pink, D. H. (2000, October). "I'm A Saboteur": Profile on John Taylor Gatto. *Fast Company, 40*, p. 242. Available at www.fastcompany.com/magazine/40/wf_gatto.html

25. Illich, I. (1971). *Deschooling Society*. London: Marian Barrows, p. 29.

26. Flett, G. L., & Hewitt, P. L. (2002). *Perfectionism: Theory, Research and Treatment*. Washington, DC: American Psychological Association, p. 19.

27. Sandel, M. (2004, April). The Case Against Perfection. *The Atlantic.com*. Available at http://www.theatlantic.com/doc/200404/sandel

28. Gonder, P. O. (1991). *Caught in the Middle: How to Unleash the Potential of Average Students*. Arlington, VA: American Association of School Administrators, p. 3.

29. DeWitt, S. (2006, September 8). Blog post from "Stacey DeWitt on Real Parenting." Available at http://www.connectwithkids.com/blogs/stacey/?page_id=2

Chapter 3

1. I believe this quote is from Jellema, W. (1986). The Legacy of Rip Van Winkle. *New Directions for Higher Education, 1986*(54), p. 5.

2. Lackney, J. (2007, May). What's next. *NEA Today*. See http://www.nea.org/neatoday/0705/coverstory1.html#jeffrey

3. David Rose, talk to the board of the Arthur Vining David Foundation, Jacksonville, FL. March 2008.

4. Sizer, T. (2004). What High School Is. In D. George & J. Trimbur (Eds.), *Reading Culture*. New York: Pearson Longman, p. 109.

5. Wagner, T. (2008). *The Global Achievement Gap*. New York: Basic Books, p. 75.

6. Marzano, R., & Kendall, J. (2007). *The New Taxonomy of Educational Objectives* (2nd ed.). Thousand Oaks, CA: Corwin.

7. Elmore, R. F. (2008). Classroom lecture, Harvard Graduate School of Education; Pianta, R., et al. (2007, March 30). Opportunities to Learn in America's Elementary Classrooms. *Science Magazine, 315*.

8. Herron-Wheeler, A. (2008, April). End of a Public School Career Renews, Not Destroys, an Interest in Studies. *The Free Lance-Star*. See http://fredericksburg.com/News/FLS/2008/042008/04172008/371882/index_html?page=2

9. Haber, C. (2004). *Schooling as Violence*. New York: RoutledgeFalmer.

10. Engler, B. (2007). Why Growing Companies Need Versatile Employees. *Caliper Online*. Available at http://www.caliperonline.com/clients/cs_diesel.shtml

11. Gallagher, B. (2007). Why Growing Companies Need Versatile Employees. *Caliper Online*. Available at http://www.caliperonline.com/clients/cs_diesel.shtml

12. Gatto, J. T. (2006). *The Richest Man in the World Has Some Advice About College* . . . Retrieved December 2, 2008, from http://www.homeschoolnewslink.com/homeschool/columnists/gatto/v8i3_richest.shtml

13. Gardner, H. (1983). *Frames of Mind*. New York: Basic Books.

14. Dweck, C. (2006). *Mindset*. New York: Random House.

15. Walser, N. (2008, September/October). Teaching 21st Century Skills. *Harvard Education Letter*, p. 1. See http://www.edletter.org/current/index.shtml#21stcenturyskills

16. Murdoch, S. (2007). *IQ: A Smart History of a Failed Idea*. Hoboken, NJ: John Wiley.

17. Lawrence-Lightfoot, S. (2003). *The Essential Conversation*. New York: Random House, p. xvi.

18. Bowles, S., & Gintis, H. (1977). *Schooling in Capitalist America*. New York: Basic Books.

19. Oakes, J. (2008). Keeping Track: Structuring Equality and Inequality in an Era of Accountability. *Teachers College Record, 110*(3), pp. 700–712. Retrieved July 2, 2008, from http://www.tcrecord.org, ID Number 14610; Au, W. (2005). Power, Identity and the Third Rail. In P. C. Miller (Ed.), *Narratives from the Classroom* (pp. 65–85). Thousand Oaks, CA: Sage.

20. Noguera, P. (2008). *Unfinished Business: Closing the Racial Achievement Gap in Our Schools*. San Francisco, CA: Jossey-Bass.

21. Brantlinger, E. A. (2003). *Dividing Classes: How the Middle Class Negotiates and Justifies School Advantage*. New York: Falmer.

22. Baez, B. (2006). Merit and Difference. *Teachers College Record, 108*(6), 996–1016. Retrieved December 8, 2007, from http://www.tcrecord.org, ID Number 12515.

23. Bowles, S., & Gintis, H. (2001, March). *Schooling in Capitalist America Revisited.* Paper presented at the annual meeting of the American Educational Research Association, Seattle.

24. Morrison, K. A. (2007). *Free School Teaching.* Albany: State University of New York Press, pp. 21–37.

25. Abramson, L. (2007, October 19). *Experimental School Gets Rid of Classes, Teachers* [National Public Radio series on Innovative Trends in High Schools]. Available at http://www.npr.org/templates/story/story.php?storyId=15322289

Chapter 4

1. Leick, N., & Davidsen-Nielsen, M. (1991). *Healing Pain.* London: Routledge, p. 1.

2. The quotes in this section are based on my conversations with Dr. L. Todd Rose in May 2007 (in person) at the Harvard Graduate School of Education and from a published account of his childhood in Brooks, R., & Goldstein, S. (2002). Todd's Story. In *Nurturing Resilience in Our Children* (pp. 261–287). New York: McGraw Hill.

3. Ibid.

4. Stoop, D. (1996). *Forgiving Our Parents, Forgiving Ourselves.* Ventura, CA: Regal Books, p. 202.

5. Leick, N., & Davidsen-Nielsen, M. *Healing Pain,* p. 156.

6. Mooney, J. (2007). *The Short Bus: A Journey Beyond Normal.* New York: Henry Holt, p. 51.

7. Flynn, K. (2008, May 24). It's Time We Put Some Responsibility Back on the Students. *The Flint Journal.* Flynn is a columnist for *The Flint Journal,* writing about education and related topics. She's also the author of *Kids, Classrooms, and Capitol Hill,* published in July 2008.

8. Connolly, L. (2007, September-December). Quotes from unpublished undergraduate paper, Wheaton College, Norton, MA.

9. Mooney, J. *The Short Bus,* p. 21.

10. Ibid., p. 22.

11. Mooney, J. (2007). *How I Channeled My Energy into Success.* See http://www.additudemag.com/adhd/article/2520.html

12. Ibid., p. 56.

13. Mooney, J. (2008). *Life on Your Terms.* See http://www.additudemag.com/adhd/article/3599.html

14. Mooney, J. *The Short Bus,* p. 51.

15. The quotes here are based on interviews with Bernard Gassaway in May 2008 and from Gassaway, B. (2006). *Reflections of an Urban High School Principal.* Jamaica, NY: XenoGass ALG.

16. Gassaway, B. (2006). *Suicide by Educator.* See http://www.bernardgassaway.com/SuicidebyEducator%20April%202007.pdfS

17. Gassaway, B. (2008, February 22). Teachers. *Teachers College Record.* Retrieved May 13, 2008, from http://www.tcrecord.org, ID Number 15025.

Chapter 5

1. Stoop, D. (2003). *Forgiving the Unforgivable.* Ventura, CA: Regal Books, p. 74.

2. Ibid., pp. 78–79.

3. Bandura, A. (1986). *Social Foundations of Thought and Action: A Social Cognitive Theory.* Englewood Cliffs, NJ: Prentice-Hall.

4. Worden, J. W. (2001). *Grief Counseling and Grief Therapy: A Handbook for the Mental Health Professional.* New York: Springer.

5. Stoop, D. *Forgiving our parents, forgiving ourselves,* p. 172.

6. Mooney, J., & Stanberry, K. (2008). Jonathan Mooney on Goal Setting and Motivation in Teens with LD or AD/HD. *Great Schools Online Newsletter.* See http://www.schwablearning.org/articles.aspx?r=527

7. Stoop, D. *Forgiving the Unforgivable,* p. 98.

8. Leick, N., & Davidsen-Nielsen, M. *Healing Pain,* p. 166.

9. Mooney, J., & Stanberry, K. Jonathan Mooney on Goal Setting.

10. Project Eye to Eye partners with local communities, public and private schools, universities, and local businesses to bring labeled adults with learning disabilities into the lives of labeled students with learning disabilities.

Chapter 6

1. Wagner, T. (2008). *The Global Achievement Gap.* New York: Basic Books.

2. Elmore, R. F. (2008). Classroom lecture notes, Harvard Graduate School of Education, Cambridge, MA. Elmore was discussing modal patterns of instruction cross-culturally based on the 2007 TIMMS [Trends in International Mathematics and Science Study]. See also Stevenson, H. W., & Stigler, J. W. (1994). *The Learning Gap.* New York: Touchstone Books.

3. Hill, H. C., Rowan, B., & Ball, D. L. (2005, Summer). Effects of Teachers' Mathematical Knowledge for Teaching on Student Achievement. *American Educational Research Journal, 42*(2), 371–406.

4. Meighan, R. (2005, July/August). An Education Fit for a Democracy. *Life Learning.* See http://www.lifelearningmagazine.com/0508/JulyAug05.pdf

5. Rose, D. (2008, March). Lecture at the Universal Design for Learning conference, Harvard Graduate School of Education, Cambridge, MA.

6. *Learning to Change/Changing to Learn* [Video prepared by Consortium for School Networking on Advancing K-12 Technology Leadership]. (2008, May). See http://www.youtube.com/watch?v=tahTKdEUAPk

7. Pink, D. *A Whole New Mind.*

8. See http://thefischbowl.blogspot.com/2007/09/is-it-okay-to-be-technologically.html. This was one of the most-read blogs on the *Teacher Magazine* Web site in the past 12 months.

9. Levine, A. (2006). *Educating School Teachers.* National Center for Policy Analysis, Washington, DC. See http://www.ncpa.org/sub/dpd/index.php?Article_ID=12670

10. Ball, D. L., & Cohen, D. K. (1999). Developing Practice, Developing Practitioners: Toward a Practice-Based Theory of Professional Development. In L. Darling-Hammond & G. Sykes (Eds.), *Teaching as the Learning Profession* (pp. 3–32). San Francisco: Jossey-Bass; Charner-Laird, M. (2007, April). *Ready and Willing: Second-Stage Teachers and Professional Collaboration.* Paper presented at the annual meeting of the American Educational Research Association, Chicago.

11. Cookson, P. (2005, October). The Challenge of Isolation. *Teaching Pre K-8.* See http://findarticles.com/p/articles/mi_qa3666/is_200510/ai_n15667671

12. Wagner, T. *The Global Achievement Gap,* pp. 135–136.

13. Levine, A. *Educating School Teachers*.

14. Medina, J. (2008). *Brain Rules*. Seattle, WA: Pear Press. See accompanying DVD, in which John Medina speaks about his "12 Brain Rules," and www.brainrules.net

15. Ibid., p. 70; Wodka, E. L., Mahone, E. M., Blankner, J. G., Gidley Larson, J. C., Fotedar, S., Denckla, M. B., & Mostofsky, S. H. (2007). Evidence That Response Inhibition Is a Primary Deficit in ADHD. *Journal of Clinical and Experimental Neuropsychology*, 29, 345–356.

16. Medina, *Brain Rules*, p. 1.

17. Rose, D. H., & Meyer, A. (2000). *The Future Is in the Margins: The Role of Technology and Disability in Educational Reform* [Report prepared for the U.S. Department of Education, Office of Special Education Technology]. Washington, DC: U.S. Department of Education.

18. Medina, J. *Brain Rules*, p. 70.

19. Ibid., p. 66.

20. See, for instance, Center for Applied Special Technology Web site, http://www.cast.org/index.html

21. What Is Universal Design for Learning? See http://www.cast.org/research/udl/index.html

22. See the CAST Web site, and specifically the "What Is Universal Design for Learning?" page, for more information and the research that underlies their principles. Available at http://www.cast.org/research/udl/index.html

23. Bransford, J. (2008, April). Quoted in G. Rubenstein, Reinventing the Big Test. *Edutopia Magazine*, p. 36.

24. Ibid.

25. Hehir, T. (2008, July). Institute presentation, Universal Design for Learning, Harvard Graduate School of Education, Cambridge, MA.

26. Barringer, M. D. (2008, February). *From Teaching to Learning*. Keynote Address to the annual meeting of the Association for Supervision and Curriculum Development, New Orleans.

27. Toffler, A. (2007). Future School: Reshaping Learning from the Ground Up [Interviewed by J. Daly]. See http://www.edutopia.org/print/3149

28. Locker, F. M., & Olson, S. (2008). Flexible School Facilities. Retrieved December 2, 2008, from http://www.designshare.com/index.php/articles/flexible=school=facilities/1/

Chapter 7

1. Lawrence-Lightfoot, S. (2003). *The Essential Conversation*. New York: Random House, p. xviii.

2. Waller, W. (1965). *The Sociology of Teaching*. Chicago: Science Editions.

3. Nowen, H. J. M. (1979). *The Wounded Healer*. Garden City, NY: Image Books.

4. Elmore, R. (2004). *School Reform from the Inside Out*. Cambridge, MA: Harvard Education Press.

5. Mathews, J. (2007, August 14). Teachers in Trouble, Parents Ignored, Part 1. *Washington Post*. Available at www.washingtonpost.com/wp=dyn/content/article/2007/08/14/AR2007081400362.html

6. Moore, D. (2001, July/August). Changing the Ground Rules. *Shelterforce Online*. See http://www.nhi.org/online/issues/118/Moore.html

7. Henderson, A. T., Mapp, K. L., Johnson, V. R., & Davies, D. (2006). *Beyond the Bake Sale*. New York: New Press.

8. Goodman, E. (2008, January 23). City Parents Boycotting Added Tests at 2 Schools. *The New York Times*. See www.nytimes.com/2008/01/23/nyregion/23boycott.html

9. Matthews, J. *Teachers in Trouble*.

10. Becker, H. J., Nakagawa, K., & Corwin, R. (1997). Parent Involvement Contracts in California's Charter Schools: Strategy for Educational Exclusion or Method of Improvement? *Teachers College Record, 98*(3), 511–536; Hoover-Dempsey, K. V., & Sander, H. M. (1995). Parental Involvement in Children's Education: Why Does It Make a Difference? *Teachers College Record, 97*(2), 310–331.

11. Fine, M. (1993). Apparent Involvement: Reflections on Parents, Power and Urban Public Schools. *Teachers College Record, 94*(4), 682–729. Retrieved July 15, 2008, from http://www.tcrecord.org, ID Number 147; Payne, R. K., & Krabil, D. L. (2002). *Hidden Rules of Class at Work*. Highlands, TX: Aha! Process.

12. Oakes, J. (2008). Keeping Track: Structuring Equality and Inequality in an Era of Accountability. *Teachers College Record, 110*(3), 700–712. Retrieved November 15, 2008, from http://www.tcrecord.org, ID Number 14610; Murdoch, S. *IQ: A Smart History of a Failed Idea*.

13. Alvy, K. T. (2008). *The Positive Parent*. New York: Teachers College Press, p. 1.

14. Dweck, C. *Mindset*.

15. Ibid., p. 6

16. Stevenson, H. W., & Stigler, J. W. (1992). *The Learning Gap*. New York: Touchstone.

17. Duckworth, A. L., Peterson, C., Matthews, M. D., & Kelly, D. R. (2007). Grit: Perseverance and Passion for Long-Term Goals. *Journal of Personality and Social Psychology, 92*(6), 1087–1101.

18. Bronson, P. (2007, February 12). How Not to Talk to Your Kids: The Inverse Power of Praise. *New York Magazine*. See http://nymag.com/news/features/27840

19. Pohlman, C. (2008). *Revealing Minds*. San Francisco: Jossey-Bass, p. 225.

20. Fried, R. L. (2001). *The Passionate Learner*. Boston: Beacon Press.

21. Ibid., p. 75.

22. Post on All Kinds of Minds discussion group site. (2004). Available at http://www.allkindsofminds.org/forums/ShowPost.aspx?PostID=1113

23. Llewellyn, G. (1991). *The Teenage Liberation Handbook: How to Quit School and Get a Real Life Education*. Eugene, OR: Lowry House.

24. Llewellyn, G., & Sliver, A. (2001). *Guerrilla Learning*. New York: Wiley.

25. Lawrence-Lightfoot, S. *The Essential Conversation*, p. xviii.

26. Hallowell, E., & Ratey, J. (1994). *Driven to Distraction: Recognizing and Coping with Attention Deficit Disorder from Childhood Through Adulthood*. New York: Pantheon Books.

27. Hallowell, E., & Corman, C. (2006). *Positively A.D.D.: Profiles of Successful Adults Who Have A.D.D.* New York: Walker Books.

28. Hallowell, E. (2008, June 1). Eagle Hill graduation talk. Unpublished.

29. Hastings, R. P., Allen, R., McDermott, K., & Still, D. (2002, September). Factors Related to Positive Perceptions in Mothers of Children with Intellectual Disabilities. *Journal of Applied Research in Intellectual Disabilities, 15*(3), 269–275.

30. Hanos-Webb, L. (2005). *The Gift of ADHD*. Oakland, CA: New Harbinger.

31. Fried, R. L. *The Passionate Learner*, pp. 83–85.

Chapter 8

1. Gassaway, B. (2008, February 22). Teachers. *Teachers College Record*. Retrieved May 1, 2008, from http://www.tcrecord.org, ID Number 15025.

2. Palmer, P. J. (2007, November/December). A New Professional: The Aims of Education Revisited. *Change*. Available at www.carnegiefoundation.org/change/sub.asp?key=98&subkey=2455

3. Ibid., p. 4.

4. Ibid.

5. Witcher, A., & Onwuegbuzie, A. J. (1999). *Characteristics of Effective Teachers: Perceptions of Preservice Teachers*. Paper presented at the annual meeting of the Mid-South Educational Research Association, Point Clear, AL. (ERIC Document Reproduction Service No. ED 438 246).

6. Thibodeau, G. P., & Hillman, S. J. (2003, Fall). In Retrospect: Teachers Who Made a Difference from the Perspective of Preservice and Experienced Teachers. *Education*. Retrieved December 2, 2008, from http://findarticles.com/p/articles/mi_qa3673/is_1_124/ai_n29032707

7. Rowan, B., Correnti, R., & Miller, R. J. (2002). What large-scale survey research tells us about teacher effects on student achievement: Insights from the *Prospects* study of elementary schools. *Teachers College Record, 104*(8), 1525–1567. Retrieved November 16, 2008, from http://www.tcrecord.org, ID Number 11041.

8. Rowan, B. (2002). Teachers' work and instructional management, Parts I and II. In W. K. Hoy & C. G. Miskel (Eds.), *Theory and Research in Educational Administration* (pp. 129–168). Charlotte, NC: Information Age Publishing.

9. Ibid., p. 147.

10. Ibid.

11. See the National Board for Professional Teaching Standards Web site, http://www.nbpts.org

12. See the Democratic Education Web site, www.democraticeducation.com/essay-miller.htm

13. Based in part on Miller, R. (2007). What Is Democratic Education? Written for a proposed book on democratic schools, available on Ron Miller's Web site, http://www.pathsoflearning.net/articles_What_Is_Democratic_Education.php

14. Essays and Articles on Democratic Education, part of the AERO education network. See http://www.democraticeducation.com/essays.htm

Chapter 9

1. Prensky, M. (2008, June/July). Young Minds, Fast Times. *Edutopia Magazine*, pp. 33–36.

2. Yazzie-Mintz, E. (2008). *Voices of Students on Engagement: A Report on the 2006 High School Survey of Student Engagement*. See http://ceep.indiana.edu/hssse/pdf/HSSSE_2006_Report.pdf

3. See http://www.indiana.edu/~ceep/hssse/pdf/hssse_2004_overview.pdf

4. Elmore, R. F. (2009). Schooling Adolescents. In R. M. Lerner & L. Steinberg (Eds.), *Handbook of Adolescent Psychology* (3rd. ed.). Hoboken, NJ: John Wiley.

5. Brownmiller, S. (2000). *In Our Time: Memoir of a Revolution*. New York: Dial Press, p. 21.

6. Clark Pope, D. (2001). *"Doing School": How We Are Creating a Generation of Stressed Out, Materialistic, and Miseducated Students.* New Haven, CT: Yale University Press.

7. Leggiere, P. (2002, January/February). Questioning Authority: Denise Clark Pope Says That Our Schools Are Turning Out "Organization Kids." *The Conference Board Review.* Available at http://www.conference-board.org/articles/atb_article.cfm?id=63

8. The Chicago Women's Liberation Union. (1971). How to start your own consciousness-raising group. Available at http://www.cwluherstory.com/CWLU Archive/crcwlu.html

9. Tom Skiba asked to be identified by his real name. His honors thesis, *Understanding Students with Dyslexia in Higher Education,* is available for school discussion groups and Tom himself is willing to speak to audiences about his journey in understanding himself as a student with learning differences. His contact information is: Tom Skiba, 147 Lawnwood Ave., Longmeadow, MA 01106.

10. Skiba, T. (2008). *Understanding Students with Dyslexia in Higher Education: A Grounded Theory Approach.* Unpublished undergraduate honors thesis, Wheaton College, Norton, MA.

11. Ibid., pp. 35–36.

12. Ibid.

13. Ibid., p. 74.

14. *The Problem We All Live With.* See http://www.whatkidscando.org/specialcollections/student_research_action/multimedia.html

15. Proposition Better Buildings was a $2.4 billion bond that California voters approved in order to improve the physical structure of high schools throughout the state. "Schools in the inner city were continuously overlooked and ignored. SCYEA documented, with student surveys, the fact that there was an urgent need for vast repairs in all south Los Angeles schools. SCYEA found itself competing with schools in the Valley for school repair funds. While South Los Angeles schools needed funding to make vital repairs to plumbing, lighting, tiling, and roofing, schools in the Valley wanted it for unessential items such as pool filters. SCYEA actively informed students about Proposition BB and alerted them to the fact that south LA schools were not being prioritized in the funding allocation process, taking pictures of the harsh conditions to further substantiate their claims. SCYEA organized students, community members, and decision makers in support of its cause. Its efforts successfully garnered $153 million for repairs in south Los Angeles schools. SCYEA was featured in local print and television media, received national attention in *People Magazine,* and was featured on the Oprah Winfrey show." See http://socal4youth.org/story.php?story=8&print=1

16. "The Fremont 911 campaign led to another significant victory for SCYEA. Fremont High School was not putting students first. Students were retaking classes that they previously passed, while classes needed for college admission were not available. They also were enrolled in unnecessary 'free period' classes such as service or allowed to go home early in the day. Students were forced to learn in overcrowded classrooms, unable to hear what teachers had to say or to be active participants in the learning process. FREYEA (the HSOC at Fremont) demanded change. It surveyed over 1,000 Fremont students in order to substantiate their demands. It then organized over 200 students to protest school conditions and demand immediate action from the school board. SCYEA won two major demands at Fremont. First, each student received a full record and accounting of his or her academic standing in relation to graduation

requirements and University of California admission requirements. Second, each student was guaranteed a meeting of no less than 20 minutes long with an academic counselor to review his or her cumulative card/transcript, progress toward graduation, and CSU and UC admission eligibility." See http://socal4youth.org/story. php?story=8&print=1

17. SCYEA currently is engaged in its "Equal Access to College Prep Classes" campaign. "There is a 66% "push-out" rate in the seven south L.A. schools and nothing is being done to prevent this by the district. Further, only 2 out of 10 south Los Angeles high school graduates attend a 4-year university. South L.A. students are being tracked into low-wage labor, prison, and the military. Counselors often force students to enroll in vocational classes (auto mechanics, cosmetology) instead of college prep courses. At Fremont High School alone there are nine cosmetology classes offered and only four chemistry classes. SCYEA demands that every student be placed on a college prep track! Each student deserves the opportunity to be prepared to complete high school and go on to a 4-year university!" See http://socal4youth.org/story. php?story=8&print=1

18. Blog post from the SCYEA Web site, April 25, 2006. See http://blog.myspace. com/index.cfm?fuseaction=blog.view&friendID=67928720&blogID=114058570

19. Wasley, P. (2007, October 12). Home-Schooled Students Rise in Supply and Demand. *Chronicle of Higher Education.* Available at http://chronicle.com/weekly/v54/ i07/07a00102.htm

20. Llewellyn, G. (1998). *The Teenage Liberation Handbook.* Eugene, OR: Lowry House.

21. Meighan, R. An Education Fit for a Democracy.

22. Ibid.

23. Gates, B. (2005). A Call to Action, Part 3. Opening plenary session at the National Education Summit on High School. Available at www.achieve.org/node/767

Index

About the Author

Kirsten Olson is a writer, an educational consultant, a national-level Courage To Teach facilitator (www.couragerenewal.org), and principal of Old Sow Consulting. A frequent lecturer and presenter, Olson has also been a visiting assistant professor at Wheaton College in Norton, MA, and is the author of *Schools as Colonizers* (2008), a book that reconsiders the educational ideas of the radical school critics of the 1960s. She received her doctorate from the Harvard Graduate School of Education in 2005 and was an English major at Vassar College.

Olson's work as an educational consultant focuses on instructional improvement and leadership development to better support all learners. She has been a consultant to the Bill and Melinda Gates Foundation, to the Kennedy School at Harvard University, and to many large public school systems and charter schools. She also writes for *Education Week, Educational Leadership* and *Teacher Magazine*.

Olson can be reached at www.kirstenolson.org, where stories about school wounding, healing, and standing up to old school culture are being collected and featured. Please join us there.